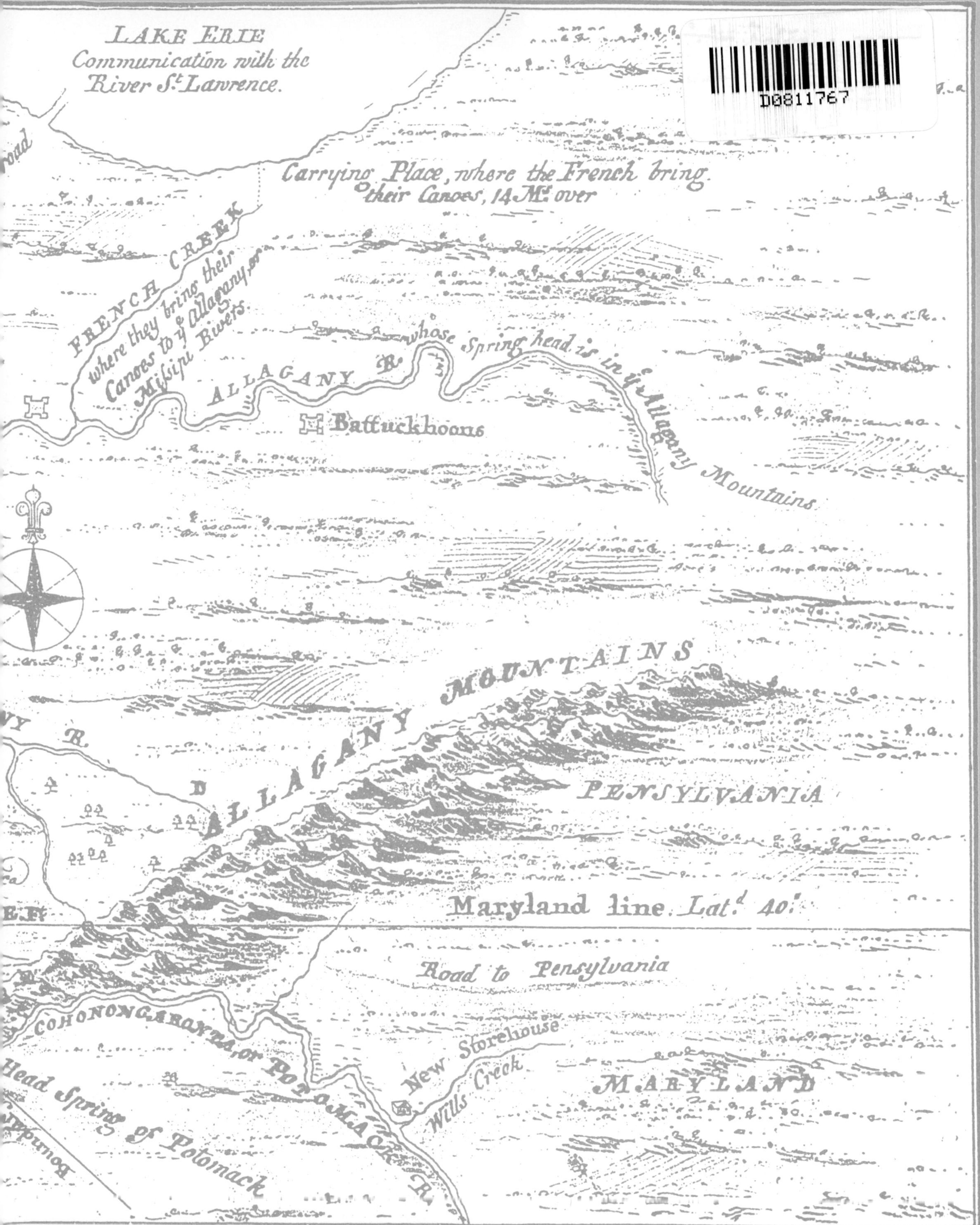

LAKE ERIE
Communication with the
River St Lawrence.

Carrying Place, where the French bring
their Canoes, 14 Ms over

FRENCH CREEK
where they bring their
Canoes to ÿ Allagany or
Misisipi Rivers.

ALLAGANY R.

H Battuckhoans

whose Spring head is in ÿe Allagany

Mountains

ALLAGANY MOUNTAINS

PENSYLVANIA

Maryland line. Latd 40°

Road to Pensylvania

New Storehouse

COHONONGARONTA or POTOMACK R.

Wills Creek

MARYLAND

Head Spring of Potomack

THE
ALLEGHENY
RIVER

THE ALLEGHENY RIVER

Watershed of the Nation

photographs by JIM SCHAFER
text by MIKE SAJNA

A Keystone Book

The Pennsylvania State University Press
University Park, Pennsylvania

A Keystone Book is so designated to distinguish it from the typical scholarly monograph that a university press publishes. It is a book intended to serve the citizens of Pennsylvania by educating them and others, in an entertaining way, about aspects of the history, culture, society, and environment of the state as part of the Middle Atlantic region.

Library of Congress Cataloging-in-Publication Data

Schafer, Jim.
    The Allegheny River : watershed of the nation / photographs by Jim
Schafer : text by Mike Sajna.
        p.   cm.
    A Keystone book
    Includes bibliographical references (p.   ).
    ISBN 0-271-00836-9 (alk. paper)
    1. Allegheny River (Pa. and N.Y.)—Pictorial works. 2. Allegheny
River (Pa. and N.Y.)—Description and travel. 3. Allegheny River
Valley (Pa. and N.Y.)—Pictorial works. 4. Allegheny River Valley
(Pa. and N.Y.)—Description and travel. I. Sajna, Mike.
II. Title.
F157.A5S34   1992
974.8′6—dc20   91-43332
                                                            CIP

Published by The Pennsylvania State University Press,
Suite C, Barbara Building, University Park, PA 16802-1003

Typeset by Coghill Composition Company
Printed and bound in Hong Kong by Everbest Printing Co., Ltd.

It is the policy of The Pennsylvania State University Press to use acid-free paper for the first printing of all clothbound books. Publications on uncoated stock satisfy the minimum requirements of American National Standard for Information Sciences—Permanence of Paper for Printed Library Materials, ANSI Z39.48–1984.

Frontispiece: Headwaters, Potter County

For my parents, Mike and Leona, who have always been there despite everything.

—Mike Sajna

To the memory of my father, Fred Schafer, who introduced me to the wonders of rivers and streams—and to the river itself, may it always have friends and allies to work on its behalf.

—Jim Schafer

Bank grasses

CONTENTS

Farm country, Clarion County

PREFACE

Rivers have served as symbols for the flow of life probably since *Homo sapiens* developed language and began telling stories. James Joyce had Dublin's River Liffey to guide him in telling his tale of civilization in *Finnegans Wake*. Hermann Hesse's Siddhartha first encountered enlightenment along a river in India. Ernest Hemingway's Nick Adams sought refuge from a world gone mad in World War I on the "Big Two-Hearted River."

If the story of the United States were to be told by river, one could hardly imagine any waterway filling the role better than the Allegheny River. The Father of Waters—the Mississippi—is too far west to capture the colonial years. The Ohio would be only a minor waterway without the flow of the Allegheny feeding it. The Hudson is too closely linked to New York, and the Potomac to Washington, D.C. They all lack the Allegheny's access to the heartland. And the Columbia, the Missouri, and the Colorado are too far west and lack a connection to the east.

But the Allegheny has touched it all. Its waters have confronted glaciers and nourished extinct species and ancient peoples. They have carried missionaries of God and missionaries of empire. They have witnessed the massacre and mistreatment of Native Americans by whites, and the massacre and mistreatment of whites by Native Americans. They played a part in the birth of the nation and then carried the first settlers of that nation into its unknown regions. Along its length have lived, traveled, or worked presidents, inventors, folk heroes, outlaws, writers, artists, industrialists, assassins, and poor immigrants. The Allegheny has seen the birth or blossoming of great industries, such as iron, steel, aluminum, and oil. And it has suffered greatly at their hands and been reborn with their decline. What other river can boast so many and so far-flung connections to the course of the United States over so long a period of time?

As a native of western Pennsylvania, I have been aware of the Allegheny River and gazed on its waters as far back as I can recall. But as any psychologist will explain, there is a vast difference between being aware of something and truly knowing it. I had no idea how very little I truly knew about the Allegheny until that dreary fall afternoon when Jim Schafer first appeared on my porch carrying his light table and file folders stuffed with slides.

At the point he stepped through my door, Jim had been photographing the Allegheny on and off for more than three years. The idea had been inspired by his father, who had introduced him to the river and had died a couple of years back. Jim had been working on the project in his spare time, with only a vague goal of eventually doing a book. But when he had enough slides to express himself and was ready to talk, publishers were generally not interested in talking to a photographer without some kind of text. So he had taken his slides to *Pittsburgh Magazine*—for which he had done work in the past and for which I write an outdoors column—looking for a writer. The people there gave him my telephone number.

Bending over the light table listening to Jim make his pitch, I was quickly struck by how close our experiences with the Allegheny were and how similarly we viewed the world. The idea for the book had come to Jim out of boyhood years spent hunting and fishing with his father along the river around Tionesta. I had started deer hunting with my dad only a few miles farther up the Allegheny in Tidioute at about the same time and was presently writing a book about those experiences. As a native of the Pittsburgh area, Jim also had known the lower river for as long as he could remember, and we both were acquainted with many other sections of the river.

As Jim and I continued to talk, we agreed that most people we knew were only aware of certain stretches of the river. Pittsburghers, for instance, tend to look on the Allegheny as beginning at Kinzua Dam and know little about New York's Allegheny or Potter County's Allegheny. We wanted to expand people's horizons, but in a different way—not, like most books about rivers, by simply putting in a canoe at the headwaters and photographing and writing about what we saw on the way downstream. We wanted to explore the river in different seasons and by different means. We wanted to look at its present and its past, its problems and its promises. We wanted to talk to people who made their living on the river, to people who used it as a playground, to people who worried about it, loved it, lived along it, and drew inspiration from it.

Accomplishing our goal took dozens of trips, running from a couple of hours to several days, to the river and to the towns and the country surrounding it. We made those trips alone, together, and with other people. We went by canoe, by towboat, by pleasure boat, by excursion boat, on foot, by car, and by plane. We visited in the spring, the summer, the fall, and the winter; in the snow, in the rain, and in the sun. This book is the result.

Every book is subjective, and no book is ever more than 75 to 90 percent complete.

Something new and interesting always seems to pop up after it is in the stores. And as for rivers, the early Greek philosopher Heraclitus said you can't step into the same river twice. So even though the book we have produced can never be complete—nothing as alive as a river can ever be written about or photographed in any definitive matter, because it changes too much from day to day, hour to hour—we believe we have created an honest portrait of the Allegheny we have known and hope it matches the perceptions of some other people who know and love the river.

Although Jim's name and my own are on the title page, this book would not exist without the support and encouragement of dozens of other people. In recognition of their help, we would like to thank, first of all, everybody who met with us and talked about the Allegheny and its people, history, and environs. They are the individuals who appear throughout the book and who know the river, or at least aspects of it, far better than either of us might ever hope to. Their stories are interesting, exciting, mesmerizing, inspiring, fun, depressing, thoughtful, hopeful, serious, frightening, amusing, silly, troublesome, and generally full of the fabric of life, and we feel richer for having known every one of them. Thank you all once more.

In addition to those who appear in the text or in photographs, we would like to thank Bruce VanWyngarden, editor of *Pittsburgh Magazine*, who recommended that Jim and I talk; Sanford Thatcher, director of Penn State Press, who was not afraid to take a chance on our idea; Peggy Hoover, who was an understanding but demanding manuscript editor with an awesome attention to detail; and production manager Janet Dietz and designers Megan Youngquist and Steve Kress, for their guidance, expertise, and willingness to listen.

Other people who deserve thanks for their help include Bill Randour of the Western Pennsylvania Conservancy; Cheryl Stewart-Miller of the H. J. Heinz Company; Bob Van Grootenbruel of Fahringer, McCarty, Grey, Inc., for his help with maps; Tom Greenley of the Forest County Sports Center for his guidance; amateur historian Frank Church of Greensburg for background and location help. The historical photographs are from the various sources indicated, with special thanks to Ruth Heasly of the Venango County Historical Society; Derek McKown of the Warren County Historical Society; and the staffs of the Pennsylvania Room of the Carnegie Library, the Historical Society of Western Pennsylvania, the Darlington Collection of the University of Pittsburgh, the Drake Well Museum, the Pennsylvania Lumber Museum, the Potter County Historical Society, the Seneca-Iroquois National Museum, and the Foxburg Public Library.

The map on the front endpaper shows how the British "Captain Snow" saw the Allegheny River in 1754 in relation to the rest of the area. The original, in the Library of Congress, is reproduced here, by permission, from *Early Maps of the Ohio Valley* by Lloyd A. Brown (University of Pittsburgh, 1959). The map on the back endpaper, courtesy of the Darlington Collection of the University of Pittsburgh, was produced by Father Joseph Pierre de Bonnecamps after his 1749 voyage down the Allegheny with

Céleron. It shows the Allegheny, as Bonnecamps saw it, from Warren downriver. Warren is where Plate 1 was buried, and present-day Pittsburgh is just upriver of Plate 3. The modern map that follows this preface is based on a map that was provided courtesy of the Western Pennsylvania Conservancy.

Very special thanks is owed to Rebecca Cook for being an inspiration, John Schafer for his canoe livery service, and especially Peggy Schafer, who refused to give up on her husband's dream.

—Mike Sajna

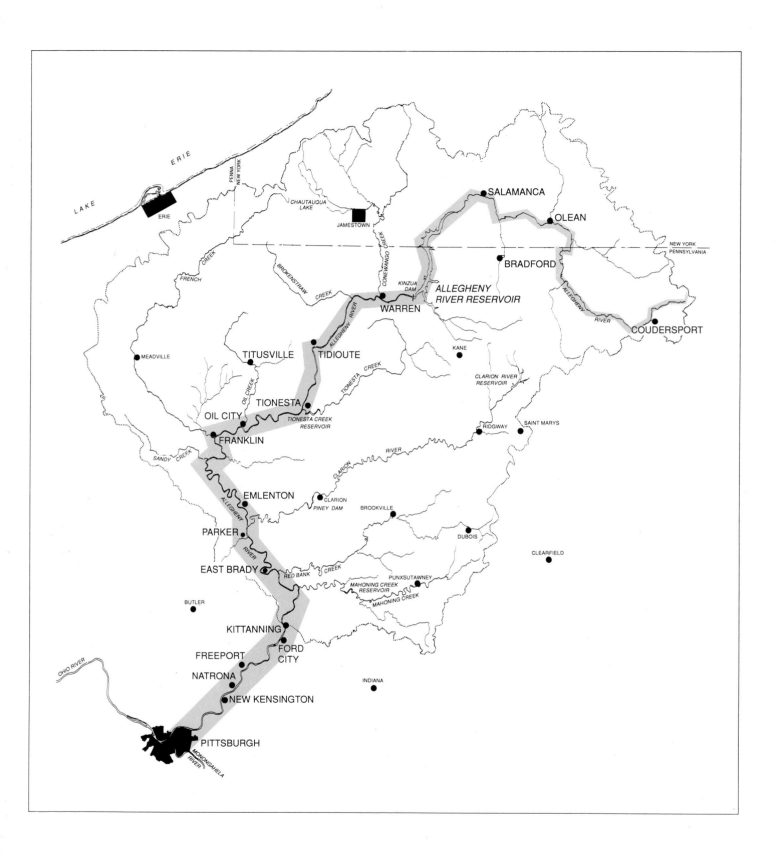

LAKE ERIE

ERIE

PENNA
NEW YORK

FRENCH CREEK

CHAUTAUQUA LAKE

JAMESTOWN

BROKENSTRAW CREEK

CONEWANGO CREEK

KINZUA DAM

SALAMANCA

OLEAN

BRADFORD

NEW YORK
PENNSYLVANIA

ALLEGHENY RIVER RESERVOIR

ALLEGHENY RIVER

WARREN

MEADVILLE

TITUSVILLE

TIDIOUTE

KANE

ALLEGHENY RIVER

TIONESTA CREEK

CLARION RIVER RESERVOIR

COUDERSPORT

OIL CREEK

TIONESTA

OIL CITY

TIONESTA CREEK RESERVOIR

FRANKLIN

RIDGWAY

SAINT MARYS

SANDY CREEK

RIVER

CLARION

EMLENTON

CLARION

PINEY DAM

BROOKVILLE

ALLEGHENY

DUBOIS

CLEARFIELD

PARKER

RIVER

EAST BRADY

RED BANK CREEK

BUTLER

PUNXSUTAWNEY

MAHONING CREEK RESERVOIR

KITTANNING

MAHONING CREEK

FORD CITY

FREEPORT

INDIANA

NATRONA

NEW KENSINGTON

OHIO RIVER

PITTSBURGH

MONONGAHELA RIVER

Captain Fred Way, age 89

1

GENERATIONS

At age eighty-nine his once catlike riverman's walk has turned into a shuffle, and the skin that weathered more than seven decades of wind and sun on the river has faded to a pale parchment. Arthritis has taken its toll of his hands, too, he points out as we shake. The only way he can write now is with a typewriter, he says, and then leads me into the living room and excuses himself to return to his basement office and turn off his typewriter. He has been working on the next issue of *S&D Reflector*, the magazine of the Sons and Daughters of Pioneer Rivermen.

Left alone in the living room, I find it is impossible to politely sit and wait. The passion of a lifetime is simply too powerful to resist. Everywhere are photographs, paintings, drawings, and models of riverboats. On the table against the wall is the tray given him as "Pittsburgh's Riverman of the Century," and not far away is the life-achievement plaque he received from the National Rivers Hall of Fame. On the back wall are two huge bookcases packed with volumes on rivers from Pittsburgh to New Orleans and west over the Rockies—probably more river books than in the Carnegie Library a few miles up the Ohio River in Pittsburgh. I notice several have his name—Frederick Way Jr.—imprinted on the spine, including *The Allegheny*, the book that has brought me to his sprawling Victorian home in Sewickley, Pennsylvania.

"There are hundreds of rivermen," he wrote in that 1942 work, "who have gazed up the Allegheny River and have remarked, 'Someday I'd like to go up there and come down in a skiff.' " He added:

> It is a mysterious sort of place, and vague tales come wafting down from explorers who have been up there, of boundless fish, primitive forests, majestic mountains, and queer names like Kinzua, Tionesta, Tidioute, and Corydon. We hear of summer camps, and oil country. A glance at a map discloses an Indian reservation bordering the shores. Wild country—adventurous country! Boulders big as a pilothouse and thundering rapids! People getting upset out of small boats in treacherous currents and—as happened in one case—airplanes scouring the river for bodies in inaccessible places where there are no railroads, highways or means of getting in. Desolation and eagles' nests. Pine trees atop rugged cliffs. Bears and wolves and ducks so tame they will not move or fly until you can nearly hit their tails with oars! Inquisitive deer standing along shores looking at a white man for the first time! A strange place, indeed, this big Allegheny River. Strange and untamed and little explored. Curious that such a place should exist so close to civilization and still be untouched. Miles and miles of pioneer river with absolutely no sign of human handiwork. This, in part, is the Allegheny. The Ohio River is not like this; neither is the Monongahela. Neither is the Beaver, nor the Muskingum. The Allegheny River is a breed of its own, and it should remain so!

I am still engrossed in the books and awards when he returns, automatically picks up his worn pipe from the coffee table, and finds a seat at the end of the couch. Quickly, I explain what I am doing and how I had read his book and would like to hear more about the Allegheny River he has known. He listens, eyes sparkling with delight as bright as the sun dancing on the Ohio River visible through a front window, and then touches a match to his pipe.

"The Allegheny," Captain Way says, chuckling. "Well, it hasn't changed much since I came down it the first time—that is, it's still all primitive up above East Brady."

Although years of hunting and fishing in northern Pennsylvania have shown me an Allegheny worlds removed from the one at Pittsburgh, the idea that a river in a region

Young Captain Fred Way

as battered and bruised by industry as western Pennsylvania remains primitive still seems incredible. The captain's first trip down the river was in 1918 on a steamboat built by a man in the Forest County town of West Hickory who wanted to reenact voyages of the *Nellie Hudson*, the *Kittanning*, the *Tidioute*, and other steamboats that worked the river in the nineteenth century. The last time he made the trip he was well past sixty years of age. Altogether, he has come down the Allegheny a dozen times in boats he has built, gone up it to Kinzua Dam on three or four other occasions, and once went all the way to Olean, New York, which made him the first and last person to accomplish that feat since the 1830s (Kinzua Dam now bars the way).

The trip he wrote about in *The Allegheny* occurred in May 1938, when, with Frank Morrison, a college student playing hooky, he put his eighteen-foot yawl *Lady Grace* in the river at Olean and shoved off for Pittsburgh. People up that way were not used to seeing such a large boat on their little Allegheny—"impracticable as though the *Queen Mary* were lying at Fort Benton, Montana, and had steam up and expected to go down the Missouri with about two feet on the marks"—and a good portion of the town turned out to watch the start of the trip. Girl Scouts ran along the bank, and a reporter stood by waiting for an accident at the first rapid a short distance ahead.

The *Lady Grace* made it through that first rapid leaving only green paint on the rocks, but quickly smashed her propeller on a submerged boulder in the deep water below. Over the next week it took them to reach Pittsburgh, Captain Way and his partner would meet one of the last lumbermen to float log rafts down the river, draw the silent attention of suspicious Indians, have all their food stolen, collide with islands, become the first boat to pass through Lock 9, run aground, and hit so many rocks and snags that

The *Lady Grace*

4

Warren

the bottom of the *Lady Grace* became a mass of splinters and had to be replaced when they got back to Pittsburgh.

"I figure a steamboat had actually gone clear up to Olean twice," Captain Way says as we talk of the trip he made up the Allegheny to Olean. "A boat named the 'New Castle' and one named the 'Allegheny,' back in the 1830s. So, I built a little stern-wheeler and reenacted the voyage. I wanted to go up the river. Anybody can come down the river. And I had no guarantee I was ever going to make it to Olean, but I kept on plowing and after about eight or ten days lo and behold there was Olean looking at me."

That *Lady Grace* (Captain Way built several boats and named them all after his late wife) also played an important role in Edwin L. Peterson's exploration of the Allegheny River, described in his 1958 book *Penn's Woods West*. "Three piercing blasts shattered the quiet of the River," Peterson wrote of the captain's appearance. "We turned and looked downstream. There in the sunlight, her stern wheel a glistening arc of drops, came the 'Lady Grace.' She looked young and fragile, a youthful sister to a 'Nellie Hudson,' a miniature too small to be out on the Allegheny River alone even in broad daylight."

Captain Way had a broad grin on his face as he pulled alongside the wharf to pick Peterson up in East Brady back in 1958. His accomplishments at that point included not only the trip downriver he describes in *The Allegheny* and his run up to Olean, but also piloting a river steamboat from San Francisco through the Panama Canal into the Gulf of Mexico and then up the Mississippi and the Ohio to the Allegheny. "That man knows every fellow who ever got his feet wet in the Allegheny," Peterson noted.

"Then I built another one, a good-sized one," Captain Way continues telling me. "It was thirty-eight feet long with a stern wheel and all enclosed with smokestacks on it.

5

Winter night, Venango County

It looked like an old-time steamboat. Kinzua Dam had been built in the meantime [1966], so I couldn't go any farther than that. I went up and looked at Kinzua Dam and then turned around and came back.

"But that caused a big stir up the river." He laughs. "It had a gasoline engine, but a lot of people thought there was a real steamboat coming because I had to go up in cold weather when I had water to float on, and I had a stove inside piped out through one of the smokestacks, and coal smoke was coming out. Some lady called up the newspaper in Warren and said, 'There's a steamboat coming up the river—and I mean a steamboat! It's got a paddle wheel on it and it's smoking!' Well, they thought she was putting them on, but they sent somebody down to take a look, and then they put it on the radio. They ended up with the roads blocked on both sides of the river all the way to Warren. Really made a grand entrance."

"They had regular steamboat service clear to Warren in the oil days," the captain adds, "and, well, even after that. The last steamboat to Warren was along in 1870 or somewhere about there. That was the only way people could come and go. All the original oil out of the oil fields up there was brought down in boats."

After numerous trips up and down the river, Captain Way sought to have his pilot's license extended up the Allegheny from the Ohio River, where he had been running boats between Pittsburgh and Cincinnati since 1924. When he approached the proper officials about the idea, they told him to draw a map of the river and they would extend his license. They balked, though, when he asked that it be extended to Olean. At the time, the early 1960s, there was a great deal of controversy about the building of Kinzua Dam, so the phrase "to the head of navigation on the Allegheny River" was substituted for "Olean." When Captain Way asked what that meant he was simply told: "Wherever you go." After the dam was finished, that meant Warren.

Allegheny National Forest, Warren County

Ice-covered trees near Tionesta

Venango County

Indian God Rock

Tadpoles at Emlenton

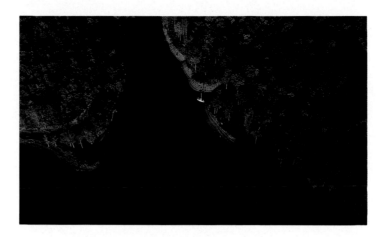

Allegheny Reservoir

"I was up to the ground-breaking for the dam," said the captain. "They ran a special train up from Oil City—fourteen cars—which blocked the whole downtown Oil City when they were loading. We wandered up there to the site, and they had the state police all around there. They thought the Indians might stage a demonstration because they were against the dam. It was going to cover up their happy hunting ground up there."

He laughs. "While they were all watching the bushes, looking for Indians, somebody stole the silver shovel they were going to turn the first sod with. They never did find it. They hollered over the loudspeaker, 'Whoever's got it better put it down, because we're going to get you.' But they never did. That tickled me."

As we talk, a rough portrait of the Allegheny River begins to emerge from Captain Way's stories of riverboats, ice tough enough to travel from Oil City and Brady's Bend to New Orleans, nick-of-time rescues, surprise encounters with famous names, battles over locks and dams and bridges, and a family history that reaches back to the western Pennsylvania of 1797. From my own, mostly book-fueled, memory flash images of glaciers, an unknown people, mysterious petrographs, canoes, David Zeisberger preaching to the Indians, George Washington nearly drowning, British soldiers being burned at the stake, Philip Tome and Chief Cornplanter, canals to Erie, Colonel Edwin Drake, Johnny Appleseed, Simon Girty, John Wilkes Booth, floating brothels, the Johnstown Flood and the Saint Patrick's Day Flood, a curse on Kinzua Dam, Hurricane Agnes, racing sculls, Formula One speedboats, symphony concerts, Seneca bingo, deer, trout, smallmouth bass, walleye, and "God's Country."

"You go up that river, you're on your own," Captain Way tells me, and then adds, "One way to make a lot of friends is to get in trouble with a boat. Everybody will come to your rescue. So I made a lot of friends up and down the Allegheny."

The friends sound fine. The trouble I hope to avoid.

11

2

POINT OF THE FORKS

Even though it's a weekday in early March, Point State Park still holds a surprising portion of the more than a million people who visit it each year. City workers with hands buried deep in trench coats push resolutely back toward the shining towers that now stand where the British once expected the French to lay siege to Fort Pitt. Others on their lunch hour stroll more casually on the grass, munching potato chips and sharing complaints. Joggers mumble greetings to each other as they head for the wall on the water's edge.

Caught in the flow, my friend Art Zielinski and I drift to The Blockhouse nearby and press against the wrought-iron fence guarding it to stare at the plastic-encased

Allegheny National Forest

Point State Park, Pittsburgh

Outline of Fort Duquesne,
Point State Park

sandstone sundial found by somebody digging on the premises. We read from a plaque that The Blockhouse is the oldest building west of the Allegheny Mountains. It is the only one remaining of five redoubts built by Colonel Henry Bouquet in 1764 to protect troops on the walls of Fort Pitt from sniper fire. Probably because we have become so much more effective at killing one another, the pitiful little building, maybe as big as a two-car garage, seems so inadequate as a place to face an attacking enemy that the very idea sends a shiver up my spine.

"One F-14 could come through here and just level this whole place," says Art, echoing the thoughts of countless people touring old battlefields and forts—which may reveal more about human aggression than it is pleasant to consider.

We stop at the stone outline of Fort Duquesne, on the lawn near the center of the park. Though it's said that a poor diet made people of the eighteenth and nineteenth centuries much smaller than today, the size of Fort Duquesne, about 150 feet square, still leaves me shaking my head. The corner bastions, jutting like arrowheads out of the main square, look barely large enough to park a car inside, yet the French once billeted more than a thousand men at the site. We walk part of the outline, stand inside it to gain a better sense of size, and then trace with our eyes the sweep of stones just beyond the fort, which mark the shoreline of 1754. Then, satisfied that we have a proper feel for the setting, we move down the steps and past the empty pool of the fountain to the tip of The Point.

More than one writer has compared The Point in Pittsburgh to the prow of a ship. It is an easy analogy to understand. All it takes is a glance up the concrete walks curving and spreading back toward the Golden Triangle. But I don't think it's very accurate. A ship carries a tremendous amount of weight with it. The people who made Pittsburgh the "Gateway to the West" were gambling to escape the stifling weight of Old World poverty and class, oppression, lost love, and as many other variations and combinations of pain and desire for adventure and riches as there were individuals who made the journey. Standing at The Point, one gets the urge to step out on the water and continue alone, leaving behind the ship of the past for a dream of something new and better. Downriver from The Point lie the Northwest Territory of Ohio and Michigan, the Louisiana Purchase of St. Louis and New Orleans, the goldfields of Colorado, the Spanish

The Point, 1932

15

Territory of Texas, Mexico, and California, vast and fertile plains, mountains where no one had ever trod, the wonders of the Yellowstone country, and whatever people had the courage to make for themselves.

"Well, there's the river," Art says. At The Point there is only "The River," for nobody can say exactly where the currents of the Allegheny and the Monongahela combine to become the Ohio on any given day—at least not since the fall of Pittsburgh's overripe steel mills has cleaned up a Monongahela that once ran as a dark stain of acid-mine drainage, mill waste, and almost every other liquid or semi-liquid pollutant humans have concocted.

"Yes, there it is," I reply, nodding, and then turn to look toward Three Rivers Stadium. "And there's the Allegheny they first came down."

Actually, nobody knows whether the first people to visit The Point came down the Allegheny or down the Monongahela—or up the Ohio. Nobody even knows who the first people to drink the waters of the Allegheny River were. "Tradition has it that there were a people here called the Allegwie for whom the Allegheny is named," explains James Swauger, curator emeritus of anthropology at the Carnegie Museum of Natural History and the man who headed the archeological dig at Fort Pitt back in the early

Confluence of Allegheny and Monongahela rivers

1950s. "We don't know anything about them as a political entity or even as a cultural people. What we have to go on, from the archeological point of view, has no relationship to any known tribe until very late times. In the archeological records, we have them in the Middle Woodland period, or Adena. We have no knowledge of tribes until, at best, the seventeenth century, when we begin to get some inkling that maybe the Iroquois groups went through, and that the Shawnee may have passed through going southeast. The Delaware certainly came over from the east in the eighteenth century. And that's about it. We have no long rendering back into prehistory."

Meadowcroft Rock Shelter, where the region's earliest known inhabitants camped along the Ohio River tributary of Cross Creek in Washington County, dates back more than sixteen thousand years. The inhabitants of the shelter probably could have seen the Allegheny River, because they were so near and would have used the rivers of western Pennsylvania for travel and to go where they could find food. But no one can answer that question for certain. Tools and other artifacts discovered at the site simply are not unique enough to say the people who used the shelter knew the river, according to Swauger. By the 1720s, though, pressure from white settlements in eastern Pennsylvania had forced members of the Shawnee and Delaware tribes to retreat to the Ohio River country.

Historians might expect the record to be better with the coming of the first Europeans, who had beautiful written languages. But it is not. Nobody knows who the first white person was to cast eyes on the Allegheny. In the mid-seventeenth century the French maintained that the famous geographer René-Robert Cavelier de La Salle floated down the river in 1669 on his way from Canada to the Mississippi and the Gulf of Mexico. That claim may be more politics than reality, though—an effort to keep the forks of the Ohio out of British hands. La Salle was a wealthy, vain aristocrat who certainly would have made sure that details of his exploits reached the court in Paris, but no diary or even a letter mentioning the trip has ever been found.

References to other explorers are scattered throughout the history books, but a complete, irrefutable written record of the first Europeans on the Allegheny and at The Point starts with the 1749 expedition of Pierre-Joseph de Céloron de Blainville and his chaplain, Father Joseph Pierre de Bonnecamps, reported in their *Account of the Voyage of the Beautiful River Made in 1749*. However, that is only the earliest reliable written record and does not mean they were the first Europeans to travel the river. Even today a person can go to the most desolate and war-torn areas of the Middle East, Africa, or Asia and find enterprising people selling water pumps, cigarettes, and especially rifles to the unfortunate inhabitants. The same was true in western Pennsylvania. Traders were probably the first white people to use the Allegheny. Father Bonnecamps even mentioned encountering at Kittanning five British traders who had come up the Allegheny from their headquarters at the great Indian village of Logstown on the Ohio near what is now Ambridge. Several miles below Kittanning, he also reported, were a group of British traders living in a "miserable cabin" but with a storehouse filled with pelts.

17

Before Céloron and Bonnecamps, the English cartographer Lewis Evans supposedly explored the region and produced a detailed account of the commerce, particularly in whiskey, between the Indians and British traders who were operating in western Pennsylvania. But some historians doubt that Evans actually saw the things he wrote about, and, like the La Salle story, his account may be more politics than truth—this time an effort by the British to keep the Ohio Country out of the hands of their French rivals. This seems especially likely because all the traders Evans mentioned suspiciously bear Anglo-Saxon surnames: Thomas McKee, John Fraiser, Paul Pierce, Hugh Crawford, Edward Ward, William Trent, and George Croghan. Evans goes so far as to mention the Céloron expedition and urges his countrymen to secure the Ohio for England. He warned that, if the French succeed, "it is not Ohio only must fall under their Dominion, but the country thence southward to the Bay of Mexico." The whole thing sounds like a political move preparing the people for another war.

"We don't really know who first came down here," Jim Swauger says. "We know only about the guys who left written records when they first came down. And, knowing the French as I do, my guess is that traders were hunting up and down the rivers for years. From my point of view, the early records begin with that Céloron expedition, but that doesn't mean there weren't some French people down here twenty years before."

No matter who first tasted the Allegheny River, Captain Way's book makes the Indians' feelings on the subject clear. The captain tells a story about a strange, unknown creature encountered one day by a hunting party. The first such creature arrived with the English settlers at Jamestown in 1607 and, according to Joseph Merrit's *Guide to the Mammals of Pennsylvania*, was quite common throughout Pennsylvania before the late eighteenth century, so the story could be true.

Reacting as people commonly do when confronted by a strange creature, one of the Indians killed it, carried it back to his village, and presented it to an elderly chief. "He squizzed up his eyes, recognized it, and deep furrows of a frown appeared above the wrinkled crow-tracks above his eyes. He made a pronouncement to this effect: 'An animal like this one was found while our venerable grandfathers lived along the Delaware. It was found just before the white man came and took our hunting grounds there. It is an ill omen.' " The mysterious creature was the rat.

On his expedition into western Pennsylvania, Céloron found little of interest in Pittsburgh. Though most histories maintain that he buried a lead plate claiming the land for the king of France at either The Point or Shannopin's Town (an Indian village up the Allegheny along Two Mile Run), his journal makes no mention of such a plate. At Pittsburgh he talks only of stopping at Shannopin's Town—where he found six frightened British traders and ordered them to leave the region.

Four years later another well-documented traveler to the region would take note of

The Point. Major George Washington wrote on November 23, 1753: "I spent some time in viewing the rivers, and the land in the Fork, which I think extremely well situated for a fort." The future first president stayed eight days at The Point on his way up the Allegheny with a warning to the French, who were building forts in northwestern Pennsylvania, that they were trespassing on land claimed by Great Britain. It was an order the French refused to heed. Four months later a small force of Virginians employed by the Ohio Company moved to support British claims by building Fort Prince George, or, as it is sometimes also called, Fort St. George at The Point.

The French response to the British move came five months later, on April 17, 1754, when a fleet of three hundred canoes and sixty bateaux (ribbed and planked flat-bottom boats wider amidship than at the bow and stern) came down the Allegheny from New France (Canada) and disgorged some fourteen hundred soldiers and Indians. Captain Pierre de Contrecoeur, commander of the force, dispatched his engineer, Captain François le Mercier, with two drummers to inform Ensign Edward Ward, the British engineer building Fort Prince George, that he had one hour to surrender. With only about forty men in his force, Ward accepted Contrecoeur's terms, dined with him that evening, and marched off the next day.

No sooner were the Virginians gone than Captain le Mercier dismantled Fort Prince George and began construction of Fort Duquesne, naming it in honor of the Marquis Duquesne, governor-general of New France. The British answered this challenge by sending now Lieutenant-Colonel Washington with a troop of Virginians to attack Fort Duquesne. The French stopped Washington at Fort Necessity in Fayette County, east of Uniontown, and forced him to sign a statement, written in French, confessing to the assassination of Captain Coulon de Jumonville in April 1754. Sensing a diplomatic coup, the French quickly circulated the "confession" among the capitals of Europe, maintaining that it proved the British were the aggressors in North America. The British responded in their typical tenacious fashion by voting 50,000 pounds to pursue a war in America and set the stage for the greatest battle western Pennsylvania has ever witnessed.

The Allegheny River played no direct role in the defeat of General Edward Braddock on July 9, 1755, but it was to the banks of the river that the Indians brought their British captives to celebrate the victory. "I heard a number of scalp halloos, and saw a company of Indians and French coming in," wrote James Smith, describing the scene after the battle in the account of his travels reprinted in John Harpster's *Crossroads: Descriptions of Western Pennsylvania, 1720–1829* (1938).

> I observed they had a great many bloody scalps, grenadiers' caps, British canteens, bayonets, &c. with them. They brought the news that Braddock was defeated. After that, another company came in, which appeared to be one hundred and

chiefly Indians, and it seemed to me that almost every one of this company was carrying scalps; after this came another company with a number of wagon horses and also a great many scalps. Those that were coming in, and those that had arrived, kept a constant firing of small arms, and also the great guns in the fort, which were accompanied with the most hideous shouts and yells from all quarters; so that it appeared to me as if the infernal regions had broken loose.

About sundown I beheld a small party coming in with about a dozen prisoners, stripped naked, with their hands tied behind their backs, and their faces and part of their bodies blacked—these prisoners they burned to death on the banks of the Allegheny river, opposite to the fort. I stood on the fort wall until I beheld them begin to burn one of these men; they had him tied to a stake, and kept touching him with firebrands, red-hot irons, &c., and he screaming in a most doleful manner—the Indians in the mean time yelling like infernal spirits.

The prisoners were actually taken to Smoky Island, which stood in the Allegheny opposite The Point until the flood of 1832 washed it away, so some of the land on which the British prisoners were horribly tortured lies under Pittsburgh's Three Rivers Stadium today.

Three more years would pass before the next British assault against Fort Duquesne on September 14, 1758. It too would end in disaster. An overly ambitious Major James Grant, the same officer who would tell Parliament during the Revolution that he would need only five thousand regular troops to make America an obedient colony once again, attempted to capture the fort with a force sent out to scout the forks and free prisoners. Outflanked by the French and the Indians moving up both rivers, he was captured while sitting on the banks of the Allegheny with his head in his hands, moaning, "My heart is broken. I shall never outlive this day."

Grant was repulsed, but the knowledge that over four thousand more British troops waited at Fort Ligonier to the east in Westmoreland County led the Indians to decide it was time to return to their villages, and Captain François Marchand de Ligneris, the French commander, to decide it was time he and his four hundred troops exercised some discretion and retreat. After setting fire to the wooden Fort Duquesne, de Ligneris sent half his force down the Ohio River to the Illinois country while he and the other half headed up the Allegheny to Fort Machault (Franklin), the nearest French stronghold. The British reached The Point on the evening of November 25, 1758. Two days later a very ill General John Forbes dubbed the land at the forks "Pittsbourgh" in honor of Britain's Secretary of War William Pitt.

Fearing a quick counterattack by the French, Captain Henry Gordon began directing work on a new fort within days after capture of the forks by the British. A month later,

21

Three Rivers Stadium and Golden Triangle

construction had progressed to the point where Colonel Hugh Mercer, who had been left in command by General Forbes, reported that the fort was "capable of some Defense, tho' huddled up in a very hasty manner."

Like Fort Duquesne, the first Fort Pitt was a small affair, holding a log house thirty-nine feet square, curtained by a stockade about one hundred feet long and four bastions, and with the whole surrounded by a ditch. After some debate over the exact site, General John Stanwix ordered construction of a second, much larger fort, and work started on September 3, 1759. This was to be Britain's Gibraltar of the West.

"Most out-of-town visitors are interested in whether the fort still exists," says John Connolly, an exhibit preparer at the Fort Pitt museum. "That's the question they ask most often. Since it doesn't exist, they go and look at the brick wall that's been reconstructed on the original site with the original firebricks that had been excavated. We tell them those bricks and The Blockhouse are original. They like that."

A project to determine the complete outline of Fort Pitt, to salvage bricks from the walls, and to collect all pre-1800 man-made objects took place under the direction of the Carnegie's James Swauger in 1953. The team met with success in locating the perimeters and salvaging the bricks but failed dismally in its search for eighteenth-century artifacts. During the previous 150 years, the area had been ravaged by fire and flood, excavated for basements, churned up by the Industrial Revolution, and then covered with fill, so a large portion of the subsurface of The Point had been removed—and with it the remnants of Great Britain's and France's struggle for North America. Not even one historical specimen was found during the dig.

While the excavation was in progress, pleas to restore the fort arose, but the state balked at the cost. Instead, the fort wall facing downtown Pittsburgh would be rebuilt using the original bricks, and the remainder of the fort would be outlined with flagstones.

"When you stand outside the Fort Pitt museum and walk away from the glass entrance, turn around and look at the doors," says Connolly. "You'll see our roof's outline is a very strange shape. That's because the museum is housed in a reconstruction of the Monongahela bastion." Fort Pitt originally had five bastions—four-sided, pointed fortifications that projected beyond the main walls of the fort—constructed so that the soldiers manning them could trap an enemy attacking the walls in a crossfire. They were named the Monongahela, the Flag, the Grenadier, the Music, and the Ohio. The Music and Ohio bastions faced the Allegheny River. Because of the cost involved, only the Monongahela bastion was reconstructed.

Fort Pitt was such a vast and powerful structure for its time that the French never dared attack it, and the Indians did so only once. That was during Pontiac's Rebellion in the summer of 1763, when the fort was surrounded for ten weeks, but only seven of its inhabitants were killed in the fighting. The siege was finally lifted on August 10, when Colonel Henry Bouquet,

Fort Pitt Museum, Pittsburgh

fresh from his victory over the Indians at Bushy Run, about twenty miles to the east, marched through the gates with drums beating and bagpipes skirling.

The rebellion was curbed but not crushed by the Battle of Bushy Run. The Indians retreated into the old Northwest Territory, where they remained until the spring of 1764—at which time, resupplied with lead and powder by French traders, they once again began venturing forth in raiding parties.

Alarmed by the renewed hostilities, colonial authorities sent Colonel Bouquet, who had returned east after lifting the siege of Fort Pitt, back to Pittsburgh. He arrived at the forks on September 18, 1764, at the head of a mile-long column of British regulars and Pennsylvania volunteers. With him he carried a bold new plan that called for, instead of the traditional strengthening of defenses, a march deep into Indian territory to free prisoners taken over the previous decade and to force the Indians to sue for peace.

For two weeks Bouquet camped at Fort Pitt waiting for a group of 250 Virginia volunteers to join his forces. While there he was forced to deal with a heavy desertion rate—he had lost seven hundred men on the march from Carlisle—first by giving two men convicted of desertion a thousand lashes each, then by ordering two others to face a firing squad. On September 26 all units were marched to the north slope of Grant's Hill, where the Allegheny County courthouse now stands. William Anderson and Francis Steedwell were executed in hopes of making "a deep and lasting impression on the minds of the troops."

Finally, on October 1, Bouquet began ferrying animals, supplies, and fifteen hundred men to a temporary camp across the Allegheny from the fort. The army marched on October 3, proceeding down the Ohio to the Muskingum River, where Bouquet built a fortified camp, conferred with the Indians, and gave them twelve days to return all captives or have their villages destroyed. To ensure compliance, the colonel pushed thirty miles deeper into Indian territory. The Indians responded by releasing 206 captives and promising to deliver more than a hundred others to Fort Pitt the following spring, a promise they kept on May 10, 1765, on the banks of the Allegheny River.

Bouquet's march into the Northwest Territory marked not only the beginning of a decade of peace on the frontier but also the decline of Fort Pitt. Within seven years the fort was ordered abandoned, and on October 12, 1772, the brick and other materials used in its construction sold for 50 pounds New York currency to William Thompson of Cumberland County and Alexander Ross, the supply officer at Fort Pitt.

Although the materials used in the fort were sold, the site itself hung on as a small military installation garrisoned first by Pennsylvanians and then by Virginians, during which time it was renamed Fort Dunmore, after John Murray, Earl of Dunmore, the governor of Virginia. In 1777 the U.S. government took over the site and erected several new buildings. Fort Pitt remained a federal military installation for the next twenty years and then the various buildings were sold at public auction.

Fort Pitt model, Fort Pitt Museum

Golden Triangle, Pittsburgh

3

CITY LIGHTS

When views of Pittsburgh are mentioned, most people picture either the dramatic explosion of the city out of the Fort Pitt Tunnels or the dazzling, eye-devouring vista that lies below Mount Washington. But on the water, in the predawn, there is an equally beautiful view, a view that belongs mainly to river people: towboat crews, fishermen, maybe a few pleasure-boaters, and those with a purpose on the edge of the river at that hour—night security personnel, police officers, the last cleaning crews. Lit with a minimum of electricity and by a sun still below the horizon, the city glows with hues of gold and yellow, and soft pinks, and shiny blues, punctuated by blocks of powerful charcoal and conservative browns indicative of the seriousness with which we treat the

Riverboat *Majestic* at Three Rivers Stadium

business going on inside. And all of it is reflected back in even greater variety and style by the bronze of the water. On a clear, soft morning in late April the feeling is one of quiet warmth and comfort, of belonging. Strange for a major city.

I am still savoring the scene and the feeling when Captain Jim Lyons arrives on board the Gateway Clipper Fleet's *Liberty Belle* toting a briefcase and a uniform sheathed in plastic. We trade introductions and greetings and then, laughing and gossiping with his three-man crew, he heads for the refreshment counter at the bow, where he pours himself a cup of coffee and continues to joke until he notices the time.

"Okay. Come on!" he shouts then. "Let's get goin'. We're goin' up that goddamn Allegheny, and you don't know what's gonna happen!"

Once above deck in the pilothouse, Captain Lyons quickly calls orders to the crew manning the lines and then slides the *Liberty Belle* sideways out into the Monongahela and swings it downriver. Within seconds, we are moving under the Fort Pitt Bridge and then rounding The Point, its fountain empty and ghostly in the new light, and passing Three Rivers Stadium, Roberto Clemente Park, and the skeletal Vietnam Veterans Memorial.

"The Allegheny is a treacherous river?" I ask in response to his earlier remark.

"I wouldn't say it's a treacherous river," he hedges, "but it's not the best river to run 'cause you gotta know where you're at—especially when you get up above Lock Four and Lock Five, where you start running into some bad places."

For thirty-two years Captain Lyons has been avoiding "bad places" on Pittsburgh's rivers. His career began in 1958 with the birth of the Gateway Clipper Fleet, and except

28

Gateway Clipper Fleet riverboat

Fountain at Point State Park, Pittsburgh

for a short period early on when he worked towboats and cut right-of-ways for a gas company, he has been with the Fleet ever since. Today, besides running regular luncheon cruises, dinner cruises, dance cruises, and the like around the city, he also handles all the Fleet's out-of-town trips, like the two-day high school prom charter we are headed for in Kittanning.

"The biggest change that's come to the Allegheny River"—he says when I ask him about the river he has known—"is the Kinzua Dam. You used to be able to go up this river, to Lock Two or any of these other locks, during the summers when we had only a little rain, and see kids out there walking on top of the dam there. There was very little water coming over. But once they put Kinzua Dam in up there you got continuous water, all of the time, and I don't see any kids walking the dams anymore. That's one of the big changes I've seen in the Allegheny River."

A reliable flow under the keel may be the biggest change in the Allegheny witnessed by Captain Lyons since the mid-1960s, but Ted Muller, associate professor of history at the University of Pittsburgh, has found plenty of others.

"For three-quarters of a century at least," he says, "Pittsburgh has looked at its segment of the rivers as not real rivers. The real rivers were out there in the country. That's where the birds and the plants are. These things inside the city are nothing but working cesspools of one kind or another. They were barriers. They were pains in the ass. They divided things. You had to get over them. They created traffic jams. They were polluted. They flooded. They did all kinds of things. They certainly were not to be enjoyed in any way."

Although Pittsburgh owes everything to its rivers, Muller says, the city is ten years behind other urban areas in the nation when it comes to use of the Allegheny and her sister rivers as recreational and environmental amenities. The Three Rivers Regatta, when it was launched in 1978 and brought the first Formula One speedboat race ever run in the United States to the Allegheny River in 1982, was a big step toward changing the public's perception of the rivers, but it is only a single event. Muller believes Pittsburgh and other towns along the lower Allegheny still have not integrated themselves with the river the way Baltimore has with the Chesapeake Bay, and Minneapolis has with its lakes. Both those cities have rimmed their waterfronts with benches, walkways, open spaces, shops, marinas, and other public facilities. Baltimore has even opened its stadium to the bay. Pittsburgh has Point State Park, but, it was never designed as a people park, according to Muller. The individuals who work and visit the Golden Triangle turned it into a people park.

To illustrate, Muller points out that most buildings in Pittsburgh face away from the river. The David L. Lawrence Convention Center, built in the 1970s, presents a windowless wall to the Allegheny only a few yards away from the river. Three Rivers Stadium, though named after the waters it overlooks, is separated from the river by a parking lot and closed off from it by walls. And then there is the simple lack of easy public access to the banks of the river.

"I live not far from Saint Margaret's Hospital in Aspinwall, straight way from the river," Muller notes. "I'm less than a half mile from the river's edge and don't even consider going to the water's edge in the evening after dinner because industry has made it inaccessible. Access does not exist. The town is completely separated from it."

River of industry, Pittsburgh

"That's the legacy of the industrial river," he continues. "We are only now coming to realize there is something more than just commercial development value here. This is an environment that is a good way, potentially, to raise the quality of our life."

Though Pittsburgh and other towns along the lower Allegheny are now generally shut off from the river, things were not always that way. Throughout much of the nineteenth century the Allegheny, as well as the much more heavily industrialized Monongahela and Ohio rivers, played an important role in the daily lives of city residents.

"Beginning around the 1850s and 1860s in Pittsburgh, we began to lose contact with the rivers as industry really started to take over the riverfronts and the first railroads came in," Muller explains. "And the canal going down the north shore of the Allegheny did the same sort of thing. But up until that point, and certainly in the areas above Pittsburgh, rivers were part of our lives. They were enjoyed in many ways—people walked along them, swam in them, rowed on them, fished in them."

One way Pittsburgh still uses the Allegheny as it did in the nineteenth century is as a source of water. Since 1828, when the city built its first pumping station, the Allegheny has fought Pittsburgh's fires, quenched its thirst, and washed its dirty laundry. Only the equipment and methods have changed.

During the nineteenth century, according to Stanley States, laboratory supervisor at the city's water treatment plant in Aspinwall, the emphasis on water at first was quantity, not quality. This became especially true after a third of Pittsburgh was destroyed by fire in 1845. The city built a series of reservoirs, and then tanks, for river water, but water from the river was pumped directly into houses without any treatment whatsoever—typical of the times. The result was a city that by 1900 was recording more than five thousand cases of typhoid fever a year.

City officials finally agreed that something had to be done to cut down on the cases of water-borne diseases, so in 1905 construction began on the Ross Pumping Station at the eight-mile marker, to avoid the discharges of industry closer to the city. Water was pumped from the river to sedimentation basins and then to a huge field of slow sand filters located where the Waterworks Mall and Saint Margaret's Hospital now stand. From the sand filters, the water was then pumped into homes, and the typhoid rate dropped to a few hundred cases a year. Chlorine was added to the process in 1910, and the emphasis has been on more and more treatment ever since.

"It's a very good raw water source for drinking water treatment," says States. "It's a very controlled river. It's one of the more controlled rivers in the United States, with nine flood-control dams and reservoirs, and eight locks and dams."

"Chemically, it's not that much of a natural river," he continues. "It's pretty well artificially controlled. It's a soup concocted by the Corps of Engineers. They have a

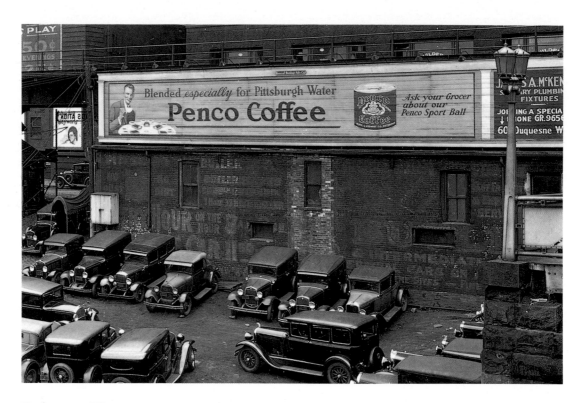

Hard water, 1932

number of chemical-monitoring stations along the river, plus they're in touch on a daily basis with a number of similar water laboratories along the river. We give them data on the chemical composition of the river each day. They pick up data from their monitoring stations, and one of the purposes of the flood-control dams and reservoirs system is to maintain water quality—and they do that by opening and closing the flood-control dams."

Historically, one of the greatest threats to the water quality of the lower river has been coal mining, particularly along the Kiskiminetas River, which flows out of the old coalfields of Westmoreland and Armstrong counties. It makes for one of the worst problems faced daily by the people who provide Pittsburgh with drinking water.

"One day a couple of years ago, I came up here and something caught my eye on the lower tip of that island," Captain Lyons says as we plow past the H. J. Heinz plant. "It was a white dress. So I picked up the glasses and looked over there, and I'll be damned if it wasn't a man and a woman—Indians—with two teenage boys, in there fishing. They had traveled down the river, right into Pittsburgh. I was really surprised."

Turn-of-the-century swimmers at Sixth Street Bridge, Pittsburgh

Herr's Island—now called Washington's Landing—where Captain Lyons had spotted the family, was for almost a century the site of an enormous stockyard used for livestock being transported on the Pennsylvania Railroad's main line between Chicago and New York. At other times it held lumber yards and oil storage tanks. Now, as headquarters for rowing in Pittsburgh, it is another step back toward the days when the river was more a part of people's lives.

No rowers are in sight as we approach the island, but on most spring and fall mornings sharp-eyed dawn commuters can catch a glimpse of racing shells and crews training on the river between the island and The Point.

"When we race against each other—whether we win, whether we lose—all of us who are involved in rowing really feel we're trying to add something to the city," says Harry Printz, former president of the Carnegie Mellon University Rowing Club. "It's a lot of fun to row, and we'd like to involve as many people as possible."

Rowing was a big-time sport in Pittsburgh from the 1860s through the 1880s, reports history professor John J. Kudlik in a Summer 1989 *Pittsburgh History* magazine article entitled "You Couldn't Keep an Iron Man Down: Rowing in Nineteenth-Century

Pittsburgh." More than ten thousand spectators often crowded the riverbanks to watch crews from across the nation compete for purses as large as $15,000. Splendid boat clubs, with reception rooms and apartments fitted with hanging oil lamps, bronze pendants, Brussels carpets, desks, chairs, and bookcases—the equal of the finest men's clubs—lined the river and produced heroes of national renown, such as Eph Morris.

An iron-puddler's helper in a rolling mill, Morris lived in Allegheny City (now the city's North Side) and competed as a member of the Clipper Club during the 1870s, when he shocked the stodgy rowing worlds of Boston and Toronto by beating their top rowers. After he defeated Boston's best in one regatta, his competitors approached him and asked, "Who are you?"

"Oh, I'm just a scrub-rower from Pittsburgh, that's all," he replied. When asked why his name had never appeared in any of the racing gazettes, he said: "Well, we don't do our rowing on paper in Pittsburgh."

The advance of industry, along with betting scandals and allegations of race-fixing, put an end to rowing in the city by the start of the Gay Nineties. It would not return for almost one hundred years—until 1984, when the Three Rivers Rowing Association was formed by a group of enthusiasts and began promoting the sport at local high schools and colleges. Schools with rowing clubs include Carnegie Mellon, the University of Pittsburgh, Duquesne University, Chatham College, the Ellis School, Central Catholic High School, North Allegheny High School, and Fox Chapel High School. In addition, there are private clubs and two annual races, the National Scholastic Rowing Championship and the Head of the Ohio, which some people believe is destined to become one of the best rowing races in the nation, possibly in the same class as Boston's Head of the Charles and Philadelphia's Head of the Schuylkill.

Upstream of the Heinz complex come the scrap yards, vacant lots, and dead manufacturing plants of postindustrial America. The Allegheny never packed the industrial punch of the Monongahela—which was once the second most heavily industrialized river in the world, second only to Germany's Ruhr River—but it has held some important industries. Andrew Carnegie, who grew up in Allegheny City, began his career on the river in the 1860s when he opened the Union Mills across from Herr's Island. Earlier, Fort Pitt Foundry was the only establishment willing to make fifteen-inch guns for the Union Army during the Civil War, and it is believed to have made 80 percent of the big guns used by Union forces in that conflict. The sound of cannons being tested by firing into the side of Coal Hill (known as Mount Washington today) was familiar to Pittsburghers of the mid-nineteenth century.

"These tests were attended by government ordnance experts, and the company officials always served plenty of whiskey with lunch," wrote Leland D. Baldwin in his *Pittsburgh: The Story of a City, 1750–1865.* "Upon one occasion, when the regular

37

Rowing, Herr's Island, Pittsburgh

Allegheny Arsenal, 19th century

company representatives had to be away, they sent a temperance man to the proving ground and he served buttermilk with the lunch. Several cannon were rejected that day, it is said.''

But the most famous early industry along Pittsburgh's portion of the river was the Allegheny Arsenal in the city's Lawrenceville section, which was named after Captain James Lawrence, the War of 1812 hero who died uttering the immortal words ''Don't give up the ship!''

Located at the site of Shannopin's Town, the Indian village visited by both Céloron and Washington, the arsenal was built in 1814 on land owned by William Foster (father of one of America's most famous songwriters, Stephen Foster) and designed by Benjamin Latrobe, who also served as architect for the south wing of the U.S. Capitol. It hosted the Marquis de Lafayette on his triumphant tour of the nation in 1825 and, during the

Civil War, played an important role in the manufacture of munitions for the Union side, spewing out some thirty thousand bullets a day. On September 17, 1862, the arsenal saw one of the largest explosions to that point in the nation's history. The laboratory blew up, killing seventy-five boys and girls who were working nearby.

While the Allegheny Arsenal is best known for its efforts in winning the Civil War, only a few years after its construction it was the launching site of an expedition that might have had an even greater effect on the settlement of the West than the Lewis and Clark Expedition. Secretary of War John C. Calhoun, worried about recent British actions in Canada, conceived the "Yellowstone Expedition" both to protect the nation's northwestern frontier and to extend the fur trade. Major Stephen Long led the expedition, which left Pittsburgh on May 5, 1819, on the *Western Engineer*.

The first recorded steamboat built on the Allegheny River, the *Western Engineer* was launched at the arsenal on March 28, 1819. The vessel weighed thirty tons and was designed to draw only about two feet of water, to help it negotiate the shallow rivers of the West. To avoid obstacles, the wheel was in the stern instead of the sides, and the pilothouse was bulletproof, to protect the crew from the hostile tribes of the Great Plains.

But the most unusual aspect of the boat was its bow ornament. "The bow of this vessel exhibits the form of a huge serpent," reported the *Niles Weekly Register*. "Black and scaly, rising out of the water from under the boat, his head as high as the deck, [this "serpent"] darted forward, his mouth open, vomiting smoke, and apparently carrying the boat on his back." The vessel would so awe the Indians, the writer concluded, that "it would require a daring savage to approach and accost her."

The boat left the arsenal on May 3 under a twenty-two-gun salute. "Great numbers of spectators lined the banks of the river," wrote the expedition's journalist, Major Thomas Biddle, "and their acclamations were occasionally noticed by the discharge by ordnance on board the boat."

From the Allegheny the two-year-long expedition continued down the Ohio and up the Mississippi to explore the Missouri and Platte rivers. The expedition was the first to ascend the Platte through what is now Nebraska and eventually went as far west as the present site of Denver, where it turned south to see the mountain Zebulon Pike had sighted during his expedition in 1806. Pike had written, "No human being could have ascended to its pinnacle." Expedition member Captain Edwin James, however, did not believe anything of the sort, and with two other men (whose names are not mentioned in the account) he set out to conquer the mountain. They were the first men to climb Pike's Peak. Major Long actually named the mountain "James Peak," so maps included with the history of the expedition bear that name.

The accomplishments of the Yellowstone Expedition received mixed reviews when they were published in 1823. The scientific work, which added sixty animals and several hundred insects and plants to the list of flora and fauna of the United States, was well received—as were the sketches and drawings, the first views of the West. However, critics believed the expedition should have accomplished much more, and they faulted Major Long for not finding the source of the Platte and for mistakenly identifying the Red River. But the greatest effect on the nation was the expedition's labeling of the Great Plains as the "Great American Desert." That simple phrase, historians now believe, blocked settlement of the region until after the Civil War.

The federal government gave the Allegheny Arsenal to the city in 1909, and the city sold the installations at auction in 1926. A half-dozen buildings of the complex survived into the 1950s, but only three presently remain: the powder magazine buried in the hillside of Arsenal Park, a building at the Clack Health Center, and the old machine shop next to the Washington Crossing Bridge.

Across the river from the Allegheny Arsenal, above Etna—a town whose once flaming, smoking industry inspired residents to name it after the volcano in Italy—lies Sharpsburg, where an even more significant and longer-lasting event than the Yellowstone Expedition got its start. Though less heralded, it was an event that altered the life of the nation every bit as much as Henry Ford's assembly line and Thomas Edison's light bulb, and it continues to touch far, far more lives around the world than either of those two inventions.

Through most of the nineteenth century, the diet of the average American consisted of such monotonous fare as bread; dried, salted, or smoked meat, like bacon or salt pork; and a few root vegetables, such as potatoes. Fresh vegetables were available only in season and only locally, and some of them—lettuce, for instance—were actually considered unmanly. By mid-winter, after the jars of preserved vegetables were exhausted, pickles were the closest thing to a salad.

Into this bland, tasteless pot stepped twenty-five-year-old Henry J. Heinz and his still-younger partner L. C. Noble in 1869. Heinz had actually begun his career as a food merchant more than a decade earlier, when as a boy of twelve he started peddling excess produce from his family's garden in Sharpsburg. His specialty became horseradish, whose pungent, sharp taste was eagerly sought both as a way to make dull food more palatable and as a medicine.

At the time, horseradish was sold in bottles that were dark green, a color chosen only because it obscured the contents. Since the contents were not clearly visible, bottlers routinely increased their profits by adding leaves, wood fiber, and grated turnip pieces to the horseradish. Heinz ended this scam by using only the whitest and best-quality roots and bottling his product in clear glass. Consumers responded by making the company one of the nation's leading producers of condiments by 1875.

Despite the appearance of prosperity, however, the Heinz company was heavily in debt. When a banking panic struck in that same year of 1875, Heinz and Noble found themselves scrambling to meet payrolls, secure loans, and pay suppliers. When their

Original Heinz plant being moved from Sharpsburg to Pittsburgh

efforts failed in December, they were forced to declare bankruptcy. After three grocers who had been friends refused to trust Heinz, he wrote in his diary: "Bankruptcy changes a man's nature. I feel as though every person had lost confidence in me and I am therefore reserved." Within four years, though, thanks to help from his family, Heinz was back on track.

Throughout the 1880s the Heinz Company continued to grow and expand its line from the original horseradish and then tomato ketchup, sauerkraut, pickles, vinegar, and red and green pepper sauce to cider vinegar, apple butter, chili sauce, mincemeat, mustard, tomato soup, olives, and the first-ever sweet pickles and baked beans, among other items. In 1886 Heinz landed a large contract with a major English food producer, and then in 1888 he purchased the twenty-two acres on the Allegheny River where the H. J. Heinz Company still stands.

George Washington and Christopher Gist crossing the Allegheny

4

HIGH STEEL
AND
SLACKWATER

"We had expected to have found the River frozen, but it was not, only about 50 Yards from each Shore: The Ice I suppose had broken up above, for it was driving in vast Quantities. There was no Way for getting over but on a Raft: Which we set about, with but one poor Hatchet, and finished just after Sun-setting. This was a whole Day's Work: We next got it launched, and went on Board of it: The set-off. But before we were Half Way over, we were jammed in the Ice, in such a Manner that we expected every Moment our Raft to sink, and ourselves to perish. I put-out my setting Pole to try to stop the Raft, that the Ice might pass by; when the Rapidity of the Stream threw it with so much Violence against the Pole, that it jirked me out into ten Feet Water: But I fortunately

saved myself by catching hold of one of the Raft Logs. Notwithstanding all our Efforts we could not get the Raft to either Shore; but were obliged, as we were near an Island, to quit our Raft and make to it.''

If it had not been for the presence of Wainwright's Island—or Garrison's Island, as it was also called—the Allegheny River might have claimed the life of George Washington and sent him into history as an ordinary Virginia planter and minor military officer instead of the ''Father of His Country.'' On December 30, 1753, on his way back to Virginia after informing the French at Fort LeBoeuf in northwestern Pennsylvania that they were trespassing on British land, Washington nearly drowned in the river, and his guide Christopher Gist nearly froze. The pair put in around the Sharpsburg Bridge, spent a terrible night on Wainwright's Island as the river froze over, and then the next day walked across the river, coming ashore near where the Washington Crossing Bridge and Lock 2 now stand.

The Allegheny River holds eight sets of locks and dams, stretching from Lock 2 at the 6.7-mile marker in the Highland Park section of Pittsburgh upstream to Lock 9 at the 62.2-mile marker a few miles below the town of East Brady. The system makes the river navigable to commercial traffic for a distance of 72 miles, but a boat as large as the *Liberty Belle* can reach only the 69.9-mile marker, at which point the low span of the East Brady Bridge puts an end to its progress.

Low bridges on the Allegheny were once a source of great controversy and even a rebellion of sorts. From before the Civil War until after World War I, the bridges limited

Fishing near the Seventh
Street Bridge, Pittsburgh

Lock 2, Pittsburgh

River salvage

steamboat service, hampered commerce, and stunted industrial development on the river. "We see on the Allegheny River the only steel boat-building establishment in Pittsburgh," Major William Sibert of the Corps of Engineers would tell the Engineers Society of Western Pennsylvania in 1902, "launching the hulls of its boats and floating them under the Union Bridge, and then building the upper part on the unobstructed river below. We see manufacturing plants on the Allegheny hauling their products by wagon

48

to the Monongahela or Ohio River for shipment to lower Mississippi River points, paying half as much for this hauling as it costs to transport the same material two thousand miles to its market."

According to Leland Johnson in *The Headwaters District: A History of the Pittsburgh District U.S. Army Corps of Engineers,* the Allegheny bridge controversy began in 1849 when river people in Wheeling, West Virginia, responded to complaints by Pittsburgh industrialists and government officials that a suspension bridge over the Ohio River at Wheeling needed to be raised. The Wheeling people handed Congress a petition demanding that the bridges over the Allegheny be raised higher too: "Aqueducts and three bridges have been erected across the Allegheny supported by innumerable piers so constructed that boats and rafts cannot be navigated amongst them without danger to life and property, and these bridges and aqueducts are so low that steamboats cannot pass under them in any stage of the river, while at high flood the water reaches the woodwork of these structures, which completely shuts off every description of navigation, even descending rafts and keels."

For fifty years Wheeling and Pittsburgh traded insults, and the problem of low bridges on the Allegheny was ignored until the Allegheny River Boatmen's Association, founded in 1897, finally took the case to the U.S. Army Corps of Engineers in 1900. Led by Captain William B. Rodgers, the association pushed both for the raising of the bridges over the Allegheny and for slackwater navigation to Oil City.

Major Sibert responded to a series of meetings on the problem in 1904 by recommending that the federal government order the raising of the bridges. The Union Bridge Company, owners of the span nearest the mouth of the river, answered with a court fight, the best result of which may have been that it kept lawyers off Pittsburgh's rivers for years. After counsel for the company complained that the hearings were a mockery because they allowed testimony from "the ignorant class of people that generally composes the body of rivermen in the United States," the river people let the lawyers know what they thought of them and what might happen if they were seen along the river.

Legal and political maneuvering would continue the controversy into the twentieth century, until Secretary of War Newton Baker and Corps Commander Lansing Beach arrived on the scene. After a secret tour of the Allegheny in 1917, Baker returned to Washington and issued an order to raise the bridges, stating, "I have confident feeling that the future of the city of Pittsburgh is of tremendous importance to the Nation, that by the order which I am now making I am freeing a great natural highway to contribute to the further expansion and growth of the city, and freeing the Allegheny River from obstructions which have until now prevented it being used, as it ought to be used, as a valuable part of the harbor of the city and a valuable artery of trade."

Hoping a change in administration would rescind the order, opponents of raising the bridges delayed action until after the next election. The order was not rescinded, however, and in a speech to city fathers and business leaders at the Duquesne Club on January 25, 1923, General Beach delivered the following ultimatum:

> The War Department has been long suffering—very patient—but this is at an end. It has become tired of asking the County Commissioners: "What have you done?" Now we will tell them what to do.
>
> The plans for the Seventh and Ninth street bridges must be in the hands of my department by March 1. If they have complied, they will be instructed on or before April 1 what further the department will require. If they fail to comply with this order, legal proceedings will be immediately begun to enforce them. This will mean a fine of $20,000 per month, which Allegheny County can shoulder until they have been carried out.

When General Beach returned to inspect the bridges in July, work was already under way to raise them higher. By 1929 all the bridges had been moved, rebuilt, or modified to clear an adequate channel for navigation.

Why the Allegheny River's lock and dam system begins with Lock 2 instead of Lock 1 is one of life's little mysteries for most residents of western Pennsylvania. Actually, there was once a Lock 1. It stood near Herr's Island—where its ruins are still visible on the banks around the Heinz complex—from 1902 until the opening of the Emsworth Lock and Dam on the Ohio River in 1938 created slackwater to Pittsburgh and made Lock 1 redundant.

The idea of building locks and dams on the Allegheny goes back to 1828, when state engineer Edward F. Gay proposed construction of eighteen locks and dams stretching from the mouth of the Kiskiminetas River upstream to French Creek. Nine years later the Corps surveyed the Allegheny from Franklin to the mouth of Potato Creek in McKean County and concluded: "If the Allegheny River is improved from Olean to Pittsburgh, a water communication is opened for a distance of more than 12,000 miles, extending into the heart of one of the most fertile regions of the globe, on which Europe might comfortably rest all her nations."

The Pennsylvania legislature in 1845 urged state congressmen to support federal improvement of the Allegheny to Olean, but questions of constitutionality—whether the river was the responsibility of the state or the federal government—and political factionalism kept any action from taking place for four decades. Finally, in 1878, a temporary sandbag wing dam was built at Garrison Ripple on the upper end of Herr's Island to permit boat access to the Allegheny Arsenal during low periods, and then, in 1880, plans for a lock and dam at Herr's Island were endorsed.

Opposition by property owners who feared they would lose access to the river and

Sixteenth Street Bridge, Pittsburgh

by the city of Pittsburgh, whose officials feared a dam would increase flood crests and ice problems, kept construction on Lock 1 from starting until 1893. Numerous floods and a tornado interrupted work on the project and kept it from being completed until 1902, when it became the second concrete river lock built in the United States.

Authorized to extend the river's lock and dam system to West Monterey at mile point 80.5, the Corps of Engineers had Lock 2 at Aspinwall and Lock 3 at Springdale under way by 1903. The present facility at Highland Park replaced the original Lock 2, in 1934, and the one at Cheswick replaced the Springdale lock that same year. Lock 4 at Natrona and Lock 5 at Freeport went into operation in 1927; Lock 6 at Clinton in 1928; Lock 7 at Kittanning in 1930; Lock 8 at Templeton in 1931; and Lock 9 at Rimerton in 1938.

Captain Way and his companion Fred Morrison are credited with taking the first boat "through" Lock 9 during their 1938 trip downriver from Olean, a moment he records in *The Allegheny*:

> Below East Brady we watched with some enthusiasm for Dam Number 9 and slackwater. We slipped down along the huge timber dike at Red Bank, sounding about eight inches of water the full of its length, and Bud pointed—There it was. A mass of concrete construction clear across the river. Progress had climbed up, or else we had floated down to progress. "Below there it will be easy sailing," we concluded. But too soon.
>
> A figure of a man was silhouetted high on a concrete pier. His arms were waving. His voice came floating up the river to us. "Go back—don't come down any further!" In sheer perplexity we let the current carry us along.
>
> "River's blocked—you can't get through!"
>
> For a fact, the York Construction Company had built piers across the Allegheny in such a way that navigation for even a canoe was impossible; that dam was a barrier of no mean proportions. We had come down from dreamland to present-day reality. Behind, far, far behind, were the deer and bears and Cornplanter Indians. Bleak hillsides now; no more pine and oak. And a modern dam planted square across the river. Sixty-two miles to Pittsburgh.
>
> We eased to shore alongside some piling at the dam. "Have to go back where you came from," said the workman. "Can't go through a spillway that'd wreck your boat."
>
> Then a busy little fellow in hip boots appeared. "What's going on here?" he asked. Our story was soon related.
>
> "Well, now, that's something—and we'll discover some way to get you across," said this fellow, who turned out to be E. W. Wolfe, superintendent of construction. "Unload your boat and we'll take you around on a truck."
>
> Twenty minutes later we were in the river again on the lower side of the lock. "First boat through Number Nine," commented Mr. Wolfe, "even if we did have to hitchhike you through."

The extension of a lock system to Olean probably was never much more than a dream. The creation of slackwater to Oil City, however, remained a hope until the completion of Lock 9 showed that use did not warrant a continuation of the system. Commercial traffic on the river reached 5.7 million tons in some years but averaged around 4 million tons during the thirty years after Lock 9 was completed and now runs between 2 and 3 million tons. From the perspective of the Corps of Engineers, the heavy traffic that would have justified extension of the system never materialized. From the perspective of local river people, though, the Corps was "almost stupid" to expect the growth of commercial navigation on a half-finished highway.

Hydro dam construction

Even though hopes of extending the Allegheny's lock and dam system beyond East Brady died before World War II, controversy of another sort continues to surround the facilities—this time in the form of hydroelectric generating stations.

"In the Pittsburgh area we have a power glut," notes Tom Proch, an aquatic biologist with the Pennsylvania Department of Environmental Resources who has been involved with the issue. "Since the mills closed, and everything else, we have more power in the Pittsburgh area than we could ever use. In fact, the power companies are frantically trying to sell excess power out of this area or out of state."

"In particular," he continues, "what gripes me is that the hydro facilities at the wholesale cost of electricity in Pittsburgh were economically unfeasible, even with tax credits. Unfortunately, New York City—immense, powerful hungry New York City, with its inactive Seabrook plant that it won't start up for safety reasons—is now buying the power at a premium."

Hydroelectric generating facilities on the Allegheny have their roots in the oil crisis of the early 1970s. When the oil-producing nations of the Middle East placed an embargo on exports, one way the United States responded was to launch a search for alternative energy sources. Under the authority of the Federal Energy Regulatory Commission (FERC), permits for hydroelectric stations were issued during the 1970s, and tax breaks—sometimes even tax credits—were given for development of such facilities, including on seven of the Allegheny's eight locks. A license was denied for Lock 7 in Kittanning because a wildlife refuge on an island near the dam would have had to be removed to allow operation of a generating plant.

Permit-holders on the Allegheny range from Allegheny County to the City of Pittsburgh to the Borough of Cheswick to private business groups. Plans call for power generated by each station to run from 8 to 30 megawatts. Using 1 kilowatt as power for one home, Fred Hoerster, an engineer with the Corps, estimates that 8 megawatts is

Chemical spill cleanup

enough to service eight thousand homes. By comparison, the hydroelectric station at Kinzua Dam on the upper Allegheny is capable of generating 422 megawatts, or enough power to light, microwave, VCR, computer, or whatever else, 422,000 homes.

Reservations Proch and some others have about altering the Allegheny to sell power outside western Pennsylvania aside, hydroelectric facilities at the locks and dams also create environmental problems like oxygen depletion and fish kills.

"Normally, on locks and dams on the Allegheny River water is constantly spilling over the dams, which aerates the water and gives us a good dissolved-oxygen content," Hoerster explains. "As I understand it, when water is diverted through a power plant, through the turbines, it takes away some of that oxygen because it's coming through a small area and under pressure."

There are ways to pump oxygen into a plant's discharge, according to Hoerster, and permits issued by the FERC require that the water carry a minimum amount of oxygen and that operators maintain a minimum flow over the dams. However, at least on Lock 6 at Clinton, which was licensed before the environmental impact study that set the discharge minimums, problems have cropped up with the pool level.

"The habitat of Pool Six is different from a lot on the river in that it is composed of lots of wetlands," Tom Proch says. "Wetlands, of course, are important in flood protection, but most sportsmen know that's where the ducks are nesting, that's where most of your fish are spawning or spending some critical stage of their life. Wetlands, especially along major river systems, are something we have to protect. Yet, unfortunately, the hydropower dam facility at Dam Six is de-watering the pool by about two feet."

"Water drives a wetland," he adds. "Without water, a wetland does not exist. We don't know what's going to happen when you lose two feet of head to the hydrology of the wetlands."

Since fish are naturally attracted to turbulent water, where they expect to find abundant oxygen and food, the possibilities of large fish kills at the hydroelectric plants are the other great concern of such state agencies as the Department of Environmental Resources and the Fish Commission. This is particularly true because nearly every place a turbine has been installed fish have been sucked into the system and killed, and because the Allegheny is not as productive a fishery as the Monongahela and Ohio rivers, according to Proch. It produces quality fish, but its low alkalinity tends to keep numbers down.

Then too, unlike oil or chemical spills that do their damage and pass on, hydroplants are a permanent source of fish mortality. Numerous engineering studies have sought means to keep fish away from plant intakes, but solutions are rare. Screens and bars are unlikely choices because of river debris. Also, screens and bars prevent only the larger fish from entering the turbine, and survival of a species in a waterway, or at least its prosperity, depends more on the smaller fish, the next generation. With only one in a

Marina ruin, Harmar

million muskie fry surviving into full adulthood, two thousand more being killed in a hydro facility could make the difference between a river of trophy fish and one of only the rare muskie.

"Pennsylvania has paid the price for the Industrial Revolution in this country," Proch says angrily. "Coal. Steel. The mining that went with the coal, the scars we're left with. We've reaped very little reward for that. We have a mess of miners with black lung. We have a scarred landscape. And now they want to fill up these old scars with everybody else's garbage, and they're going to take our streams and screw them up to sell power to the rich and hungry again. It starts getting to me. It should have ended yesterday if everybody had been paying attention."

Lock 2 looms gray and dull pink ahead, a deserted hulk in the still-sunless early morning light, the only sense of life coming from the broad yellow and black stripes painted on the chamber ends as a caution to boaters. A few hundred yards below the lock, Captain Lyons takes the radio to alert the lock crew to the *Liberty Belle*'s approach.

"WTR 5330, the *Liberty Belle*, to Two Allegheny. *Liberty Belle* to Two Allegheny."

As we wait for a response, the captain grabs a clipboard loaded with forms and quickly fills out a report listing the vessel's name, number, length, width, depth, and other statistics required by the Corps of Engineers. When a response still has not come, he picks up the radio and repeats his call. Then he repeats it again, and a few more times, until, just as it begins to seem as if the lock is as dead as some of the industry we have passed, a harassed-sounding voice finally breaks through the silence.

"Yeah, Captain."

"Yeah, we're down below here."

"Starboard side?"

"Roger. All the time," the captain answers.

"Okay," replies the voice. The lock bubbles and then the gate slowly swings open.

The Allegheny is far more a pleasure-boating river than a commercial river. Lock 2 handles more pleasure craft than any other lock in the nation—upward of ten thousand boats a year carrying well over thirty-five thousand passengers. The preponderance of recreational traffic over commercial tonnage allows only Locks 2, 3, and 4 to operate on a year-round twenty-four-hour schedule. Locks 5 and 6 operate on a varying schedule from April through November, while Locks 7, 8, and 9 are open only during the summer months. It has been years since the last commercial tow passed through Lock 8 or Lock 9. Extensive campaigns waged during the first half of the twentieth century to extend the river's slackwater all the way to Oil City have dwindled to occasional complaints.

"Two things make the Allegheny River unique in terms of the three rivers we service out of the Pittsburgh District Corps of Engineers," says John Reed, public relations officer for the Corps. "One is that recreational use far outweighs commercial use in terms of primary consideration for the entire river. Second is that all dams on that river are what we call fixed-crest dams, which means that we probably have a higher percentage of boating accidents on that river than on the others."

A fixed-crest dam is essentially a slab of concrete laid across the river. It is difficult to see from a low-riding pleasure boat because it has no superstructure and is normally covered with flowing water. Boats that approach too close on the upstream side can be caught in the strong current and drawn over the dam. Boats that cruise too close to the face can be pulled into the wall by powerful reverse currents. The Corps has marked all dams with signs and buoys, but still people ignore the warnings or miss them or don't know what to do and are swept to their deaths on the Allegheny almost every year.

"A lot of the people we talk to come from Lake Erie and Lake Ontario," says Bob Klemz, a mechanic at Lock 2. "They'd been boating for years on the lakes, but that's different. If there is a storm on the lake, right away they dock their boat. Four hours later the storm is over, they take their boat back out and there is no problem. Well, they come down here thinking they can do the same thing," he continues. "But they don't realize you've got high water now, and you've got a stronger current. And it might stay up for five or six days. People don't realize the river is a lot different from a lake."

The Fourth of July and the Three Rivers Regatta in August are the two busiest periods for recreational boating on the Allegheny. Fireworks, Formula One races, and other events in Pittsburgh attract boaters from all along the river for days. Then, as soon as the fireworks or race ends, everybody heads home at once. Lock 2 has had as many as four hundred boats waiting to lock through after the two celebrations.

"They'll come up in droves," Klemz says, "and what happens is they all jam up and everybody wants to be first."

The lock workers have found too that most people, even experienced boaters, are not aware that vessels must be locked through in a certain order. "U.S. mail has first preference over any boat on any waterway in the United States," explains Klemz. "Then the Corps of Engineers has second preference over any boat. They're over any other government boat, the Coast Guard, anything else. Then your passenger boats have preference one way unless the boat is on a schedule. If they're on a schedule, they have preference both ways. Last come personal pleasure boats—and a lot of the recreational boaters don't know that and get upset and want to know why they can't lock through."

"For instance," adds Lockmaster Larry Scafuri, "you have a towboat with a triple, which takes about an hour and a half to lock. In the summertime, as you're locking him up you get a line of motorboats on the upper end waiting, and a line of motorboats on the lower end. Then all of a sudden comes the *Gateway Party Liner*. You've just locked this towboat, which took an hour and a half, and you got maybe thirty motorboats waiting the whole time. But you've got to lock this passenger boat first. What do you think those motorboats are going to do? They get upset. It's pure hell down here."

Working river

Pleasure boats, Oakmont

5

CROWD PLEASER

Coming out of the yawning steel gates of Lock 2, Captain Lyons swings the *Liberty Belle* for mid-channel. On one side of the river, beyond the floodplain, runs Route 28, overshadowed by towering, drill-scarred rock. On the other side stands a sheer, untouched wall of trees under which rush hour traffic is beginning to build along Allegheny River Boulevard. As I look back at the lock, it is easy to understand why almost every year boaters who ignore or are too drunk to read the warning signs or to understand the buoys strung in front of the dam are swept away. Even from the pilothouse, twenty feet or so above the river, the smooth flow over the crest of the dam gives the water the appearance of an unbroken silver-green sheet. The image of four hundred boats lined up downstream waiting to lock through, however, remains difficult to comprehend, until up ahead the marinas and boat docks start coming into view.

Back in 1955 the idea of pleasure boating on the lower Allegheny bordered on insanity. The river was essentially a sewer for the industries along its banks and almost totally inaccessible. Then, as part of Renaissance I, the rebuilding of Pittsburgh then under way, the Allegheny County Sanitary Authority was formed to look at ways to clean up the city's filthy rivers. It was as treasurer of the authority that John Connelly began to consider the recreational potential of the river and decided that an excursion boat would be a tremendous way to show off reborn Pittsburgh.

The following year, Connelly was in Chicago visiting Jack Goessling, his nephew by marriage. At the time, Goessling was piloting an excursion boat on Lake Michigan and the Chicago River. When his uncle suggested running a similar boat in Pittsburgh, Goessling liked the idea and agreed to keep his eyes open for a boat. Eventually, he came across the *Bridget Ann,* a sixty-five-foot, one-hundred-passenger fishing boat moored on Lake Erie. The two men bought the boat, and then Goessling set about piloting it to Detroit, across Lake St. Clair to Lake Huron, through the Straits of Mackinac and along the new Illinois River to the Mississippi, then downstream to the Ohio and up to Pittsburgh.

Goessling's run took almost a full month of day-and-night travel, but the *Bridget Ann* made her entrance at Pittsburgh on May 16, 1958, in time for the city's bicentennial. It was rechristened *The Gateway Clipper*—after a mad dash to the State Store for a bottle of champagne—and the next day took members of the YMCA on the first chartered cruise of Pittsburgh's three rivers.

Some twenty-five thousand sightseers rode *The Gateway Clipper* during its first season, and the boat soon came to be known as the city's official sightseeing ship. Connelly and Goessling added two more boats to the fleet in 1959, and the fleet has continued to grow. It now has six boats capable of handling twenty-five hundred passengers a day. As far as anyone knows, that makes it the largest inland water fleet of its kind in the nation.

The approaching line of docks, one dock reaching almost a third of the way out into the river, reveals exactly how recreational use of the Allegheny has grown since the start of the Gateway Clipper Fleet and adds some reality to the picture of four hundred boats lined up at Lock 2. Pennsylvania annually registers some 275,000 boats, according to Tom Qualters, supervisor of the Fish Commission's Southwest Region, and almost 27,000 of those boats reside in Allegheny County, making it run nip and tuck with Dade County, Florida (otherwise known as Miami) for the county with the most registered boaters in the nation. And of all the pools on Pittsburgh's three rivers, none is as busy as Pool 2.

The *River Belle*

"We've often said we're probably going to have to make the first two pools on the Allegheny River 'Slow No Wake,' " Qualters says, "because the docks keep coming out into the river and anybody throwing any kind of wake damages boats at the docks. Every year we have boats being thrown up on docks, and people getting thrown off docks, just from wake problems."

With only three boats to patrol all of Pittsburgh's rivers, the Fish Commission—chief enforcement agency for Pennsylvania's boating laws—has been simply overwhelmed by numbers. Qualters estimates that the three officers in charge of Allegheny County write about one hundred citations each, annually and yet barely scratch the surface where violations are concerned. On busy weekends, even with aid from the Pittsburgh Police Department's River Rescue Unit and the Coast Guard, he says waterways patrolmen are limited mostly to being traffic cops trying to keep the peace.

The size as well as the number of pleasure boats on the Allegheny also has greatly increased. From mostly small twenty-four-foot boats with a single 25-horsepower motor, and the occasional houseboat, that were using the river when Qualters started patroling it in the 1960s, cigarette boats, high-speed racing hulls, and cabin cruisers capable of traveling on open seas are common today.

By far the majority of boating law violations center on safety equipment and drinking, Qualters says. A shortage of lifesaving devices and lack of a fire extinguisher are two of the most common equipment violations. Drinking has been so bad that in the mid-1980s the state legislature enacted Pennsylvania's first boating-under-the-influence law. Fines of $250 to $5,000 have helped the situation somewhat but at the same time have contributed to enforcement problems because officers now must find a way to move and dock a boat whose operator has been arrested, and then transport that operator to a hospital for a blood test.

"Drinking is probably worse on water than it is on land," Qualters adds, "because you're out on the water with the constant rocking of the boat, constant moving, the sun, the glare, constantly beating on you. Some studies say you can be affected a lot more on water than on land. And you have a collusion on water: you can't get out and walk away. Plus there are no white lines on the water."

A fishing boat speeds by, giving rise to questions about boaters. Captain Lyons points toward the bow and the maybe fifteen-foot-long ramp suspended above it. "You have motorboats stop in front of you, run around the bow. I've had them go underneath that ramp out there."

"You're kidding!" I say, and then ask, "How much distance does this boat need to stop?"

"It depends on what type of water you're in," he explains, "whether you're traveling upstream or downstream, if the current's running, if the current's not. I'd say, from full ahead, if you're coming downstream on any kind of water you're gonna need about three or four hundred feet to get her stopped. And that all depends on how many passengers

Summer evening

you have on the boat too, and how much fuel you have, how much water you have.''

A towboat pushing barges may need as much as a quarter of a mile to stop. And when the barges are empty and floating high, a blind spot is created at the head of the tow, making the situation doubly dangerous to boats running too close.

"They sneak up alongside you," Lyons tells me. "You don't even hear them. Or else they come straight across to see how close they can get. Your heart jumps up into your throat. It just scares the hell out of you."

But not every story about boating on the crowded lower Allegheny involves drinking or recklessness. "Underneath the Sixty-Second Street Bridge," the captain says, smiling, "there were a lot of women on board. I heard everybody clapping and raising all kinds of hell. I looked down, and there comes this guy on water skis. He's bare-ass naked! They were laughing and screaming. He went up and turned around and came down again. You oughta heard them. I thought the boat was gonna roll over!"

Pittsburgh builder Joe Ross had just finished a large plan for condominiums about a half-mile away and was looking for another project to tackle when he was shown a piece of property along the Allegheny in O'Hara Township. In his mind the location begged to be the site of a marina. That was back in the mid-1980s. On the property today stands the

Sylvan Canoe Club candlelight parade

Edith Baum

Fox Chapel Yacht Club, the most elegant marina on the entire river.

"We have two hundred and fifty boaters and three hundred and fifty nonboaters," Ross says of the membership. "We have two hundred and ninety-two slips. We have wide, stable steel docks, each equipped with adequate power, telephone, cable T.V., water. We have a two-hundred-seat restaurant, and we can accommodate twelve hundred people in our banquet facility. We have a waiting list a mile long for boat slips. And—not to blow our own horn—we have the finest facility for a large area."

Seated on a bar stool, surrounded by polished oak and brass, and looking over the linen-shrouded tables of the restaurant, out the glass wall facing the river, and then beyond the deck and bandstand to the well-kept boats at the docks and finally to the peaceful wooded bluff beyond, I can't dispute Ross's claim, or imagine the industry and ruins of industry I had passed on the way to the club. I think how nice it would be to return some Friday evening during the summer with a full wallet, dine on roast duckling or maybe scampi agliata or some other dish from the club's menu, and then stroll out to the deck with a drink and settle down to enjoy the jazz artists who perform at the club's weekly concert.

"That's the wonderful thing about it. It's a very democratic membership," Ross says when asked about the type of people who belong to the club. "You can have a brain surgeon who's berthing next to a gas station owner. There are no snobs here. Boaters share a mystique. These people become very close-knit. They meet off-season as well. The socioeconomic range is from top to bottom. From a fellow who has a seventeen-foot boat with his wife and two kids, to the seventy-foot cruiser that has three bedrooms and two baths in it." He adds, "We have twenty people who live year-round here."

It holds the most boaters and the best docking facility of any stretch of the Allegheny River, but Pool 2 also is home to a relic from the days of straw boaters and white summer flannels known as the Sylvan Canoe Club. Founded by a group of engineers from the Westinghouse Corporation in 1904, the Sylvan Club in Verona is one of the oldest boating clubs on the river and the last strictly canoe club in Pool 2. The Duquesne Canoe Club, next door, founded in 1895, is the oldest boat club on the river, but its membership now consists mostly of powerboaters. The Sylvan Club has stayed with canoes, plus a few kayaks, sailboards, rowboats, and one small sailboat equipped with a motor that some of the members hope will disappear.

"Right now we are the only honest-to-goodness canoe club," says member Edith Baum. "Way back in the twenties, though, there were canoes everywhere and canoe clubs everywhere."

Edith Baum's own attachment to the Allegheny began in the early 1930s when she met her late husband, Alexander Baum, a member of the old Pittsburgh Aquatic Club and an organizer of the area's first Polar Bear Club, whose members became famous for their New Year's Day dips in the Allegheny. Alexander Baum had grown up on Pittsburgh's North Side and began canoeing the river as a child before World War I. In 1936, shortly after they married, he took Edith—who at age seventy-eight still swims regularly in the Allegheny, though she had to give up water-skiing at seventy-five when a series of strokes ruined her balance—on a two-week canoe trip from Olean to Pittsburgh.

"They were just building Lock Nine when we were coming through," she recalls. "My mother's cousin was an engineer on the job. So we had made up our minds that we were going to stop at the construction site to see him. But we got down there and the engineers were all shouting 'Stay away! Don't go!' My husband and I sized up the situation. They had the coffer dams in and all the water rushing through the one side. So he tied me with a rope to the canoe and said, 'Now do what I tell you to do, when I tell you to do it.' Once we got in that chute we went sailing. We went about a quarter of a mile down before we stopped."

"The next lock, number eight, when we pulled in"—she laughs—"the lockmaster looked over and saw me. He said, 'You mean to tell me you brought that girl through number nine!' He said the week before there had been seven canoes come through. Five of them overturned and were smashed. But my husband was an expert. He knew what he was doing."

Lee Kilgore, who at age eighty-five is the oldest member of the club, remembers when the Saint Patrick's Day Flood in 1936 poured out of the Kiskiminetas River and swept down the Allegheny to inundate towns from Freeport to Pittsburgh. A small brass plaque above the fireplace on the second floor of the Sylvan clubhouse marks exactly how high the water got.

"That was quite a thing, that flood," he says. "I can remember driving down toward Pittsburgh and going past some railroad yards down along the river. And here was a guy sitting on top a locomotive with the water lapping right up to the smokestack. He was sitting there waiting for somebody to rescue him. Houses were going down the river and trees. It was quite a sight."

Designed as a canoe club with a large, high basement to store canoes and little else that could be damaged by the high water that poured down the river every spring, the Sylvan Club survived the Saint Patrick's Day Flood in fairly good shape. The Duquesne Club next door was not so fortunate, however. It floated away.

Efforts by club members to assist the people of Verona also proved less than successful. "Two of the boys went to the clubhouse before it reached its crest," Kilgore recalls. "The water around the club was already more than knee-deep, and they took their canoes and went down the street to help people get out of their houses. But canoes don't make very good rescue boats, and, as I recall, they tipped over."

Surviving as the last canoe club on the lower Allegheny has not been easy. For a period during the 1970s, membership was so far below the seventy-person limit set by the club's charter that admitting powerboaters was considered. Then, gradually, efforts to enroll new members, including women, succeeded. In fact, the full admittance of women, who for most of Sylvan's history played only a secondary role, worked so well that Virginia McCune and Jean Rodman were each elected commodore. The membership's old attitude toward women—and its continuing feelings on liquor, which always has been forbidden on the premises—are captured in the club song:

The Song of the Sylvan Canoe Club
(Sung to the tune of ''Rum by Gum'')

We're coming, we're coming, our brave little band.
On the right side of temperance we do take our stand.
We don't chew tobacco, because we think
That the people who use it are likely to drink!

(Chorus)
Away, away with rum by gum, rum by gum, rum by gum,
Away, away with rum by gum.
The song of the Sylvan Canoe Club.

Since 1904 Sylvan's been a man's club
'Else why would the ladies prepare all the grub?
All of the members would turn into wrecks
If we ever admitted the opposite sex!

We never eat fruit cake because it has rum,
And one little bite turns a man to a bum.
Oh—can you imagine a sorrier sight
Than a man eating fruit cake until he gets tight!

Whenever we dine, we flip up our pie,
Hoping we catch it, but NOT in our eye.
Oh—can you imagine a sorrier sight
Than a pie on the ceiling that wasn't flipped right!

We never eat cookies, because they have yeast,
And one little bite turns a man to a beast!
Oh—can you imagine a sadder disgrace
Than a man in the gutter with crumbs on his face!

We never go bare-chested on the front lawn,
'Cause all the young ladies would swoon at the brawn.
Oh—what would Bill Ritinger have to say
If he ever saw Hoecker's hairy-chested display!

69

"Do you see a lot of wildlife along the river?" I ask Captain Lyons when a white heron or egret of some sort sails across the river up ahead.

"You'll see quite a bit," he answers, and then mentions deer swimming, beaver, belted kingfishers, and Canada geese sitting on bridge piers. "In fact," he adds, "some Canada geese stay here all year long now."

In spite of being the busiest section of river in Pennsylvania, Pool 2 still has an incredible amount of wildlife and natural wonders. And few people know both those worlds better than Patrick McShea, a member of the education department of the Carnegie Museum of Natural History, whose boyhood home in Penn Hills gave him almost the same view of the Allegheny River that early twentieth-century Pittsburgh artist John Kane captured in his painting *Through Coleman Hollow.* McShea has been exploring Pool 2 for twenty-five years.

"You've got great horned owls, at least one pair of pileated woodpeckers, quite a few warblers, scarlet tanagers, orioles, grosbeaks, towhees—and lots of other things are almost certainly nesting, because you see them all through the summer," McShea says. "There also must be wood ducks nesting somewhere close, either on the banks or on the islands themselves, because we've seen female wood ducks with young in July and June."

McShea, like Lyons, has encountered deer, beaver, raccoons, woodchucks, red foxes, squirrels, skunks, and other mammals common to Pennsylvania—creatures many people would not expect to find only a few miles above the Golden Triangle. He has also come across black snakes, milk snakes, garter snakes, ringneck snakes, spiny soft-shelled turtles, and several species of clams.

But perhaps the most interesting, and certainly most spectacular, wildlife on the lower river are migrating waterfowl. Pool 2 is a natural stopping spot for ducks and geese on their way south from Canada and the Great Lakes to the Chesapeake Bay. It also is used as a winter territory for a small collection of waterfowl. Goldeneyes and hooded mergansers are two ducks that spend the entire winter on the river, McShea has determined, and they are often joined for a time by common mergansers, red-breasted mergansers, scaup, ring-necked ducks, and grebes of several kinds, as well as by great blue herons, green herons, loons, and ospreys. He says some people have even seen bald eagles around Pool 2—incredible as it sounds.

"Tundra swans, often mistakenly called snow geese, are the other surprise, but they wouldn't be something you could predict in a particular year," McShea says. "If they run into a storm between Lake Erie and the Chesapeake, they'll often come down on the lower Allegheny in the hundreds, but they're usually on the river for only a few hours, until the storm clears. When they do show up, in early November, it is often spectacular."

The swans land at night and continue their journey in the morning, though, so it's usually only commuters on their way to work along roads bordering the river who see them. McShea estimates he has encountered the phenomenon about eight times. "I've

River lovers, Tarentum

seen groups as small as fifteen and as large as two thousand."

Although much of Pool 2 is lined by towns, marinas, factories, warehouses, and other development or ruins, portions of its terrain are as spectacular as its wildlife. Islands, shifting deltas, and wooded bluffs also fill the stretch and, in the spring, can be a riot of wildflowers, especially trillium.

"The trillum display along the one access road—because you are down below it and looking up at terrace after terrace after terrace of trillium—it's kind of a hanging garden effect, and it's much showier than the trillium trail over in Fox Chapel that brings in thousands of tourists," McShea says. "It's more than just more trillium. It's a different display. It's slump blocks. The whole hill has had lots of landslides—some of them probably hundreds of years ago—so it's terraced and there is trillium on every terrace."

71

Migrating waterfowl

Tundra swans, spiny soft-shelled turtles, green herons, wood ducks, and beavers are all testimony to the health of the lower Allegheny, but in a peripheral way. The lives of every one of those creatures is dependent on a clean river environment, and they are often killed by oil spills or other pollution episodes. But in a way these creatures are also separated from the water, because they are capable of walking or flying away from it.

72

Fish, on the other hand, have nowhere else to go. In the public mind the health of a waterway is most frequently associated with the size and diversity of its fish population. And in that respect the lower Allegheny of today is very different from what it was for most of the twentieth century.

Perched atop an old stool in the shed guarding the entrance to the parking lot on Pittsburgh's North Side, where he works part-time in retirement, John Gilbert recalls when he first started fishing the river around Highland Park as a youngster, before World War II. The mounts, photographs, and drawings of trophy muskie, northern pike, walleye, and largemouth and smallmouth bass covering the walls of the shed, and a calendar marked with the dates of fishing tournaments, attest both to his skill and to the great passion of his life.

"When I was twelve or thirteen we couldn't catch anything but catfish and carp," Gilbert says. "Later, about the mid-fifties, when I was working for the state highway department surveying along Route 28, I didn't realize there were any game fish around. For them, I used to go up to Kennerdell or Rockland or Oil City, Tionesta, and Tidioute because that was where it was clean enough to hold game fish. But one day I was working along Route 28 down in O'Hara Township, surveying, and I happened to walk over and look down at the river and see large fish swimming in shallow water and minnows skipping along the surface. So I crawled down the bank and snuck up real quiet and got behind a willow tree and watched them. They were largemouth bass, about ten to fifteen inches long, herding the minnows into the shore. I couldn't wait to get home and get my fishing rod. That night I must have caught fifty bass there without moving."

From that day forward, Gilbert began fishing the lower river regularly, and many times with spectacular results. During one season in the early 1960s he even took three legal muskies in the area around Lock 2. Photographs in his album include a 21¾-inch smallmouth, a beautifully marked and colored 38-inch northern pike, and a 25-inch walleye.

But large fish are nothing unusual for the Allegheny. The river, and the Allegheny Reservoir, has given up six Pennsylvania state record fish—only one less than Lake Erie. Among them are the channel catfish, 35 pounds; the flathead catfish, 43 pounds, 9 ounces; the northern pike, 33 pounds, 8 ounces; the sauger, 3 pounds, 15 ounces; the sucker, 10 pounds, 12 ounces; and the walleye, 17 pounds, 9 ounces.

"The Allegheny is unique in being a really top-notch piece of water from a fisheries standpoint," notes Rick Lorson, area fisheries manager for the Fish Commission's Southwest Region. He says the gravel shoals found in the river make excellent spawning grounds and that improved water quality has brought about an increase in the numbers of fish and species both, while an abundance of forage fish, such as gizzard shad and shiner minnows, provides a plentiful food supply for growing larger fish.

Although the increase in the lower river's game fish populations remains wonderful news, the Allegheny's proximity to millions of people has given rise to problems with fishing pressure and overcrowding. For more than twenty-five years after he spotted those bass herding minnows into shore, Gilbert shared the river mainly with a few retirees and young boys content to sit on the bank and wait for a carp or a catfish to stumble across their bait. Sport fishermen in boats were a rarity until the late 1970s, when a newspaper article alerted anglers to the fine walleye fishing available around Pittsburgh.

"We were going in there all through the winter and all summer long," Gilbert recalls. "We'd go out there and catch walleye after walleye, and nobody knew about it. Then one day we went down on a weekend in January and couldn't even find a place to park. All these fishermen had read an article in the Sunday paper and come down."

That Sunday, cars pulling boats and racing to get on the river actually caused a traffic jam at Turnpike Exit 5 in Harmarville. Within a few years, the resulting heavy pressure through the spring spawning season nearly decimated the walleye fishery, until the Fish Commission moved to close the season during that critical period.

"I've really gotten excited since I've had an opportunity to get closer in touch with the Allegheny River," says Lorson. "It's amazing to see how water quality has improved all up and down the river—and how the fishing has improved along with it. Now we have something people are able to utilize, are able to fish, and the PCB chlordane content on it is in pretty good shape right now for all species."

"It's a river that provides a lot of opportunities from a fishing standpoint," Lorson continues. "Except for the muskies, which we stock, it's pretty much sustaining itself. What we have to do is continue to watch for problems from angler overexploitation— and whether we have to come in there and protect it in one way or another, whether it be smallmouth, walleye, sauger—whatever. That is something we have to keep tabs on."

Fish and Boat Commission electroshocking

6

RIVER
OF
MIGHTY DREAMS

Several years ago a group of fifth- and sixth-grade students were polled on their greatest concerns in life. A news story reported that their lists included all the things adults usually worry about—the economy, a good job, nuclear war—but none of those was at the top. The number-one worry, by a good margin, concerned the environment. One student explained, "In the end, the environment is all we have."

I remember that story as the *Liberty Belle* pushes upriver past the silent power plant, the oil tanks, and other stands of industry at Acmetonia and Cheswick, and as the Allegheny starts to bend round Springdale, the birthplace of Rachel Carson, one of *Life* magazine's hundred most influential people of the twentieth century—that and my

The river above Kittanning

failure a couple of years ago to turn up a single copy of *Silent Spring* or any of Carson's other works in five different bookstores. Even before its arrival in stores in October 1962, *Silent Spring* had, as the *New York Times* put it, "aroused the nation like no other since *Uncle Tom's Cabin*," yet the only copy I was able to find—an old, yellowed one—was in my local library.

Lock 3, Cheswick

Rachel Carson

"It's a great mistake that people think she was against the use of all pesticides," says Evelyn Hirtle, a director of the Rachel Carson Homestead Association. "She was only against their indiscriminate use. She wanted more informed use and cautious use—when everything else has failed."

The house at 613 Marion Avenue, where Rachel Carson was born on May 27, 1907, is a long, white wood-frame affair. Additions have made it about twice the size of the four rooms the author knew when she was a child. The growth of Springdale and the hard times that plagued the Carson family have reduced the home's original sixty-five acres to a single plot of about an acre. The barn and other outbuildings disappeared decades ago. Only the variety of native plants the Homestead Association allows to flourish on the grounds conveys anything of what the property must have been like when Carson was a child. The rest is pure suburbia, edged lawns, and trimmed shrubs.

"Rachel was really quiet," Hirtle notes. "Everything we hear is that she was very quiet and shy."

The words "shy," "quiet," "gentle," and "feminine" frequently crop up in stories about Rachel Carson. They are not the words one would associate with a person who once incurred the wrath of multinational corporations and gained the attention of both President John Kennedy and Congress, and who is generally credited with launching the

Tiger swallowtail

Black swallowtail

modern environmental movement. Yet the mystery those words convey about her may explain why she continues to have an effect on people so many years after her death on April 14, 1964.

The best-known photographs of Rachel Carson add to the mystique by revealing little of the fire that burned inside. Neatly dressed in conservative suits, she looks like everybody's aunt. But if Rachel Carson had not lived, or not loved nature so dearly, and not warned the world of the dangers of DDT, many more people might be dying of cancer today, and hundreds of species of wildlife and plants might be nearing extinction even faster, making the world immeasurably poorer by unrestricted use of pesticides and herbicides.

"At school you don't get to know the shy people very well," Hirtle says. "It's the ones who are more boisterous or mischievous that you get to know. And here's a girl who didn't get anybody's attention. She communicated through her writing and came up with lasting ideas."

Nothing in Carson's childhood high on a hill above the Allegheny gave any indication of what lay ahead. She was born the youngest of three children of Robert and Maria Carson. Her brother, Robert, and sister, Marian, were eight and seven years older, respectively, and perhaps because of the age differences she grew up much closer to her mother than to either her brother or her sister. And it was from her mother that she acquired a love of nature during long walks through the family's fields and along the river.

"It was sort of a miracle that she thought so far into the future," Hirtle says. "When other people were not aware of what was happening, Rachel picked up on it. You wonder what childhood experiences led up to that."

"There is a tremendous lesson here," she adds. "You don't have to take exotic vacations to enjoy nature. People talk about going to the ocean or the beach or the mountains, but even walking in the woods or keeping your yard so you can see a variety of organisms can let you enjoy nature."

As a student at School Street School in Springdale, Carson showed the first signs of literary talent when, at the age of ten, she had a story entitled "A Battle in the Clouds" published in the *Saint Nicholas Children's Magazine*. She later went to Parnassus High School, across the Allegheny near New Kensington, where as a "good but quiet student" she earned an academic scholarship to attend the Pennsylvania College for Women (now Chatham College) in 1925.

Originally an English major, Carson switched to biology after coming under the influence of Mary Skinker, an unusual woman for those days in that she chose to forgo marriage for a career in science. At the time, Carson could never have imagined how her decision to major in biology would aid her in later life. It saved her, though, when the nation's chemical companies attacked her, after *Silent Spring* was published, as an "idealist" and a "hysterical" woman without a proper background in science. *Life* magazine countered those attacks when it published a photograph showing Carson at her microscope and pointed out that she was the first woman to work as a scientist for the U.S. Fish and Wildlife Service.

"She's a heroine in science," Hirtle adds. "There's Marie Curie and Rachel—that's it. Overwhelmingly, scientists are men. Rachel is a good example for the women's movement. Nobody has picked up on that very much."

When she was twenty-two years old, Rachel Carson left Springdale and the Allegheny Valley forever to do graduate work in genetics and teach undergraduate biology at Johns Hopkins University in Baltimore. The arrival of the Great Depression soon after forced her family to sell what was left of their farm and move in with her. During the depression she supported both her parents and, after her sister died, her children.

The house on Marion Avenue is now owned by the Borough of Springdale and maintained by the Rachel Carson Homestead Association as a tribute to a "quiet" and "shy" woman who touched the lives of every person on earth.

Industry stands on the banks of the Allegheny in the shadow of Pittsburgh's sparkling skyline, but it really grows in intensity as the river approaches New Kensington. Scarred banks and heavy barge traffic are its calling cards and stir an interesting contrast. As Springdale gave birth to one of the greatest environmentalists ever, New Kensington,

82

New Kensington

Creighton, and Natrona were the cradle of three of the greatest American industrial innovations of the nineteenth century.

Aluminum is the most common metal in the earth's crust. It occurs everywhere, but always in some form of chemical compound. From the time aluminum was first isolated by the German chemist Friedrich Wöhler in 1827, people had dreamed and experimented with practical ways to produce the metal, among them Charles Hall.

A descendant of an English family that settled in Massachusetts in 1652, Charles Martin Hall was born in Thompson, Ohio, on December 6, 1863. Soon after, his parents—the Rev. Herman Hall and Sophronia Brooks Hall—moved the family to Oberlin, Ohio, where the young Hall found his life's calling in an old chemistry book and then, when he enrolled in Oberlin College, fell under the influence of the chemist F. F. Jewett. It was Jewett who told Hall, "If anybody should invent a process by which aluminum could be made on a commercial scale, not only would he be a benefactor to the world but he would also be able to lay up for himself a great fortune." Hall's reply was, "I am going for that metal."

Even before Charles Hall was born it was well known that aluminum could be electrolyzed from fused cryolite, but the process was too expensive to be economically practical. Then Hall began to think that aluminum oxide dissolved in metaled cryolite might be electrolyzed. Using an old clay crucible lined with carbon, a plumber's torch, and carbon electrodes charged by a battery, he built his first electric furnace and made his first globules of the metal in his parents' woodshed in 1885.

Though the process proved successful, Hall, like most inventors, soon discovered the difference between creating something in a laboratory and producing it commercially. Two groups of financial backers declined to invest in the process until, in 1888, the Mellons and other Pittsburgh investors formed the Pittsburgh Reduction Company and helped the inventor erect a small experimental plant on Smallman Street in the city.

Seeking room for a commercially viable large plant—before Hall developed his process the small amount of aluminum available was viewed as a semi-precious metal and used mainly in jewelry—the company moved its operations to New Kensington in 1891. Two years later the Pittsburgh Reduction Company began rolling sheet aluminum, cutting the price of the metal from $8 a pound when Hall was working in his parents' woodshed to just 93 cents a pound. In 1895 the yacht *Defender* was fitted with aluminum sides and deck beams made by the company and won the Americas Cup for the United States.

Once described as "perhaps taking life too seriously," Hall died on December 27, 1914, never having married. Alcoa (Aluminum Company of America), as the Pittsburgh Reduction Company was later renamed, moved its reduction operations from New Kensington to Niagara Falls, Tennessee, and Canada, places where, early in the twentieth century, it could obtain cheaper electricity. Finishing operations remained in New Kensington until after World War II. Alcoa's involvement in the area now involves mainly research.

Creighton, just above New Kensington, grew up around a tavern erected there in 1792. But it gained its real fame almost a century later, when in 1883 the directors of the new Pittsburgh Plate Glass Company (PPG), seeing the coal mines on both sides of the river as an unlimited source of fuel to fire the company's furnaces, built a huge glassworks in the town.

Although glassmaking is an ancient art going back far into biblical times, it resisted automation and mass production before the center for the industry shifted to Pittsburgh, and especially until PPG built its plant at Creighton. It was in the Pittsburgh area that glass was first fired by coal and then by natural gas and many of the critical steps toward mechanization were worked out. For a time, all the machines that produced Coca-Cola bottles were made in the area. At its peak, PPG's Creighton facility included fifty buildings and employed some six thousand workers, who made the company the world's first successful producer of plate glass and the center for the manufacture of safety glass for automobiles. The mines that once drew PPG to the Allegheny Valley have dwindled to a single mine, the Newfield Mine downriver in Oakmont. The old brick mills with their high-peaked roofs, designed to dissipate the intense heat created by the glassmaking process, have been leveled and replaced with a modern plant of steel sheeting.

In Natrona, above Creighton, salt-well driller Thomas Kier and his son, Samuel, were bottling and selling "Kier's Petroleum or Rock Oil" a full decade before Colonel Edwin L. Drake struck oil with his famous Titusville well in 1859 on the Allegheny tributary of Oil Creek.

Salt was an extremely important commodity in early America. It was used to preserve meat and make dull or even spoiled food palatable. Records from Fort Pitt reveal that, in times of scarcity, salt could buy meat when money could not. In some locations west of the Allegheny Mountains, farmers were glad to trade twenty bushels of wheat for one bushel of salt.

Barges

At first, almost all the salt used in western Pennsylvania was shipped over the mountains from Philadelphia and other cities in the east. Transportation costs made the price of a bushel in the 1790s about $8. The price was cut to about $4 a bushel in 1796, when General James O'Hara, on a visit to Niagara, found salt could be brought to Pittsburgh cheaper down the Allegheny River from the Onondaga Salt Works in Syracuse, New York, than from the cities of the East Coast.

As quartermaster general of the army, O'Hara obtained a contract to supply the garrison at Oswego on Lake Ontario with provisions shipped up the Allegheny River in keelboats from Pittsburgh. Part of the contract reserved for O'Hara the barrels in which the provisions were packed. He then had two vessels built—one for use on Lake Ontario, the other for use on Lake Erie—and the road from Erie to French Creek improved.

Once everything was in place O'Hara sent his barrels to the saltworks, where they were packed and then transported by wagon to Lake Ontario. There they were loaded on his boat, taken to Niagara Falls, and then carried by wagon around the Falls to Lake Erie, where they were placed on O'Hara's second vessel and carried to Erie. At the city of Erie the barrels were once again loaded onto wagons and then taken to the headwaters of French Creek and finally to the Allegheny.

Although O'Hara's operation made salt more readily available in Pittsburgh and cut the price of a bushel in half, the great distance involved caused endless problems with storage and transportation. Then the War of 1812 brought a halt to all shipments from the Onondaga Salt Works, and the search for another supply intensified.

About the same time O'Hara was developing his trade route, a salt well was discovered on the banks of the Conemaugh River near Saltsburg. News of the discovery quickly spread, and by November 1798 William Johnston was operating a small saltworks in the vicinity. Then, in July 1812, Johnston tried and failed to drill a salt well in the location. Discouraged, he gave up on the idea until the following year, when the war pushed the price of salt sky-high. With one eye on the tremendous profits to be made, he forced an auger through more than two hundred feet of rock near where the Conemaugh River and Loyalhanna Creek flow together to form the Kiskiminetas River, and when he removed the bit from the hole he was rewarded with a stream of saltwater spouting eight feet into the air. In the decades following Johnston's success, salt wells sprung up all along the Allegheny and the Kiskiminetas.

It was as a salt-well driller that Thomas Kier struck oil in Natrona (a name derived from the Greek word for "salt") in 1849 and began marketing it as a medicinal oil and lubricant. By 1853 Kier was refining his oil for sale as an illuminant, within a year he was pumping oil out of wells four hundred feet deep, and by 1860 he was exporting petroleum to England.

It was a bottle of "Kier's Petroleum or Rock Oil," with its picture of a well spewing oil, that inspired Colonel Drake to try drilling for "black gold" in much larger amounts at Titusville.

87

Tarentum

Riverview Park, Tarentum

Tarentum, between Creighton and Natrona, is the first industrial town along the Allegheny that has avoided turning its back on the river. Instead of factories, warehouses, and other industrial concerns, which line much of the lower river, Tarentum offers a beautiful green park and a re-creation of Orr's Blockhouse, where early settlers sought safety from Indian raids.

Around Natrona the stream of industry that has followed the river from Pittsburgh breaks up into high wooded bluffs, expensive homes with manicured lawns, and flock after flock of geese. As the end of the industrial river—ahead lie only patches of industry, at towns like Freeport and Ford City—Captain Lyons explains, it seems somehow proper that the river between Natrona and Edgecliff was the location of the last ferryboat to work the Allegheny.

It was probably not long after the first white traders made their way to the river that enterprising individuals established ferry services to carry people and goods from one side of the river to the other. Leland Johnson's history of the Pittsburgh District of the Army Corps of Engineers reports that the dugout canoes used by the Native

Tarentum Point

Americans were sometimes split in half by settlers, pinned together with a crossbeam, and then covered with planking to ferry passengers, produce, and trade goods on the river. By the end of the Revolution such craft had evolved into the flatboat and become a fairly common sight.

For years Lawrence Reedy had ridden old Sammy Ross's ferry across the river from his home in Edgecliff to the Allegheny Ludlum Steel Company plant in Natrona. Without it, he and his neighbors who worked in the mill would have had a twenty-five-mile-long drive down Route 56 into New Kensington and then across the New Kensington Bridge and up Creighton Road to the plant. With it, they had a commute of six hundred feet.

"When old Sammy died," the eighty-year-old Reedy recalls, "some young fellow—I don't recall his name, but he was pretty heavyset, must have weighed near about two hundred and fifty pounds, maybe three hundred—started ferrying the workers. That was back in forty-six or forty-eight. He ferried for about a year."

The young man's career ended unexpectedly when he was caught stealing scrap metal out of the railroad cars Allegheny Ludlum used to park along the river where the

Water-skier

90

ferry landed. "The bulls caught him, and they took him and paroled him to his uncle out in Ohio, and there wasn't nobody to run the ferry," Reedy says.

Less than thrilled about the prospects of driving twenty-five miles to work every day, and sensing a business opportunity, Reedy told his son he thought they should take over the ferry. Then he drove to Pittsburgh to see a boat builder he had heard about under the 16th Street Bridge and had the man build a rowboat for him. He brought the boat back to Edgecliff and began rowing people back and forth to their jobs at the mill for twenty-five cents round-trip.

Rowing across a river as unpredictable as the Allegheny in those days, before all the flood-control projects were built, was often akin to hard labor. "Well, we don't put up with hard labor," Reedy says, "so, I said, we gotta get a motor and put it on the back of the boat." After the ferry brought in a little money, he also purchased Sammy's old shed for fifty dollars and fixed up landing spots on both sides of the river.

Business continued to be good into the early 1950s, when Reedy decided he needed something bigger than a rowboat to serve his customers. After testing the design on the Chesapeake Bay, he purchased for $3,500 a twenty-foot boat that could haul a dozen passengers, and then built a plywood cabin on top of it to shelter the passengers from the weather. Because a license was required to operate such a large motorized craft, Reedy went down to the Coast Guard office in Pittsburgh to apply for one and learned he would also need insurance to cover his passengers.

"They didn't say anything. I didn't buy it," he says, when asked about insurance on the rowboat. "I just kept on goin'."

"I went for insurance for it—one hundred thousand dollars," Reedy says. "The man from the insurance company came out, I took him in that boat over to the other side, and he said, 'I am sorry. I can't give you the insurance.' I said, 'Why?' He said, 'What if an old man got on there and fell overboard and drowned?' I said, 'How's an old man gonna fall over four feet of side? Somebody's gonna have to push him over. He can't fall over. You know that yourself. Try to fall over.' But they wouldn't give it to me, so I couldn't run that boat."

And so two hundred years of ferryboat history on the Allegheny River slipped into extinction in 1956, pushed by insurance problems and then the opening of the Tarentum Bridge, which cut the trip from Edgecliff to Natrona from twenty-five miles to just five.

Above Natrona, railroad cars headed downriver are the only blot on the scene, and they remain so until we approach Freeport, once the home of another of the Allegheny's great dreamers.

David Alter was born in Allegheny Township on December 3, 1807. His parents, John Alter and Eleanor Sheetz Alter, had moved from Philadelphia to western Pennsylvania in 1800. The Allegheny Valley was wilderness at the time, and Alter's early

David Alter

schooling was poor, limited to two books—a biography of Benjamin Franklin, who was once a landowner in the area, and a book on electricity—and a few simple electrical devices.

Whether his talent had always been in electricity or was driven there by his extremely limited educational resources it is impossible to say. But Alter found a calling in the electricity book and electrical devices, and inspiration in the life of Franklin. He entered the Reformed Medical College in New York City when he was twenty-one years old, graduated three years later, and began a life of scientific experimentation that, though he was equipped with only crude prisms, lenses, and other apparatus he made himself, led him to an incredible array of inventions and discoveries.

"Medicine was his vocation," Francis Harbison wrote in his 1941 book, *Flood Tides Along the Allegheny*, "but chemistry and electricity were his avocation and to them he gave his heart to the sacrifice of his profession." Harbison listed some of David Alter's accomplishments:

> He contrived an electric telegraph in 1836 which he installed between his house and workshop. It was undoubtedly the first of its kind. He applied for a patent four years before Morse was granted one, but it was refused on the ground that "the idea was absurd and chimerical." He built a small electric motor in 1837. He built a telegraph that could be made to speak—the telephone of later invention—which he installed upon his grounds in Freeport. He built an electric buggy, a forerunner of the automobile. He experimented with daguerreotypes and invented a rotary retort for the extraction of coal oil which was being operated when Drake discovered oil and made its use unprofitable. He invented a process to extract bromides, hitherto expensive and scarce, from the waste of salt wells along the river. He discovered the spectrum analysis in 1853. If not the first, his was the second mind to grasp the wonders of the new science which enabled men to investigate the chemical nature of substances independently of distance by means of luminous radiations, so as to chemically analyze the sun and other heavenly bodies.

Harbison's claim that Alter invented the first telegraph may not be correct. Although his telegraph, which consisted of seven wires, each deflecting a needle, was among the first successfully used, there is evidence that one was being built in Alabama in 1828.

Still, there is no denying Alter's genius. Along with all his major inventions and findings, he also made an electric clock and a model of an electric locomotive. Like Charles Martin Hall, though, he had no talent for marketing his inventions. His one try at commercial success came with his coal-oil process and ended when Drake drilled his well and made oil plentiful and cheap. Alter died in poverty on September 18, 1881, perhaps the saddest of the Allegheny dreamers.

Commission to the Corps of Engineers to the Department of Environmental Resources—in other words everyone who should know—has labeled the Kiskiminetas a "polluter," nature has begun to show it is not quite ready to give up on the river. And, even without any help from the government, nature has once again begun to prove it can correct our worst mistakes, given time and half a chance.

"There is some naturally occurring mine drainage phenomenon going on right now that might be related to a water cycle," says the DER's Tom Proch. "Water cycles occur over long geologic periods of time, and when we're in them we really don't know."

"What do you mean by water cycles?" I ask, puzzled.

"The way water flushes in a mine, or the way groundwater behaves," he explains. "All these goodies occur on scales of time of hundreds of years. We only really see small sections of that, so it's hard to say where we're at. But the Conemaugh River, which with the Loyalhanna forms the Kiski, is improving fairly rapidly in water quality, and it's an acid-mine-drainage-affected stream. We don't know why it is improving. There's not a whole lot of reclamation being done."

Russell Stutzman, another aquatic biologist with the DER, and the Fish Commission's Rick Lorson both agree with Proch that the water quality of the Kiskiminetas is improving. They say they began hearing stories about fish being caught in the river during the late 1980s—something simply unheard of, or even dreamed of, for more than a hundred years. "I was amazed when we electrically shocked it to stun the fish so we could capture the fish for a census," Stutzman says. "We were constantly pulling out fish. My arms got sore."

John McAdams is a fisherman who lives above the river outside Saltsburg and manages a tackle shop in Greensburg. He says customers first came into the shop with stories about catching perch in the Kiskiminetas in 1988. Having fished at the outflow of Loyalhanna Dam about five miles upstream of the town since the late 1960s, the following season he decided to try his luck on the Kiski.

"We've taken perch," he says. "During the summer we take largemouth and smallmouth bass. I've caught northern pike. I had one day of five northerns running up to thirty-seven inches. We've caught channel catfish and catfish and a couple of sauger. The guys have even picked up a few trout. And then there's all the standard panfish, bluegills, crappies. I caught a one-pound-fourteen-ounce yellow perch two weeks ago."

"The fish aren't dirty," he adds. "When we first started fishing the Loyalhanna back in the late sixties, early seventies, a lot of fish had a lot of orange on them—their protective slime, their protective coating, had an orange tint to it. These fish don't. They fight good. They're heavy. I haven't caught a thin fish out of the river."

Although the water quality of the Kiskiminetas appears to be improving, that river's standing as the worst polluter of the Allegheny remains depressing, in light of its past. It was along the Kiskiminetas that the first great migration west began, prior to the Revolution and long before the Indian threat had ended, when emigrants from the East

Coast struggled over the mountains of central Pennsylvania to gather at Johnstown. From that settlement, they floated down the Conemaugh River to the Kiskiminetas, then down the Allegheny to Pittsburgh and to the virgin Ohio Country and Kentucky beyond. And in the forests above the Kiskiminetas and the Allegheny one of the most dramatic, savage, and, through the early years of the nineteenth century at least, best-known Indian hostage incidents ever recorded on the American frontier occurred.

Massey Harbison was living with her family in the wilderness of what would be Allegheny Township on the morning of May 22, 1792, when her ordeal began. Her husband, John, was off with local scouts tracking an Indian raiding party when a hand suddenly pulled her out of bed and she was confronted with a house full of Indians.

After ransacking the cabin, the Indians sought to carry off Massey Harbison and her three sons—an infant, a three-year-old, and a five-year-old—until the middle boy began to resist. "They took him by the hand to drag him along with them," she wrote later in *A Narrative of the Sufferings of Massey Harbison from Indian Barbarity*, "but he was so very unwilling to go, and made such a noise by crying, that they took him by his feet, and dashed his brain out against the threshold of the door."

> They then scalped and stabbed him, and left him for dead. When I witnessed this inhuman butchery of my own child, I gave a most indescribable and terrific scream, and felt a dimness come over my eyes, next to blindness, and my senses were nearly gone. The savages then gave me a blow across my head and face, and brought me to my sight and recollection again.

From the cabin, the Indians herded Massey and her two remaining children toward the mouth of the Kiskiminetas and then took them by canoe to an island in the middle of Allegheny.

> Here I beheld another hard scene, for as soon as we landed, my little boy who was still mourning and lamenting about his little brother . . . was murdered. One of the Indians ordered me along, probably that I should not see the horrid deed about to be perpetrated. The other, then, took his tomahawk from his side, and with this instrument of death killed and scalped him. When I beheld this second scene of inhuman butchery, I fell to the ground senseless, with my infant in my arms, it being under me and its little hands in the hair of my head. How long I remained in this state of insensibility, I know not.
>
> The first thing I remember was my raising my head from the ground, and my feeling myself exceedingly overcome with sleep. I cast my eyes around and saw the scalp of my dear little boy, fresh bleeding from his head, in the hand of

one of the savages, and sunk down to the earth again, upon my infant child. The first thing I remember after witnessing this spectacle of woe, was the severe blows I was receiving from the hands of the savages, though at that time I was unconscious of the injury I was sustaining. After a severe castigation, they assisted me in getting up, and supported me when up. The scalp of my little boy was hid from my view, and in order to bring me to my senses again, they took me back to the river, and led me in knee-deep; this had the intended effect.

Revived, Massey was taken across the Allegheny and overland toward Butler. "I now felt weary of my life, and had a full determination to make the savages kill me, thinking death would be exceedingly welcome, when compared with the fatigue, cruelties and miseries I had the prospect of enduring." Hoping to end her pain with a quick tomahawk blow, she dropped the large powder horn she had been made to carry and refused to pick it up. Instead of killing her, though, one of the Indians picked up the horn and accused the brave who had made her carry it of being lazy.

Emotionally and physically exhausted, Massey spent her first night in captivity tied down on a blanket. She dreamed of escaping to Pittsburgh but awoke only to have her ordeal continue the next morning when

> [The Indian] who was the murderer of my last boy took from his bosom his scalp, and prepared a hoop, and stretched the scalp on it. Those mothers who have not seen the like done by one of the scalps of their own children (and few, if any, ever had so much misery to endure) will be able to form but faint ideas of the feelings which then harrowed up my soul!! I meditated revenge! While he was in the very act, I attempted to take his tomahawk, which hung by his side and rested on the ground, and had nearly succeeded, and was, as I thought, about to give the fatal blow; when alas! I was detected.

Again instead of killing her, the Indian only cursed her and then moved away and continued to stretch her son's scalp on the hoop.

Following a quiet day, during which the Indians divided their plunder, Massey was moved deeper into the woods for the second night. The next morning, after the guards had been changed and those who had been on watch during the night were asleep, she made her escape.

Striking out on what she thought was a course for home, Massey walked and ran into the afternoon until she discovered she was actually heading away from the Allegheny and Pittsburgh. Her bare feet bleeding and full of thorns, she was sitting on a hill and waiting for night, when she spotted the North Star and planned her route for the next day. Then she made a bed of leaves and laid down to sleep with her infant son, neither having eaten anything in two full days.

The next day passed uneventfully until the evening, when she put the baby down and he began to cry. Afraid the noise might alert the Indians searching for her, she scooped up the infant and held him to her breast, quieting him in time to hear footsteps approaching. Desperate, she looked around for a hiding place and spotted a large fallen tree. Hurrying to it, she burrowed deep inside the top, which was still thick with leaves.

> The footsteps I heard were those of a savage. He heard the cry of the child, and came to the very spot where the child cried, and there he halted, put down his gun, and was at this time so near, that I heard the wiping stick strike against the gun distinctly.
>
> My getting in under the tree, and sheltering myself from the rain, and pressing my boy to my bosom, got him warm, and most providentially he fell asleep, and lay very still during the time of my danger at that time. All was still and quiet, the savage was listening, if by possibility he might again hear the cry he had heard before. My own heart was the only thing I feared, and that beat so loud, that I was apprehensive it would betray me. It is almost impossible to conceive, or to believe, the wonderful effect my situation produced upon my whole system.
>
> After the savage had stood and listened with nearly the stillness of death, for two hours, the sound of a bell, and a cry like that of a night owl, signals which were given to him from his savage companions, induced him to answer, and after he had given a most horrid yell, which was calculated to harrow my soul, he started and went off to join them.

On the fifth day of her ordeal, Massey reached Pine Creek at what is now Etna and came upon some moccasin tracks she followed to the Allegheny, where she became alarmed and retreated upriver toward Squaw Run above Sharpsburg. There, when she stopped to assess the situation, three deer came running toward her followed by a pack of dogs. Not knowing whether the hunters who came after the dogs were Indians or settlers, she hid behind a log, where her will was tested once more.

> I did not go clear to the log; had I done so, I might have lost my life by the bites of rattle-snakes; for as I put my hand to the ground, to raise myself that I might see what was become of the hunters, and who they were, I saw a large heap of rattle-snakes, and the top one was very large and coiled up very near my face, and quite ready to bite me. This compelled me to leave this situation, let the consequences be what they might.

Sometime the next day, she stumbled on a cattle path, which she followed to an uninhabited cabin. Feeling hopeless and exhausted, she concluded she "would enter and

As the Allegheny tributary that reaches the farthest east, the Kiskiminetas River was the first waterway west of the Allegheny Mountains to be declared legally navigable. In 1771 the Pennsylvania Colonial Council declared it a public highway and forbade obstructions that might prevent navigation by "his Majesty's liege subjects." About 1790, work began to clear boulders from the channels so that farmers along the Kiskiminetas, the Conemaugh, and the Loyalhanna could ship their crops to Pittsburgh.

Location also made the Kiskiminetas River a major link in an enormously expensive—some say nearly mad—but nevertheless ingenious scheme to link Pittsburgh to the Atlantic Ocean. Authorized on February 25, 1826, and completed in 1834, the Pennsylvania Canal was the state's answer to a threat by the Erie Canal to deflect western commerce to New York and the Great Lakes. Rails were laid from Philadelphia to Columbia on the Susquehanna River, where canal boats took over, carrying goods and passengers up that waterway, then down the Juniata River to Hollidaysburg in Blair County, where the genius of the canal builders was sorely tested.

Because water rarely flows uphill and mountains are not easily moved, when the Pennsylvania Canal reached Hollidaysburg a way had to be found to transport boats, cargo, and passengers almost thirty-seven miles to Johnstown, where the Conemaugh River could be picked up for the trip on to Pittsburgh. The answer was the Allegheny Portage Railroad, an engineering marvel of the period that used ten inclined planes, horses, and stationary steam engines to haul railcars loaded with canal boats over the mountains, an ascent of 1,172 feet at Johnstown and 1,399 feet at Hollidaysburg.

"Occasionally the rails were upon the extreme verge of a giddy precipice," Charles Dickens would write on a trip he took on the Pennsylvania Canal in 1842. He continued:

> Looking from the carriage window, the traveler gazes sheer down, without a stone or scrap of fence between, into the mountain depths below. . . . It was very pretty traveling thus at a rapid pace along the heights of the mountains in keen wind, to look down into the valley full of light and softness; catching glimpses, through the treetops, of scattered cabins; . . . men in their shirtsleeves, looking on at their unfinished houses, planning out tomorrow's work; and we riding onward, high above them, like a whirlwind.

The Western Division of the canal followed the Conemaugh and then the Kiskiminetas to Freeport, where it crossed the Allegheny on an aqueduct and proceeded down the west bank of the river to Pittsburgh. There another aqueduct carried it back across the Allegheny into the city at the corner of 11th Street and Penn Avenue, then through a tunnel under Grant's Hill to the Monongahela River. Passenger fare on the canal between Philadelphia and Pittsburgh cost $12 and the trip took four days. During the first year the canal was open, an estimated twenty thousand passengers and fifty thousand tons of freight passed over it. Pennsylvania had originally budgeted $26 million for its construction, but subsequent losses and expenses brought that figure up closer to $40 million. The Pennsylvania Railroad, authorized by the legislature in 1846 and completed to Pittsburgh in 1852, was the death knell for the canal. The railroad actually ended up purchasing the canal for $7.5 million in 1857, burying it in, and using the grade to lay tracks.

"While a financial failure from the state's point of view, the canal from the city's point of view was very successful commercially in expanding the amount of trade the city was able to do across Pennsylvania," says University of Pittsburgh historian Ted Muller. "In essence, it accentuated our gateway role by vastly improving overland travel through Pennsylvania."

Allegheny fog

Fishermen near Kittanning

Warm water from the Kiskiminetas and Buffalo Creek opposite it mix with the cold mountain flow of the Allegheny to make the river a haven for fog. Nearly impenetrable clouds often fill the valley from crest to crest, shutting out the rays of the morning sun, casting a damp chill on everything it touches, and causing a quickening of the heart in river people.

"From here down it was so damn bad I could hardly see anything," Captain Lyons recalls about one of his early encounters with Allegheny fog. "I could see the tops of the trees every once in a while—that was it. My brother was on board. I said, 'If we ever get down out of here without running into something it's going to be a miracle.' But we made it."

Massey Harbison's descendant Francis Harbison paints a vivid portrait of the Allegheny's fog in his 1941 book on his ancestors and the settling of the region, *Flood Tides Along the Allegheny*:

The dense vapors shut out the rays of the sun and cast a damp chill on all within its embrace, while to those upon the highlands it is as a mysterious silent river with billowy waves that move but do not flow, now foaming upward, now subsiding, but filling the valley to its bordering hilltops, and then inexplicably vanishing as the sun moves toward its zenith.

Instinctively trusting Captain Lyons's abilities, I feel no fear as we pass through the cloud enveloping the river and as trees, banks, and rocks emerge as in an English horror movie, but the gradual stretch of a line of red buoys in the haze makes me curious.

"You said earlier the channel is tough. So the bad thing about navigating on the Allegheny is the channel and fog?" I ask.

"The channel isn't," the captain answers. "But you get high water through here. You've got to be awful careful. You get yourself out of shape, you're in trouble. Everything is a fixed-crest dam. If you ever have engine trouble or anything and you get beyond the wall of the lock with the water moving, you're liable to go over that thing."

"But it also has a narrow channel in a lot of places."

"Yeah, you've got a lot of bad places, shallow places. You can't run anything over there," he says, motioning to the line of buoys on the starboard side. "You see all those buoys? This looks like this is big, but the water is up now. You wait until a couple feet of water drops and this all gets closer."

We make it, though, without any problems.

Towboat *Big Tom*

Dredging, New Kensington

Swinging toward midstream to avoid the powerful, swirling currents being thrown off the dam, and trying to draw a boat into the concrete wall of the lock, Captain Lyons slips the *Liberty Belle* into Lock 5 and breathes a sigh of relief.

"The water isn't coming off here too bad right now," he explains, "but you've got a helluva set here. When that water gets rough, you've got an eddy that drives you on that wall and then pulls you out and wants to stick you on that bullnose [the face of the outside wall of the lock chamber] out there. I damn near hit this thing a couple of times."

Pool 5 is the most heavily dredged pool on the Allegheny, and evidence of that activity appears soon after we are out of the lock. It comes in the form of small towboats pushing barges loaded with sand and gravel, and floating cranes hauling buckets spilling dirty water to the surface. It is not the first time we've seen dredgers at work. Davison Sand & Gravel, the largest dredging company remaining on the river, is headquartered in New Kensington, and signs of its operations cover a good portion of riverbank in that town with piles of sand and gravel, and the heavy equipment used to process it into usable material.

Glaciers scouring all the loose material from the landscape as they moved south from Canada between 350,000 and 500,000 years ago made the Allegheny a repository for some of the finest sand and gravel in the world. "The pebbles and boulders are well rounded and constitute the most conspicuous part of the formation," a 1909 U.S. Geological Survey report states. "In diameter, they range up to a foot or more, though most of them are between one and three inches. The proportions of different rocks vary. Sandstone is most abundant; quartz and igneous rocks are present in nearly equal amounts; chertz pebbles are numerous."

Glacial gravel

Since the days of Fort Pitt, people have been using Allegheny River sand and gravel for building and paving purposes. It is the foundation on which western Pennsylvania is built. During the first half of the nineteenth century, people out in the river gathering stones were a common sight, and by 1850 stones had become so scarce around the city that they had to be imported from upriver. "Many flatboats come down the Allegheny from a considerable distance up the river, laden with paving stones," reported the *Pittsburgh Gazette* on July 29, 1850. "Almost all in the immediate vicinity of the town have been picked up, and persons contracting for grading streets have experienced great difficulty in obtaining them at high prices."

Sand was collected from bars and shoals and along the banks during low-water periods. Early methods involved simply driving a wagon into the river or floating a small flat, which workers with shovels would then fill. As the business grew, larger flatboats and guipers (a kind of barge) replaced the wagons and flats. Then, in 1852, the first steam-powered sand digger appeared.

Davison Sand & Gravel's beginnings go back to 1854, when J. K. Davison and Edward Davison Jr. started J. K. Davison & Brother. "None of the pioneers in the sand business in the Allegheny Valley worked harder than Edw. Davison, Jr.," wrote Serepta Kussart in her 1938 book *The Allegheny River*, adding:

> As a young man he gathered sand along the river banks, and from bars and islands, shoveling it into small flats. Early sand operators were accustomed to build wing dams or breakers of stone and clinkers at the heads of islands. When the river rose, sand sifted through, settling behind the wing dams, where it was easily obtained, when the water subsided. The Davisons owned the towhead at Nine Mile Island, Allegheny River, and boated sand from there in flats or guipers to Pittsburgh, to sell for building purposes.

The Davison brothers were among the first to use mechanical diggers on the river and were the main suppliers of the sand used in Pittsburgh's first water-treatment plant at Aspinwall.

By the turn of the century, dozens of dredging companies were operating on the river and removing more than one and a half million tons of sand and gravel annually from the Allegheny and the lower Monongahela. Occasionally the operators would turn up some unexpected objects. In a 1921 report, Captain Philip Pfeil, president of the Iron City Sand Company, mentioned finding a mastodon's tusk opposite the 40th Street Bridge, and an old bronze cannon, lead-ringed cannon balls, and loads of arrowheads and flintlock rifles from around The Point.

Although dredging for sand and gravel has been going on along the Allegheny River for two hundred years, the resource is a finite one. At the moment, no more gravel-bearing glaciers are on the way. And environmental concerns designed to preserve the river for increasing recreational use have severely limited areas where dredging is permitted. In the early 1980s the DER halted all dredging in the upper river above Lock 9, and the Fish Commission successfully sought a moratorium on dredging in ecologically sensitive Pool 6, so it's difficult to say how much longer the business might continue.

"Basically, they're now dredging missed areas," says Ed Smith, a biologist with the Corps of Engineers who worked with the dredgers to prepare an environmental impact study at the start of the 1980s. "For example, where a submerged river crossing has been abandoned, they go to that area and pick up that sand and gravel." He continues:

> Because of the great cost involved, because it is difficult to find suitable dredging areas, they now tend to target their dredging more to the needs of specific customers. And, quite frankly, PennDOT [the Pennsylvania State Department of Transportation] was the prime customer for river and sand gravel. They had very demanding criteria for the aggregate used in road surfaces, for skid resistance. And basically the criteria were written by PennDOT to specifically favor river sand and gravel. For purposes of highway construction, the bank sand and gravel apparently do not have the quality of the river sand and gravel.

One major conclusion of the impact study was that submerged areas from a depth of six feet in to the bank need to be protected because this littoral zone is essential both to prevent erosion and for fish spawning purposes. To preserve these areas and to ensure that banks do not start sliding into the water, dredgers are now required to keep a minimum distance from the bank of twice the depth of dredging. So if a dredger is going down twenty-five feet, he must stay at least fifty feet away from the normal pool shoreline.

The Corps of Engineers, the DER, the Fish Commission (which is paid a small royalty by the dredging companies), and other government agencies also oppose removing sand and gravel down to bedrock. The bottom of the river is relatively flat. Dredging makes pits of cold, anaerobic water in which fish and other aquatic life cannot exist. The problem is aggravated during times of high water, when the fine particles left by dredging are stirred up and resuspend, creating a veritable desert on the river bottom.

"We don't want them to strip that riverbed down to bedrock," Smith says. "We don't want that to happen. That resource belongs to all the residents of the commonwealth, not just to private dredging companies. It also is a source of armor along the river bottom which helps in times of flood. We think there should always be a certain depth of that material left for future generations."

From the old Schenley Distillery just above Lock 5, once the pride of Allegheny whiskey—now "a warehouse or something," Captain Lyons says—the valley turns

Commercial freight

mostly to woods marked by rail lines and dotted by patches of summer homes and the squatter shacks of fishermen. Booms for corralling oil from a recent spill surround the mouth of tiny Knapp Run but fail to keep a brown scum from leaking into the river. Still, the scum doesn't seem to bother the three anglers sitting on the bank only yards above the mouth.

At Clinton, more substantial and expensive houses reclaim the low side of the river to look out at another wooded bluff. Captain Lyons points to a large red-brick home with

Ford City and Ford Cliff

gazebos, a trimmed lawn running down to the water, and eight white columns with a gigantic boat wheel standing at the center. The house was built by an old riverman who owned a towing company, the captain tells me, and we try to estimate the wheel's diameter, guessing from seven to eight to ten feet and finally fifteen feet. It's difficult to believe that anyone could handle such a wheel, until Captain Lyons explains how most of it would have been buried below deck. He then radios ahead to Lock 6.

The bend of Logansport and Cadogan appears and slips by as a collection of somewhat reclaimed strip mines and slag piles. Their ugliness is surprising so far out in the country, away from a town and approaching the beginning of the primitive Allegheny. Then ahead looms Ford City, its century-old glass plant overlooked by a church steeple and shadowed by ultramodern plate-glass walls—panels from "PPG Place," PPG Industries' glittering, award-winning corporate headquarters in Pittsburgh. I wonder whether the walls were erected to test their endurance before they were carried downriver to the Golden Triangle. The contrast between old industrial and new high-tech western Pennsylvania is striking and has been explored in some depth by Ford City native and writer Peter Oresick in his 1990 book *Definitions* and in such poems as "Landscape with Unemployed," "The Annual PPG Pensioners' Picnic," "The Social Impact of Corporate Disinvestment," and, below, "After the Deindustrialization of America, My Father Enters Television Repair."

> Here there were Indians, mound builders.
> Here, an English fort, a few farmers.
> And here the industrialist settled his ass,
> John Ford on the river dredging sand
> for making glass. Plate glass.
> (Why should America buy from Europe?)
> Some half dozen years, German engineers, and hundreds
>   of Slavic peasants.
>
> Grandfather sat on his samovar,
> warming himself and making excuses,
> but finally, he set off.
> Got a room, became a shoveler.
> Got a wife, a company house.
> Ford City: a valley filling with properties.
>
> No one got along—
> Not Labor and Capital, not Germans and Slavs,
> not husbands and wives, for that matter.

He continues:

> The factories today are mostly closed down,
> or full of robots or far off in Asia.
> Ford City lives through the mail:
> compensation, a thin pension,
> and, of course, Social Security.

Oresick was drawn to explore his home town through poetry in the early 1970s when he first left the Allegheny Valley to attend the University of Pittsburgh. In the classroom he found he had a real love for poetry, and then, as he came to know more and more people of different backgrounds, his appetite for Ford City's history and people grew.

"The whole town was really cut from the same cloth," he says. "Everybody I knew, everybody's dad, worked in the plant. There was no other economic life. Likewise, everybody I knew was Catholic and from some East European background: Polish, Slovak, Ukrainian. It was community in a really true sense—there were no classes.

115

There were three or four doctors in town, but their kids didn't go to our school. There were maybe seven or eight blacks in my graduating class of 250. So it was a very comfortable, decent, hardworking, classic American small town. And that fascinates me. And I kind of knew it, but I didn't really know it until I had gotten into an urban setting that was much more diverse."

"I have a lot of respect for that culture I grew up in," he adds, "what people did there and how they made a life. So for a long time I've been interested in trying to capture that and typify it in my poetry, catch the soul of it somehow—a sense of what people did, how they worked, the ethnic things, their religious sense of life."

Ford City is named for Captain John Ford, the founding father of Pittsburgh Plate Glass Company, who decided to expand his company's glassmaking operations northward, up the Allegheny, in 1887, after the company's success with its facility at Creighton. At the peak of its Ford City operations in the late 1940s, the plant employed almost four thousand people. The good times continued, more or less, until the late 1960s, when, in a story played out in many old-line industrial towns throughout the nation, management and labor clashed over the issue of new technology and profitability.

Management saw the technology as a way to improve efficiency, reduce costs, and increase dividends, while the unions saw it as a threat to jobs and to a way of life. Between 15 to 20 percent of the jobs at the Ford City plant were expected to be terminated by the change in manufacturing methods. After a long and heated debate, the union voted against installing the new float glass system in the plant. Management reacted by installing the system in another facility, shutting down the plant's furnaces and sending employment on a downward spiral to less than five hundred people, who now work fabricating glass made at other plants into building components.

As a new college graduate in the summer of 1974, Oresick's first job was helping demolish the glass tanks and furnaces where his grandfather worked when he came to western Pennsylvania from Russia shortly after the turn of the century until his retirement during the Eisenhower years.

"We went on these trucks into a cavernous old section of the plant that had the old high ceilings and various glass panels to let light in," he recalls. "There was a large crane running down the center, and silo-like tanks made out of iron, where they had stored things. My first job involved putting this rope around my waist and walking out on the beams. Somebody had already marked with chalk where they were going to cut with a torch. My job was to take a wire brush and go to all the chalk marks and scrape them down so the guy with the cutting torch could make a clean, quick cut."

In good weather, during breaks, Oresick often took a sandwich and walked down to the Allegheny, a river he didn't realize existed until he was about ten years old because the plant ran the entire length of Ford City and sealed it off from the water. From the bank he watched the workers in other sections of the plant and thought about his town. Years later he would write in "The Annual PPG Pensioners' Picnic":

116

We watched the valley stretch
below us and the river wind away for miles and the bats
shriek and dip below the bridge.
We crossed ourselves, moaning "God preserve us!"
under the moon rising small and thin,
as the mill fumed, as the town glimmered, as the star ignited
above it, burning like a carefully carried candle.

A row of red-brick houses with oddly slanted roofs gives Kittanning something of the air
of a Mark Twain town. They might be quaint now, I think with Oresick's poem in mind,
but in the past they were probably the "company houses" for the poor Slavic peasants
who found their way into the town's foundries, collieries, and brickworks. I like the feel,
though, and it certainly does fit, since Kittanning may be the oldest continuously
occupied site on the entire Allegheny River.

Lock 7, Kittanning

Delaware Indians were the first documented residents of the town, whose name has been translated to mean "place of the great river." Pushed west by Europeans seeking land in eastern Pennsylvania, the first Delawares are believed to have arrived on the site in 1724 or 1725. The explorer Céloron, hoping to gain the support of local Indians against the British, stopped at the town, which he called "Atticke," in 1749 and wrote:

> The village is of twenty-two cabins. M. de Joncaire [whom he had sent ahead to scout] told me that a chief with two young men, who had stopped on their discovery, seeing few accompanying him, came to him and demanded the motive of his voyage, to which he replied that I had come to speak to the natives of la Belle Rivière and give spirit to the children of the Governor who lived there. He engaged this chief to take charge of some strings of wampum which I had given to him to take to the lower villages, and to tell them to keep themselves tranquil on their mats, that I only came to treat of affairs which will be of advantage to them.

Six years later, during the French and Indian War, Céloron's visit bore fruit when Kittanning became the center for Indian attacks against English settlers. Raiding parties from the town ventured so far and wide that both Pennsylvania and Virginia put a price on the heads of their leaders, Shingas and Captain Jacobs ("Captain" being used to mean "Chief"). When Delawares from the town ravaged villages along the Juniata River and the Conococheague Creek in south-central Pennsylvania in 1755, a contingent of troops was assembled under the command of Colonel John Armstrong and dispatched from Fort Shirley in Cumberland with orders to destroy Kittanning.

From his camp on Blanket Hill east of the town, Colonel Armstrong sent troops forth to surround Kittanning on the night of September 8, 1756. At dawn he struck and, with an estimated three-to-one superiority and surprise on his side, quickly had much of the town ablaze. Captain Jacobs, after ordering his women and children to flee into the woods, made his home the center of resistance. When its bark covering was set on fire and he was called to surrender, he is said to have replied "I eat fire" and fought on until he "tumbled himself out at a Garret or Cock loft Window, at which he was Shot."

Faced with the approach of Indian reinforcements from across the Allegheny, Colonel Armstrong retreated to Blanket Hill—so named because his troops left their blankets there when they departed to attack Kittanning—where he found most of the rear guard he had left at the camp dead after provoking an attack from a small group of Indians camped nearby. Of his force of about three hundred men, seventeen were killed, thirteen were wounded (including Colonel Armstrong), and nineteen were listed as missing. The Indians lost a similar number. Although the casualties were small compared with what the world has since come to accept, the battle brought to an end Kittanning's role as a center for Indian attacks on the frontier. But before that end, the town was for a short time the home of one of the most complex and notorious characters of

KITTANNING OR ATTIQUÉ
INDIAN TOWN
WAS LOCATED ON THIS RIVER FLAT
THE CHIEF SETTLEMENT
AS EARLY AS 1727
OF THE LENNI-LENAPE OR DELAWARE INDIANS
IN THEIR EARLY WESTWARD MOVEMENT
FROM THE SUSQUEHANNA RIVER
BECAME THE MOST IMPORTANT INDIAN CENTER
WEST OF THE ALLEGHENY MOUNTAINS
DESTROYED
SEPTEMBER 8, 1756
BY
COLONEL JOHN ARMSTRONG
AND HIS 300 FRONTIER TROOPS
FROM THE CUMBERLAND VALLEY

MARKED BY
THE PENNSYLVANIA HISTORICAL COMMISSION
AND THE ARMSTRONG COUNTY HISTORICAL SOCIETY
1926

Historic Indian town, Kittanning

Revolutionary War America, a man who today has been forgotten but who through the nineteenth century was a near mythical figure of Billy the Kid or Jesse James proportions.

The second of four sons born to Irish trader and farmer Simon Girty Sr. and his English wife, Mary Newton, Simon Girty was born along the Susquehanna River near Harrisburg in 1741. His father was killed in a drunken brawl with an Indian known as "The Fish" when Simon was about nine years old. A year later his mother married John Turner, another farmer living in the area.

While extremely difficult by today's standards, life for Simon and his new family remained ordinary until the defeat of General Edward Braddock by French and Indian forces in 1755. Emboldened by the victory and encouraged by the French, Native American tribes throughout the state went on the warpath, raiding settlements from the Delaware to the Ohio. When Indians approached the Turner farm along Sherman Creek, the family sought refuge with other settlers in Fort Granville, on the Juniata River near Lewistown. There they remained for several days, until it appeared their crops would rot in the fields and they were forced to send out armed troops to harvest them. At that moment the Indians struck.

Though greatly outnumbered, the settlers inside the stockade managed to fight off the attackers, until the commander was killed and the walls of the fort were afire. Finding resistance no longer possible, they agreed to accept an offer by the French commander of the Indians to surrender. Instead of the fair treatment they expected from their fellow white, however, two of the settlers were quickly killed and others were beaten senseless. The commander then turned all the prisoners over to the Indians, who immediately began taking them through the forest toward Kittanning. There, as revenge for the deaths of braves at Fort Granville, John Turner was tortured to death in front of his family. Simon Girty was adopted by the Senecas, with whom he would remain until 1759, when he was released at Pittsburgh under the terms of the Treaty of Easton.

Before Pontiac's Rebellion in 1763, trading with the Indians was the primary occupation of most Pittsburgh residents, and the knowledge of Native American customs and language Simon Girty acquired during his years with the Senecas quickly earned him employment as an interpreter for local traders after his release. It was Girty who supposedly translated "Logan's Lament," the speech Chief Logan made after his family had been murdered by whites and that led Thomas Jefferson, in "Notes on Virginia," to compare the chief to the great Roman orators. The chief said:

> I appeal to any white man to say if ever he entered Logan's cabin hungry, and I gave him not meat; if ever he came cold or naked, and I gave him not clothing.
> During the course of the last long and bloody war, Logan remained in his tent, an advocate of peace. Nay, such was my love for the whites, that those of

120

my own country pointed at me as they passed, and said, "Logan is the friend of the white man." I had even thought to live with you, but for the injuries of one man, Colonel Cresap the last spring, in cold blood, and unprovoked, cut off all the relatives of Logan; not sparing even my women and children. There runs not a drop of my blood in the veins of any human creature. This called on me for revenge. I have sought it. I have killed many. I have fully glutted my vengeance. For my country, I rejoice at the beams of peace. Yet, do not harbor the thought that mine is the joy of fear. Logan never felt fear. He will not turn on his heel to save his life. Who is there to mourn Logan? Not one.

Girty's most important role as an interpreter and liaison between the Indians and the whites occurred during the spring and summer of 1776, when the Continental Congress, fearing a British and Indian alliance that could crush the Revolution on the frontier, sent Philadelphia trader George Morgan to Pittsburgh to negotiate a treaty that would keep the Indians neutral. Morgan hired Girty and sent him up the Allegheny with a peace belt for the tribes of the Six Nations in New York. The treaty the two men put together was finalized at Fort Pitt on November 7, 1776. It was the first of almost eight hundred treaties the United States negotiated with the Indians—all of which it would break—and it kept most of the Indians from joining the British during the Revolution.

What caused Girty to turn against the colonists, side with the British, and lead Indian war parties against Americans living on the frontier is difficult to say. Girty himself was unable to read or write and so left no written record, but over the years he gave a variety of reasons in conversation. The most common explanation at the time was that he had become a "white savage" during his stay with the Senecas and could no longer function as a white man. But that is probably little more than prejudice speaking, for while Girty never forgot the wild, free life he led with the Indians, and often went on visits to their camps, he also made many friends among the whites in Pittsburgh.

Willshire Butterfield's 1890 *History of the Girtys*—perhaps the best and most objective study of Simon Girty and his brothers—concludes after looking at the stories that grew up about the frontiersman that Girty may simply have made too hasty a decision and have fallen under the sway of traders Alexander McKee and Matthew Elliott, two ardent Tories who lived in Pittsburgh, and simply made a bad choice. "Beyond this it were vain to speculate," Butterfield maintained.

Whatever the reasons behind Girty's switch in loyalties, the fact is that he left Pittsburgh for Indian country and British-held Detroit with McKee, Elliott, and four other men during the night of March 28, 1778. Although they were not the only residents of Pittsburgh to desert to the British side during the war, their departure aroused the most concern because of their close ties to the Indians. "Of those men who had eloped but a few days since," wrote General Edward Hand, commander of Fort Pitt, after McKee, Elliott, and Girty departed, "the worst might reasonably be expected; their disaffection to the United States, their disposition to act hostile, the influence they would have over the minds, at least, of many of the poor Indians, the means they would have at command for the purpose of enforcing their evil designs, might be calculated on with certainty."

Through the remainder of the Revolution and the Indian wars that followed, Simon Girty would be involved in numerous raids on settlements in western Pennsylvania, Virginia, Ohio, and Kentucky. While he no doubt occasionally took part in, or at least witnessed, acts of great cruelty against whites loyal to the United States (the best known of which was the torturing to death of Captain William Crawford), on other occasions he stepped forward to save white captives, such as scout Samuel Kenton.

The picture of Girty is further complicated when it is considered that Kenton was a brave man who had once fought with Girty and who successfully ran the gauntlet in four different villages after his capture, while Crawford was the leader of a militia troop that had slaughtered almost a hundred peaceful Christian Indians, mostly women and children, at Gnaddenhutten in the Ohio Country. The only crime of the Indians was that a raiding party had ridden through their mission village with a white woman they had kidnapped in Kentucky. Buttefield wrote:

> Brought in by the savages from the woods, as were Simon Girty and his brothers James and George, after the French had been driven from the Ohio, only the first named was of an age sufficient to engage in any regular employment, and even he had only reached eighteen; all were left, of course, to shift for themselves; however, when arriving at manhood, it is probable that they might have settled down to something like ordinary business habits had their lots been cast away from the western border; but, remaining in Pittsburgh, then a rough frontier settlement, is it to be wondered at that their lives were shaped by their surroundings?

Blind and full of gloom, Girty died on his farm in Essex County, Canada, on February 18, 1818, ending another of the incredible stories that began along the Allegheny River.

"This is a *bad* area." Captain Lyons sighs as he wrestles with the wheel to counter a head wind strong enough to hold straight the wind sock at the upper end of Lock 7 at Kittanning. "Almost hit fishermen in the night here," he adds. "They come out without lights, and you don't see them until the last second. Same thing with canoes."

We make it into and through the lock without a problem, and then around the bend lies the end of our trip. A support crew of waiters, waitresses, and kitchen workers arrives in a van belonging to the Gateway Clipper Fleet as we reach the marina. They look like recent high school graduates, or maybe college students taking a semester off, and quickly sprawl out on the grass of the bank to watch Captain Lyons fight the wind for the right angle. It takes several tries, but the captain finally manages to nose the *Liberty Belle* up to the bank. Quickly the crew runs to secure the boat against the wind while the service crew hurries aboard.

"I hope I helped you out," Captain Lyons says once his boat is secure and we shake hands. "Good luck," he adds, and I recall Captain Way's remark about finding friends along the Allegheny. Then, as I enter Kittanning, I wonder what lies ahead on the second river, the primitive river.

Primitive river

Sunset from Brady's Bend overlook

8

SWEET TRACT OF LAND

East Brady is generally viewed as the beginning of the primitive Allegheny or the end of the civilized slackwater river, depending on one's point of view. But above Kittanning, where Jim Schafer joins me to explore the river by car, the Allegheny rapidly begins to lose people. Collections of worn frame houses and trailers cling to the banks with a hint of Appalachia in places with names like Tarrtown, Mosgrove, Bridgeburg, French's Corners, Reesedale, Rimer, Cosmus, Wattersonville, Van Buren, and Philipston. Industry barely hangs on, in the form of a couple of sand and gravel plants, a fertilizer plant, a power station, and railroad tracks.

Steel tracks or, just as likely today, abandoned railbeds are nothing unusual along

Fog-filled Mahoning Creek
meets the Allegheny at Reesedale
power plant

Pennsylvania's waterways. Rugged mountains made rivers and streams natural highways not only for flatboats and packets but also for the railroads, since the riverbanks held the most level land. The state legislature approved the building of a railroad from Pittsburgh up the Allegheny to Warren and New York as early as 1837. After the usual delays such projects always encounter, the Allegheny Valley Railroad was opened to Kittanning in 1856 and then, spurred on by oil, to Oil City in 1870, where it branched out on feeder lines throughout northern Pennsylvania.

While river valleys may have been the easiest place to lay rails across mountainous Pennsylvania, tough construction problems still cropped up. And few were more difficult than the problems the builders of the Allegheny Valley Railroad faced along the river

126

between Emlenton and Franklin, a stretch where the Allegheny uses up 35 of its 325 miles to cover 15 miles as the crow flies. Captain Way wrote in *The Allegheny*:

> To accomplish this it goes off on a leisurely excursion around broad bends, sometimes aiming for the Gulf of Mexico, oftentimes for the Atlantic seaboard, once or twice for Lake Superior, and for a mile or so very certainly toward the North Pole. While engaged upon this serpentine adventure, the river is buried deep in yawning mountain gorges. . . . The railroad which parallels the Allegheny most of the distance from Pittsburgh to Oil City takes one look at this primitive chaos and disappears through a tunnel for other fields to cinder. Once in a while an engine pops out of the hillside to survey the situation and scurry away again.

The hide-and-seek trains of the Allegheny Valley Railroad have long gone, but the narrow, trackless 3,500-foot-long Kennerdell Tunnel and the shorter Rockland Tunnel, with their tiny alcoves where workers once squeezed for safety out of the way of passing trains, remain as ghostly witnesses to the era.

As Jim Schafer and I cruise in our car along Route 68 toward East Brady, a blue-and-gold Pennsylvania Historical and Museum Commission marker alerts us to another railroad link—Brady's Bend Iron Works. Built in 1839 along Sugar Creek, the marker says, the four furnaces and rolling mill that made up the ironworks were the first to produce iron

Kennerdell Tunnell

rails west of the Allegheny Mountains. Before the Civil War, the Brady's Bend Works and another ironworks in Johnstown produced about one-seventh of all the rails manufactured in the United States. The Brady's Bend operations ceased in 1873, I read, and then slip the car back into traffic. A few moments later we are crossing the Allegheny on one of those wonderful old steel bridges that still appear with a certain frequency along the primitive river.

Geologists say that Brady's Bend, near the center of which stands the town of East Brady, is one of the finest examples of an entrenched meander—essentially a sharp bend in a river or stream overlooked by a high trenchlike wall—found anywhere in Pennsylvania. Six miles long, the bend is only a half-mile wide at its neck and dwarfed by five-hundred-foot-high bluffs. Winding quickly through East Brady, past the sign announcing the town as the home of Buffalo Bills quarterback Jim Kelly and the nineteenth-century facades of its business district, we climb Route 68 until the scenic overlook Jim has often mentioned appears.

"There *is* a monument to a hang glider!" I exclaim, laughing, as we walk toward the rail-guarded edge of the bluff.

"I told you there was," Jim answers, a slight frustration showing. "Nobody ever believes me. They must think I make it up or something."

I never thought he made it up, but I'd never expected to find a stone marker topped by a bronze plaque. From the way Jim had talked about people flying off the bluff on hang gliders being killed, I'd expected to find a homemade affair of some sort, like one of the little white crosses groups place along roads to mark where somebody was killed by a drunk driver. Now, as Jim describes how hang-glider pilots once used a wooden ramp to launch themselves off the bluff, until the state or county or somebody put a stop to the practice and built the overlook, I read the quotation on the plaque—"You haven't lived until you've looked down on a hawk"—and smile.

Strolling along the walk at the edge of the bluff, we watch a houseboat and jet skier at play in graceful wakes on the river below and stare out over the heat-hazed mountains. Jim explains how the main part of the bend is out of sight downriver, and then I think of the story about Captain Samuel Brady leaving his footprints on a rock at the edge of the bluff. Legend has it that they were left when he jumped off the bluff to escape pursuing Indians.

A glamorous figure to settlers and a demon to their enemies, Captain Brady became one of the best-known Indian fighters of the Revolutionary War era after his father and brother were killed in two separate Indian raids in central Pennsylvania in 1778. Blaming Chief Bald Eagle for the deaths, and vowing revenge, Brady chased the chief up the Allegheny after a series of raids against settlements in Westmoreland County. He finally caught up with the chief near the bend that now bears his name. Captain Brady's men struck at dawn, killing Bald Eagle in the ensuing fight and forcing Seneca Chief Cornplanter to swim for his life. According to a report filed by Colonel Daniel Brodhead,

Brady's Bend

Brady's commander, Brady's forces also retook "six horses, the two prisoners, the Scalps & and all their plunder" and "all the Indians Guns, Tomahawks, Match Coats, Mocksins, in fine everything, they had except their Breech Clouts."

Born atop the Allegheny High Plateau—the coldest region of Pennsylvania—fed by dozens of icy tributaries, and aided by a shallow, placid, meandering nature, the Allegheny River may be one of the great ice factories of the world. Stories about it appear in numerous narratives by early travelers, beginning with the day in 1753 when it nearly claimed the life of George Washington. And no place along the river is more famous for its ice than Brady's Bend.

Gazing down from the heights at the great bend, it's easy to see why East Brady has become famous for its ice jams. All it takes, it appears, is a cold snap that freezes the water along the banks and narrows the channel a bit. Then a piece of ice breaks loose upriver, swings a little wide, and catches. Soon another piece jams up against it, and then another and another, until for hundreds of yards around the bend the river is a solid mass of tightly packed jagged white ice. Brady's Bend ice jams are so famous along the river that Pittsburgh television stations routinely send crews out to film them, especially in the spring when they are about to break up—an event that will bring out residents of East Brady even in the middle of the night. Captain Way has captured the event in *The Allegheny*:

> The river stirs uneasily at first, winces, then with no warning whatever delivers itself of ice, drift, flotsam and jetsam, trees, logs, houses, barns, haystacks, cornshocks, barrels, dead pigs, bloated horses, boxes, barrels, packing crates, and other impedimenta which it has warehoused during the winter—all of this hodgepodge starts moving to the tune of thunderous cannonading of ice jams breaking, and one jam swoops down upon another, and with continuing crashing and rending the mighty discharge is on its way, now taking bridges, piers, sometimes whole villages, with the natives of the bottom lands fleeing for the hills and terrified livestock jumping fences and racing away for Egypt or anywhere, so as to be shed of this cataclysm. "The Allegheny's bust loose!" This cry is passed from mouth to mouth, and hurries over telegraph wires, and shortly every owner of floating property the entire length of the Ohio River, some 1,000 miles long, is suddenly busy getting his houseboat, or raft, or steamboat, or fleet of barges out of the road of this demon of destruction. For oftentimes the full force of this upheaval runs at brim tide for several days, and the broad Ohio proves a meager plumbing system to handle this cosmic diarrhetic discharge. Not until the Mississippi is reached does the destruction cease, and sometimes not even then—for case-hardened blocks of Allegheny ice have serenely sailed by New Orleans at intervals.

Ice damage, East Brady

"I remember," Captain Lyons told me about his own experience with Allegheny ice when we were aboard the *Liberty Belle*, "the second year I was here there was some tremendous ice come out of this river. It laid down between Sixth and Seventh Streets. There were chunks as big as this boat. It was into June laying on there—and I mean it was *big* ice!"

At a crossroads somewhere above East Brady we turn off Route 68 toward Kissinger's Mill and then toward West Monterey. Larry Scafuri, lockmaster at Lock 2, had told me about a "castle" along the river there that we want to see. What we soon find, though, is the primitive Allegheny. Quiet and serene, watched over on one side or the other by soaring green walls descending straight to the water, and touched only by a few summer homes and hunting camps, it's almost impossible to believe such a piece of river has been allowed to exist in crowded Pennsylvania.

Mouth of Redbank Creek

132

"I cou'd say much here in Praise of that sweet Tract of Land," Edwin Peterson, in his book *Penn's Woods West*, quotes explorer Gabriel Thomas as writing about another piece of country in 1698, and then adds, "Indeed, he could have. To have this River makes the people of Penn's Woods West among the luckiest in the world. Centuries later the casual canoeist could still say much in praise of the valley and the River and 'that sweet Tract of Land' through which they wander." Like Peterson, I'm glad Jim and his camera are along both to praise and to provide proof that such a place remains in Penn's Woods West. As in describing the force that drives the earth, words alone seem pitifully, woefully, inadequate.

Delighted at the sight and idea, though, and hopeful about plans to make the stretch part of the federal Wild and Scenic Rivers Program, we drive on. The paved road becomes dirt, then gravel, then ruts eroded into bedrock. When it narrows so that weeds close in on both sides of my subcompact and stand like a row of wheat down the center, we choose another road to the right, which takes us away from the river, and then another that leads to a paved road we guess will take us to West Monterey. We choose correctly and follow it into the village past the now-expected trailers, spreading Victorian homes, and occasional brick ranches of the primitive river.

On the river's edge we meet a high-school-age girl walking her dog and, feeling somewhat silly, ask her if there's a "castle" in town.

"It's down the road, but I don't know how you get over there," she responds, smiling.

Surprised, we follow the pavement to its end and find ourselves staring across the Allegheny at a beautiful, well-kept red-brick Victorian house with a turret and shining roof that must be "the castle." Scafuri had told us it was once a speakeasy, and it certainly seems to fit the idea. I wonder whether it might have been "Hogan's Castle"—the "gymnasium" Ben Hogan, the "wickedest man in the world"—built to cater to the after-hours fancies of oil-field roughnecks during the oil industry's boom years after the Civil War.

A native of Syracuse, New York, Ben Hogan began earning his title as a boy when he stole several dozen art books from an elderly clergyman, tore out the prints of classical Grecian statues, and sold them as "dirty pictures" to his friends. From that promising start he went to New York City, where he gave boxing lessons and fought small bouts for money. Shortly before the Civil War he headed south, where he murdered a gambler in New Orleans and was offered a suspended sentence if he would join the Confederate army. He agreed to do so, and then deserted the next day and headed for Mobile, Alabama, where he murdered two other gamblers and fled.

Always in search of a quick dollar and ready to play one side against the other, Hogan worked as a spy for both the North and the South during the war. He also tried his hand at blockade-running and piracy. Captured by federal troops, he was sentenced to death for his crimes, but then saved by a general pardon issued to Confederate supporters by President Abraham Lincoln after Robert E. Lee's surrender at Appomattox Courthouse.

Like a fly to sugar, or other less socially acceptable substances, Hogan soon found his way to the Allegheny River and Pithole City, a now extinct oil boom town near Oil City. Broke when he arrived in town, he took a job as "business manager" at Emma Fenton's establishment. There he met French Kate, "a startlingly beautiful brunette with dead-white skin," wrote Hildegarde Dolson in her 1959 book *The Great Oildorado*, ". . . a haughty Romanesque nose, full pouty lips, a bosom made for cleavage, and a voice like a sliding trombone." In partnership with Kate, Hogan hired fifteen women "gymnasts" and opened his first "gymnasium": Hogan's Lager Beer Hall. His "girls" were able to converse in six different languages, and the beer hall was an immediate success, earning Hogan and Kate a thousand dollars a day. In fact, it was so popular that customers had to be barred at gunpoint once the hall filled up.

When the Pithole bubble burst, Hogan and Kate moved downriver to Parker's Landing, where they opened, on the Allegheny just beyond the jurisdiction of town authorities, the Floating Palace, another "gymnasium," where according to Dolson, "members of both sexes may enjoy wholesome exercise, using the different parts of the body in such a way as to bring all the muscles into play." In three years they made $210,000 by encouraging customers to slip out of their hot clothes and join Palace females for a swim in the river.

After a run of ice destroyed the Floating Palace, Hogan headed for the new town of Petrolia, on the edge of which he opened his "castle." The new establishment served as his base of operations, but business often took him out of the Allegheny Valley. On one of his trips to New York, he found himself on Broadway with a couple of hours to kill and wandered into a theater. Instead of the dancing girls he expected, however, he found on stage Charles Sawyer, a "converted soak," with a Bible. After reading a few passages from the Bible, Sawyer launched into the tale of how he had been rescued from the gutter. Hogan listened and fell. At the end of the service he signed a pledge of abstinence and spent that night in his hotel room on his knees asking for divine salvation. He emerged the next day to say: "Peace fills my soul chock-full and I feel awfully happy."

A reporter for the *Oil City Derrick* recorded Hogan's return to the Allegheny in the January 26, 1880, issue when he wrote:

> The Trinity M.E. Church was crowded last night with all that could possibly get in, a great portion of the audience standing in the aisles and the back part of the room, down to the head of the staircase.
>
> The meeting was opened with prayer by the Rev. Craft and Ben Hogan came forward and addressed the crowd for nearly two hours. His talk was principally of

Ben Hogan's Floating Palace, Parker's Landing

his old life and his reformation and the sincerity of his repentance. He speaks of his being converted weeks before his wife "English Jenny," and his efforts to have her follow him. At the conclusion of his remarks, the choir sang, "Where is my wandering boy?"

Later, when I try to find out whether the house across the river really is Hogan's castle, nobody seems to know. An old-timer remembers only that it used to be owned by a man named Bailey. Then, finally, the librarian at the Foxburg Public Library tells me the house was built by Job Sedwick, a cabinetmaker, and that the only reason it's called "the castle" is its turret. But in the end it doesn't matter. The Hogan story is a good one, and it belongs to the Allegheny.

Hometown pride

Like East Brady, Parker is also at the end of a steel bridge. Another relic of the oil days, the town distinguishes itself from other such settlements along the river by its billing as "the smallest city in the United States." Settled by William Parker, who came to the area from Washington County shortly before 1800, its location at the mouth of Bear Creek ties it and the Allegheny to one of the most hazardous waste sites in the nation.

Bruin Lagoon lies in the Butler County town of Bruin along the South Branch of Bear Creek about seven miles off the Allegheny River and the town of Parker. Created by the Bruin Oil Company in the 1930s and used for the disposal of wastes from the production of white mineral oil, paraffin wax, and other petroleum products for more than forty years, the lagoon is filled with so much acidic sludge, oil, grease, solvent, and heavy metals that in 1984 it was ranked third among 538 Superfund sites on the Environmental Protection Agency's National Priorities List of Hazardous Waste Sites.

Partially situated in the one-hundred-year floodplain, the lagoon is separated from the South Branch of Bear Creek by a twenty-five-foot-high dike of clay and shale supported by riprap, gabion cages, and concrete barriers. Behind the dike lie four acres (approximately two million gallons) of sludge, about three thousand gallons of which once escaped into Bear Creek and the Allegheny River in 1968, leaving a trail of dead fish all the way beyond Pittsburgh and fouling the water of the Ohio River to Cincinnati.

"It ends up," says the DER's Tom Proch, "that Bruin Lagoon is full of detergents. The one time it broke and leaked, it essentially created a foam slick from here to Cincinnati—it's just so concentrated. There was ten feet of foam over most of the dams. You couldn't see the dam. There was just big foam piles. This stuff got churned up as it went over the dams and just created these piles."

Treatment was prohibitively expensive, so in 1989 a two-year $4 million project was launched to improve containment of the waste. The cleanup procedure, completed late in 1990, involved boring into the dump to vent explosive and toxic gases and then passing the methane gas and the hydrochloric and sulfuric acid mists produced through scrubbers to remove the pollutants. Bulldozers then mixed soil and lime into the toxic sludge to solidify and neutralize it. When that was completed, the lagoon was capped with dirt and a plastic sheet to prevent rainwater from flushing out the contaminants. Whether the procedure is comprehensive enough to work continues to be debated.

Driving past the fenced-off site of rusted storage tanks, brick ruins, bulldozers, cranes, and mountains of raw earth, we find it surprising how many homes stand near the lagoon, the third most poisonous piece of earth, that we know of, in the entire nation. I have to wonder where the people in the town get their water, how much more hazardous scientists will find the property to be in the future, and how much longer we will continue to do such things to ourselves in the name of jobs and progress.

Parker—or rather the railroad-bridged mouth of the Clarion River a short distance upstream of the town—also stands at a unique natural point along the Allegheny River, the spot where the lower Allegheny was linked to the middle and upper rivers about a half a million years ago.

"The Monongahela was the main drainage river in the Pittsburgh area," explains John Harper, chief of the Oil and Gas Geology Division of the Pennsylvania Geological Survey, about western Pennsylvania's original river system. "It came up the present Monongahela channel. At Pittsburgh it ran up what is now the Ohio channel. At Beaver it ran up what is now the Beaver River channel and on up through Sharon and into Ohio, draining into Lake Erie. The Ohio River we know from East Liverpool on to Beaver was simply a tributary stream. The true Ohio River of Cincinnati and Louisville and so forth was part of a major drainage system in Ohio that was not related to the Pittsburgh river."

"The Allegheny River was a tributary of the Monongahela," Harper continues. "But there were three Alleghenys. There was what we would now call a 'lower' Allegheny that started up in Elk County. The Clarion River, Red Bank Creek, the Kiskiminetas were tributaries of that lower Allegheny. It flowed down into the Monongahela. So it did what the whole Allegheny is doing now. The 'middle' Allegheny started

"The meltwaters from the glaciers came down the Allegheny River carrying with them all the sediment and stuff of that sort," Harper says. "You can pick up all sorts of Canadian and New York rocks that have been transported down here by the glacier, and then the river brought them down as far as Pittsburgh."

Gravel from the "old" Monongahela and the "new" Allegheny mixed and compacted around what is now Pittsburgh. The city's Squirrel Hill, Greenfield, Highland Park, and Allegheny Cemetery areas were once islands between the two rivers. The towns of Rankin, Swissvale, Edgewood, and Wilkinsburg on the eastern edge of Pittsburgh, and the Homewood-Brushton, East Liberty, Bloomfield, Shadyside, Oakland, the Hill District, and Schenley Heights sections of the city are all built on a dry riverbed, as is the heart of downtown Pittsburgh, the Golden Triangle. "As a matter of fact," says Harper, "the Cathedral of Learning at the University of Pittsburgh, when it was built, had to be stabilized a certain way because of the thickness of the riverbed sediments underneath it."

Pittsburgh's ancient riverbeds make the only direct natural overland route toward The Point from the east. The first roads and railroads into the city used them, as does the present Port Authority Transit's busway. Accessibility fostered the urbanization of the areas lying along the old river valley far earlier than urbanization of the hills on which Greenfield, Squirrel Hill, and Hazelwood are situated and the high ground between Allegheny Cemetery and Highland Park.

"There is no fourth river in Pittsburgh," Harper adds. "Pittsburgh's underground river does not exist. The sand and gravel under the Allegheny and Ohio rivers are the so-called fourth river, and actually they are no more separated from the flowing river of the Allegheny than the water in a bucket of sand. In a bucket half-filled with sand, the water in the sand is not separated from the water above the sand. It's all the same thing."

Glimpses of the path the Allegheny first took to Pittsburgh after the glaciers turned it can still be had in numerous places along the river. Known as the Parker Strath, from a typical occurrence along the river near Parker and from the Scottish word "strath" (meaning a wide, flat valley), the original riverbed is today visible as flat areas between two hundred and four hundred feet above the present river. These include portions of Troy Hill in Pittsburgh, Natrona Heights, Brackenridge, Harmarville, and on upstream at least to Parker. Gravel found in Parker Strath is identical to that lying at the bottom of the modern river so far below.

Views of the river from sections of Parker Strath are often spectacular, ranging from scenes of Pittsburgh to tractless forests. At Foxburg, above Parker, one stop also carries a warning: "Hitting of Balls off the Cliff is Unlawful and Prohibited. It Endangers Fishermen on the River." Alone—Jim back in Pittsburgh, working—I stare at the sign and then step up to the railed edge of the cliff and look down at the empty, brown

140

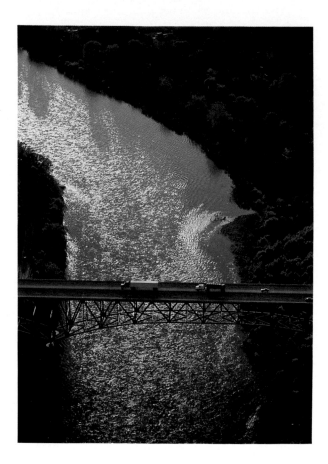

Interstate 80, Emlenton

Allegheny below. Suddenly I'm tempted to drive a ball out over the river just to see how far I can hit it. The sign is sure proof that I'm not the only one who's had that feeling. I smile to myself, and then walk back around to the front of the Foxburg Country Club's log clubhouse, the center of the oldest continuously used public golf course in the United States and home of the American Golf Hall of Fame.

Joseph Mickle Fox was a descendant of England's eminent Fox family (the founders of the Quaker religion) and a wealthy Philadelphia businessman who once owned 118,000 acres around the confluence of the Allegheny and Clarion rivers. Part of the City of Brotherly Love's Main Line society set, Fox belonged to the Merion Cricket Club in Philadelphia and as a club member journeyed to Edinburgh, Scotland, in 1884 to participate in a series of cricket matches. While in Scotland he decided to travel to St. Andrew's to see the game of golf being played. There he met Tom Morris, described in an American Golf Hall of Fame brochure as the "kindly old bearded Pro at St. Andrews," who took a liking to the young American and taught him the fundamentals of golf.

142

Equipped with a set of clubs and "gutta-percha" balls stuffed with feathers, which he purchased at St. Andrew's, Fox began playing golf on the lawns and meadows of his family's summer estate at Foxburg. Before long he decided to build a small eight-hole course on his property and to invite neighbors to join him. Almost immediately the game became so popular with residents of the area that Fox's original course could not accommodate everyone who wanted to play. Discussions were held on constructing a larger course, and Fox agreed to provide land for what was to become Foxburg Country Club. That was back in 1887, and golf has been played on the site every year since.

Appropriately enough for a course built above a river as famous for its sand and gravel as the Allegheny, the first greens at the country club were made of sand. Holes were made of quart-size tomato cans, possibly the product of the H. J. Heinz Company downriver, and long poles with burlap bags nailed to the ends were used to erase footprints after a player putted out. To keep the fairways playable, John Dunkle was hired at a salary of $15 a season to cut weeds with his scythe. In 1900 a small clubhouse was added to the course near the second tee because it was a convenient place to keep horses and carriages.

Because golf had been considered a pastime of royalty and the wealthy, it is surprising that the game got its start in the United States in such an out-of-the-way spot as Foxburg. But in the late nineteenth century Foxburg was probably the perfect incubator for the sport. The oil then being pumped from the mountains around the river had created a huge pocket of wealth in Foxburg, Parker, Emlenton, and other towns in the area. Actually, Emlenton, only three miles upriver, was at one time reputedly the richest city per capita in the world, counting seven millionaires among its population of 1,400.

Evidence that Foxburg Country Club is the oldest continuously used public golf course in the nation was presented to the United States Golf Association and published in the USGA journal in 1952. Two years later the Pennsylvania Historical and Museum Commission carefully investigated and verified the claim and then erected a marker noting the fact. A group of Foxburg boosters then organized the American Golf Hall of Fame Association, whose directors included famous newscaster Lowell Thomas. The association assembled a collection of trophies, clubs, balls, and other accoutrements of the game, which are now housed on the second floor of the clubhouse.

9

RIVER RUNNING

Standing on the bank maybe a mile below Franklin, looking out over the expanse of the Allegheny, I am struck once more with the apprehension I felt when a few days earlier Jim, his brother John, and myself finally decided to float down the river from Franklin to Emlenton and I failed to find a partner for my canoe. Everybody is always ready for an adventure until the time actually comes to do it. Being only a few steps above a beginner as a canoeist, I have to wonder whether I can handle such a large river on my own—or if it is even safe to try.

"What are the rapids like?" I ask again, as Jim and John load their canoe.

"They're not bad," Jim says reassuringly. "The only ones you might have trouble

Moonlit night, Rockland

Wild and scenic

with are the falls at Emlenton. And you can always get out and walk around them."

The word "falls" only adds to my concern, but they are thirty miles away. I tell myself Jim is right and that I can walk around any really tough spots—cross that bridge when I come to it—and then I climb into my canoe and shove off into the quiet water that lies ahead. In a moment we're rounding the first bend toward a gravel island and a riffle. I slip down onto my knees and, focusing the best I can over the bow, dip my paddle from side to side, hoping to avoid the rocks throwing current from just under the surface. We shoot past a fisherman whom luck so far has avoided and into a deep pool, where my heart settles.

146

Autumn morning

"That's about as bad as it gets," Jim tells me.

"That's it?" I say, happy and surprised. "I can handle that."

More than forty miles above Lock 9 and the end of commercial navigation, the Allegheny below Franklin quickly takes the form of a series of shallow flats and deep, lakelike pools broken by easy riffles. A steep, winding canyon too narrow to accommodate highways or large settlements limits signs of human development to summer cottages, gas and powerline rights-of-way, terraced rail beds, and, as we've come to expect, the occasional steel bridge. The mountains, in Father Bonnecamps's 1749 words, are "sometimes so high that they did not permit us to see the sun before 9 or 10 o'clock in the morning, or after 2 or 3 in the afternoon. . . . Here and there, they fall back from the shore, and display little plains of one or two leagues in depth."

One hundred and ninety years after Bonnecamps, Captain Way also wrote about the mountains and the sun in the stretch. But, reflecting the river's change from a highway into unexplored wilderness to a place of recreation, his writing is in a lighter vein:

> High outcroppings of bare rock stand solitary sentinel on the hillsides and catch the direct rays of the afternoon sun and reflect them into gloomy green vales below. At several points the sun comes up at 11:30 in the morning and sets at 1:30—so a native told us. This native was tending a "hillside" farm set at an angle of about 45 degrees. He placed his cabin at the foot of the farm; said it was a handy arrangement: on rainy days he need only look up the chimney and watch the corn grow above him. He planted the field by standing on the rooftop firing a shotgun loaded with corn kernels and with deadly aim.

Afternoon delight

Indian God Rock

No such encounters present themselves to us as we drift downriver. Besides birds and the fish we surprise in the deep, clear pools, our only companions for hours are scattered groups of other canoeists and anglers who have driven down the abandoned rail bed in hopes of bettering their chances. Then, with an island about to split the river, Jim signals for me to pull in. The current coming up on the island is too strong to handle on my own, though, and I have to let it carry me until I can turn toward a cobbled shore, where I get out and walk up the rail bed to find my companions already examining the Indian God Rock.

"In the evening, after we disembarked, we buried a 2nd plate of lead under a great rock upon which were to be seen several figures roughly graven. These were the figures of men and women, and the footprints of goats, turkeys, bears etc., traced upon the rock. Our officers tried to persuade me that this was the work of Europeans; but, in truth, I may say that in the style and workmanship of these engravings one cannot fail to recognize the unskillfulness of savages. I might add to this, that they have much analogy with the hieroglyphics which they use instead of writing."

Travelers along the Allegheny below Franklin have been fascinated by the Indian God Rock at least since Father Bonnecamps wrote those lines about the rock in 1749. During the latter half of the nineteenth century the sandstone boulder even became a popular stopping point for excursion boats. Names with dates reaching back into the 1870s, well-known logos, and other symbols—much of it meant to fool visitors by imitating what the carver believed the Indians would have cut—cover the stone and testify to exactly how big an attraction the rock has been over the centuries. The original carvings occur mainly on the face and are very faint, nearly impossible to discern—and a mystery.

"I'm the world's authority, and I have no idea what the carvings mean," the Carnegie Museum's Jim Swauger says, smiling. "I don't think anybody does. A lot of people will give you explanations. They'll tell you the snakes mean enemies, or messengers to the gods. They can be most anything you want to make up because we just don't know."

Although he has been studying Indian petrographs of the Ohio Valley for more than thirty years and has written a couple of books on the subject, Swauger says he doesn't even know how the Indian God Rock got its name. He guesses that whoever applied the name believed the symbols on it were religious, but he has no way to support that assumption. Neither can he say how old the carvings are. He doubts they go back beyond A.D. 1200, though, and believes that whoever made them stopped before the middle of the eighteenth century, when written records of western Pennsylvania that might carry explanations begin to appear. The only things he knows for certain about the God Rock, as well as other petrographs he has found in the river near Parker and in the woods above that town, are that they exist and that some of them were carved by early Indians.

"You have to remember that this part of the world was known as a great desert and people were going to stick mighty close to the streams because of the overgrowth," Swauger says, to explain how many primitive people might have passed the site and carved something on the rock. "You read the early travelers' journals and they'll speak of a squirrel being able to travel on grapevines from the Delaware to the Ohio. The sun was cut out. There wasn't much game, and the Indians—there weren't very many of them to begin with—were fairly well bound to the rivers for ordinary life. That's what I think, but I wasn't there."

As the nation most closely associated with the Allegheny River, the Iroquois would

Indian God Rock carvings

Captain Seth Eastman drawing, 1856

seem to be a logical source of the God Rock, but according to Swauger they deny any involvement. In one of his books, Swauger guessed that the carvings might have been done by a proto-Shawnee people, but a Shawnee friend of his claims the Shawnee people never created such carvings. Swauger, however, has seen a Shawnee walking stick with carved figures similar to some of the petrographs along the Allegheny. But he cautions that he's also seen similar figures carved on items from Africa and Australia. "There are only so many ways you can carve a man," he points out.

One story Swauger can refute with certainty, though. Some locals like to say the stubs visible in the God Rock were the remains of iron spikes left by French trappers, who used them to tie up their canoes. Swauger only laughs and says, "I put them there." He and an assistant drove them into the rock in the mid-1950s so they could study the carvings on its steep face without falling into the river.

Our—at least my—luck with unexpected encounters increases dramatically when I walk back to my canoe and suddenly spot two bare bottoms staring at me. Believing they must be in the middle of a wilderness, two women from one of the canoe groups we had passed earlier have decided to answer the call of nature on the edge of the rail bed. They giggle when they see me, and one of them scurries to cover herself. The other just continues to laugh. For my part, I smile and lie—say I am not looking. But they are both too beautiful to avoid, and I briefly fantasize trading Jim and John for either one until some huge offensive lineman of a guy crawls up over the steep bank looking for them and my canoe seems to be a safer option.

Bank prowler

Golden shores

Back in the canoe, I find that the apprehension I originally felt when I looked out over the river with the idea of tackling it myself has given way to boredom. Instead of becoming fearful of the approaching sound of rushing water, my ears search for it, seeking a push to end my constant paddling and a counter to the wind fighting to turn my empty bow.

At one rock-lined bend I rig my fly rod with a popping bug and flip it toward the bank. Instantly a smallmouth bass rises and takes it. For a moment after I release it, I picture one fish after another falling to my popper, but that soon gives way to the usual reality. Catch a fish on the first cast, and chances are good that's the only fish you'll see all day. Again and again I cast into the bank, spin the canoe around, paddle back upstream, and drift down to do it over again. I try poppers and dry flies and streamers, then switch to my spinning rod and jigs. Nothing. I finally slip the rod under the canoe's cross braces and paddle on.

Smallmouth stalkers

Small cottage communities cling to both sides of the Allegheny until we reach the bend at Brandon, where the appearance of Kittanning State Forest clears the west bank of human habitation. In the 1970s the state purchased more than three thousand acres along the stretch, with the idea of creating Allegheny Gorge State Park. The land had been heavily used in the past, first for subsistence farming, then for charcoal and iron manufacturing, and more recently for oil and gas drilling. Funds to develop the tract never became available, however, and the land became a state forest instead. With an adjoining tract of State Game Lands 39, some four thousand acres covering six miles of riverbank have been preserved in a wild state for future generations.

A primitive camping area stands within the forest above Kennerdell and is marked with a rustic sign. But another twenty miles or so of river lie ahead of us before we reach Emlenton, and we decide to paddle on past the town until we spot a suitable level spot on the eastern bank, where we turn ashore. Then, while I work with the tent, Jim and John concoct a dinner of noodles, rice, carrots, potatoes, and canned chicken, which we wash down with beer and top off with apple cake and a bottle of bourbon passed back and forth—a better meal than any of us had expected, we agree.

Then we're brought to our feet by the sudden sight of two brightly colored ultralight planes skimming down the center of the river. They are moving too fast for Jim to photograph, but the sun is more than cooperative and ends the day on film, glowing a deep orange and pink above two anglers in a bass boat.

Heads buried under sleeping bags to escape the day's initial light for as long as possible, at first we refuse to acknowledge Jim's call. We can hear splashing, but we'd also heard it before he arose and decided to try his luck. We think it belongs to fish far out in the river and not to one on the end of his line.

"He just wants us to get up," John says with a groan.

"I know." I groan too.

"I'm telling you guys, I got one!" Jim calls again.

"Yeah, yeah. Sure," John answers, sounding like a brother who has heard the story before.

"No, I mean it! It feels like a nice one too!"

"We're not getting up," I shout back.

But Jim won't stop calling, and finally I crawl out of my sleeping bag and through the door of the tent. Outside, the river is a solid bank of fog. Even Jim standing next to the canoes on a rock about twenty feet away is hazy. The fish, though, comes across clearly.

"Holy cow!" I exclaim.

"I told you it was a nice one."

"You're not going to believe this fish," I tell John. "You better get out here."

Power-boating below Kennerdell

The fish, a smallmouth, measures eighteen and a half inches. Mentally comparing it with a similar fish I saw caught on Lake Erie, I guess it to be about four and a half pounds. Then our excitement dies. It has taken the crayfish plug Jim was using so deeply it is bleeding from the gills. There's no way it would live if released. It has to be finished off. Jim does his duty, then places it in the cooler for John to take home. We eat our breakfast of coffee and apple cobbler depressed by the loss.

After a full day of nearly constant paddling, our arms and shoulders are feeling the results of too much time spent at desks. Our spirits too are somewhat less than elated about facing another seventeen miles of seemingly flowless pools that, Jim informs us, still lie ahead. This is especially true when we realize that soon we will have to load our canoes on Jim's car, which we'd left at Emlenton, and then drive back to Franklin to pick up John's truck so he can head home to Butler, and my car so I can head for Irwin. This complicates things, but since we all live in different areas it was the only way we could arrange the trip. We waste little time over coffee, quickly break camp, and shove off.

As we canoe around the bend below Kennerdell, Jim points out the location of the Kennerdell Railroad Tunnel, then we drift apart. Jim begins directing John to spots he wants to photograph, while I fall into the peace of canoeing alone, taking in the mountains and the edge of the river, waiting for whatever might happen along. It's a pleasant and relaxing way to pass the morning, though later I know I'll be hoping for company.

When the light climbs too high for good photography, we paddle closer and lash our canoes together. The arrangement works well on the quiet water, and we settle back to swap stories about college and business, beer, books, hunting, fishing, and women. The sound of rushing water makes us wonder whether we should separate for the "rapids" ahead, but when we reach them they look no worse than what we have already conquered, and we decide to stay tied together. We return to our stories and make the run without the slightest problem.

Near Rockland Station, in a series of loops, the river flows first to the northeast, then to the southwest, then almost directly north and almost directly south. The shifts in direction reveal the struggle between the Allegheny and the terrain when the glaciers turned and joined it. As we enter the loops, Jim, like Bonnecamps and Captain Way before him, relates tales of the sun shining on a person's back at one point along the stretch and on his chest at another. When he mentions he has a compass in his pack, we tell him to take it out so we can trace the changes, but we soon become totally confused, unable to agree from one moment to the next where north is, until we simply give up.

The constant change in direction also plays tricks with the wind. One time it blows from behind us, next time it is a head wind. Most of the time, naturally, it seems to be a head wind. We have to dig our paddles deep to make progress, and what should be fun becomes work. Then, when the wind shifts to our backs Jim holds up his shirt, and we spontaneously begin to rig sails, slipping the paddles through the arms of our shirts and holding them aloft. The rig works, and we sail on laughing and joking, until we reach the next loop and the wind rushes toward us again.

Such changes in direction also make it difficult to gauge where we are on our journey—or where the falls at Emlenton might lie. Jim tells us we are getting close so many times without reaching anything that we begin to tease him about it. When the falls finally appear, we run them without even untying our canoes, and then wonder why such an inconsequential rush of water earned the title "falls." Maybe in higher water they rate such a classification, but now they're no different from a half-dozen other pieces of fast water we had encountered on the way. Jim maintains they are the falls, but we have to wonder for a while, until we are far into another pool, and then the smell of petroleum overcomes everything and a refinery appears, welcoming us to Emlenton. It is a smell the Allegheny will soon know well.

Soft-shelled turtle

Midnight near Kennerdell

10

OILDORADO

Its wide, pleasing main street, Norman Rockwell courthouse, and beautiful Victorian homes bear little hint that the town of Franklin, at the confluence of French Creek and the Allegheny, stands at the center of one of the longest, richest, and most uproarious histories of any portion of western Pennsylvania. Céloron paused at an Indian village of "only nine or ten cabins" he found nearby in 1749. Seven years earlier, the English trader John Frazier is believed to have arrived at the site and remained until the French drove him out in May 1753. That same year George Washington and Christopher Gist stopped at the settlement to warn the French they were trespassing on British land and the French first expressed their determination to fight for North America.

Venango County Courthouse, Franklin

"We found the French Colours hoisted at a House from which they had driven Mr. John Frazier, an English subject," Washington noted in his journal.

> I immediately repaired to it, to know where the Commander resided. There were three Officers, one of whom, Capt. Joncaire, informed me, that he had the Command of the Ohio: But that there was a General Officer at the near Fort, where he advised me to apply for an Answer. He invited us to sup with them; and treated us with the greatest Complaisance.
>
> The Wine, as they dosed themselves pretty plentifully with it, soon banished the Restraint which at first appeared in their Conversation; and gave a License to their Tongues to reveal their Sentiments more freely.
>
> They told me, That it was their absolute Design to take Possession of the Ohio, and by God they would do it: For that altho' they were sensible the English could raise two Men for their one; yet they knew, their Motions were too slow and dilatory to prevent any Undertaking of theirs. They pretend to have an undoubted Right to the River, from a Discovery made by one La Solle 60 Years ago; and the Rise of this Expedition is, to prevent our settling on the River or Waters of it, as they had heard of some Families moving-out in Order thereto.

During the winter of 1753–54 the French built and stocked storehouses around Frazier's cabin, and then in 1755 they began erecting a stockade they dubbed "Fort Machault." It was to Machault that half the French troops at Fort Duquesne fled when General John Forbes captured the forks of the Ohio in 1758. Soon after, the Indians advised the French to abandon Fort Machault because "it was not strong enough to resist the English," according to a traveler quoted in *A Traveler's Guide to Historic Western Pennsylvania* (1954) by Lois Mulkearn and Edwin Pugh. In the fall of 1759, British troops occupied the site, finding "nothing but the remains of a reduced fort and about 44 houses, with one swivel and a quantity of broken gun barrels and old iron."

Fort Venango was built by the British to replace Machault in 1760. Timber for it was floated down French Creek from Fort LeBoeuf (Waterford, in Erie County), where the French had left behind a large supply of boards when they retreated from that fortification. The original garrison sent from Fort Pitt consisted of about a hundred and fifty men. A long period of peace, however, caused the British to reduce the garrison "to just enough to keep up Communication, there being nothing to fear from the Indians in our present Circumstances," in the words of one officer. The Senecas attacked Fort Venango during Pontiac's Rebellion in June 1763, massacring the detachment and burning the fort to the ground.

The young United States took its turn at the juncture of French Creek and the Allegheny when it replaced Fort Venango with Fort Franklin in 1787, naming it—because it was "in the state of Pennsylvania"—after that most famous of all Pennsylvanians,

Benjamin Franklin. By 1794 the installation had fallen into a "wretched state of defense," but when the Senecas threatened the installation in June of that year, it was rebuilt in just four days. A garrison was maintained at the fort until 1796, when another fort, Old Garrison, took its place and was maintained as a refuge against Indian raids until it was abandoned in 1799.

The reason Native Americans settled at the site of Franklin and the French, British, and Americans fortified it was, of course, geography. French Creek and the Allegheny River were major highways through the wilderness of western Pennsylvania. As early as 1753 the French undertook a snag-clearing project to improve navigation along French Creek, and the British used the stream to transport troops in 1759. That expedition lost such a large number of boats on snags and in the rapids that Colonel Henry Bouquet was forced to undertake his own snag-clearing operation in 1761.

After the Revolution, American pioneers moved into the French Creek basin in great numbers and immediately began sending flatboats laden with whiskey, beans, furs, salt, and lumber down the stream and river to Pittsburgh. General James O'Hara used the stream to bring salt from Syracuse, New York, to Pittsburgh in 1796. Records show that on November 23, 1809, more than fourteen thousand barrels of salt were stacked at Waterford waiting for a rise in French Creek. The huge flatboats used to transport goods on the stream were themselves floated down the Allegheny for use by coal miners along the Monongahela River. To river people, the term "French Creek" eventually came to mean a sturdy wooden barge.

Such a lively commerce naturally drew many characters to the region, including one of the most famous names in American folklore—Johnny Appleseed.

"An actual person as well as a folk hero," the historical marker in Franklin points out, Johnny Appleseed's real name was John Chapman. He was born in 1775 on a farm in Springfield, Massachusetts, and educated at Harvard. While in college he became interested in the teachings of the Swedish scientist and mystic Emanuel Swedenborg, who maintained that the infinite, indivisible power and life within all creation is God and that the trinity of soul, body, and mind is disturbed by people's misuse of their own free will.

As a follower of Swedenborg, Chapman was sent to preach in settlements along the Potomac River in Virginia. There he heard stories of the fantastic country and opportunities awaiting the adventuresome west of the Allegheny Mountains. With Abraham Buckles he set out for Pittsburgh in 1788 and then up the Allegheny to visit an uncle who lived near Olean. The uncle was gone, but his cabin stood intact, and the two friends established themselves as settlers.

On that trip up the Allegheny from Pittsburgh to Olean, Chapman noticed the absence of fruit trees in the surrounding country. He found one neglected orchard near rapids, towing the boats up, unloading, then returning to bring up the rest of the cargo. In spite of bodies scratched and bruised, clothes torn by brambles, muscles burning from fatigue, Marcus Hulings and his sturdy sons beat their way up French Creek, delivering the naval stores and ordinance to Commodore Perry in time for him to finish and arm his ships.

Without the Allegheny, French Creek, and the Hulingses, Perry may never have been able to report: "We have met the enemy and they are ours, two ships, two brigs, one schooner, and one sloop."

Following the War of 1812, the Allegheny River–French Creek route became a major link in western Pennsylvania's transportation network. By 1827 it was so important to commerce that the state sought to stabilize it by constructing the French Creek Canal. The project dammed the stream in eleven places to furnish slackwater from Franklin to Meadville, where a feeder canal to Conneaut Lake diverted water from the stream to the lake to supply the Erie Extension Canal, which linked the Ohio River with Lake Erie via the Beaver and Shenango rivers.

Despite the high hopes accompanying the opening of the French Creek Canal in 1834, major commerce never developed on the canal. Captain Way says the plan misjudged the volume of the stream and that only two canal boats used the waterway before it drifted into oblivion around the middle of the nineteenth century. But by that time the fortunes of Franklin, French Creek, and the Allegheny River in Venango County had shifted in another direction, one that is still driving the world today.

From about the eighth grade on, the photograph seems to appear in one American history book after another. A tall, lanky gentleman dressed in top hat and frock coat stands in a field of weeds. Behind him is a crude-looking wooden derrick with an equally crude shack attached. "Drake's Well," the caption might read. "In 1859 Colonel Edwin Drake drilled the world's first oil in Titusville, Pennsylvania."

Strolling through the park surrounding the Drake Well Museum at Titusville on the banks of the Allegheny River tributary of Oil Creek, I recall the photograph and how exciting I thought it was that Pennsylvania had been the location of such a monumental event. Fed by a diet of old movies on wildcatters, I had expected the first oil well to have been drilled in some other place, such as Texas. I pause to look at the rough-hewn, gray-weathered re-creation of Drake's Well and, as often happens at famous sights, feel somewhat disappointed. Once more, reality fails to measure up to legend.

Stepping inside the re-created well, I think only of the old chicken coop my grandfather had when I was a child. The structure is a universe apart from the modern steel rigs and ocean-drilling platforms that appear on the evening news every time there is a crisis in the Middle East, but in a way that seems fitting, because the true story of

166

Edwin L. Drake also is a universe apart from those schoolboy history books.

One of the most common and greatest misstatements in American history is that Drake *discovered* oil. Oil as a substance has been known at least since the time of ancient Rome and the Caesars. More recently, in North America, Seneca Indians spread blankets on the rainbowed oily surface of streams throughout northwestern Pennsylvania and western New York and then wrung out the liquid for use as liniment and medicine, in tribal ceremonies, and as a base for war paint. French missionaries in the seventeenth century near Cuba, New York, told of finding springs of "thick and heavy water, which ignites like brandy and boils in bubbles of flame when fire is applied to it." In 1755 the British cartographer Lewis Evans wrote "Petroleum in Pensilvania" across his map of the region. And in 1785 General Benjamin Lincoln, surveying land for grants to Revolutionary War soldiers, wrote:

> In the northern part of Pennsylvania, there is a creek called Oil Creek, which empties itself into the Allegheny, on the top of which floats an oil, similar to what is called Barbadoes tar, and from which may be collected, by one man, several gallons in a day. The troops, in marching that way, halted at the spring, collected the oil, and bathed their joints with it. This gave them great relief, and freed them immediately from the rheumatic complaints with which many of them were affected.

Settlers in colonial Pennsylvania learned about oil from the Indians and began trading in it. Almost every household had a supply of "Seneca oil" and, like the Asians Marco Polo knew back in the thirteenth century, used it to cure the ills of both humans and animals. In hot weather, farmers even lathered their teams with crude oil to keep the flies away.

Lower on the Allegheny, in Natrona, Thomas Kier, looking for a way to make a profit from the oil seeping into and fouling his salt wells, began marketing "Kier's Petroleum or Rock Oil, Nature's Remedy, from Four Hundred Feet below the Earth's surface" a full decade before Drake drilled his well. Kier hawked his product from gaudy green-and-red wagons with paintings of a "Good Samaritan" administering the balm to a wounded soldier lying under a palm tree, and accompanied by a circular flaunting pictures of Indian chiefs, derricks, and health-flushed maidens. At fifty cents a half pint, Kier recommended three spoonfuls a day and claimed:

> The lame were made to walk. Cases that were pronounced hopeless and abandoned by Physicians of unquestioned celebrity have been made to exclaim, "This is the most wonderful remedy ever discovered." Ingredients blended together in such a way as to defy all human competition. Several who were blind have been made to see.

At the same time Kier was huckstering his cure-all, lumberman Ebenezer Brewer

Rouseville

skimmed five gallons
to his son, Francis, a
patients. Dr. Brewer
surprising success. Th
who tried it and agree

Brewer's flask wa
students, George Biss
visit and noticed it. B
flask. A seeker of fo
advancing Industrial I
and contacted Jonatha
by Dr. Brewer, Bisse
along Oil Creek and c
share.

Villagers in Titu
chuckled over the sch
son to stay away. "N
alone that I now say
already ruined you, tl
merchant whom Bisse
the Brewers: "From
confidence in them as

In hopes of gaini
Benjamin Silliman Jr
report, which he refi
wanted, concluded: "
Company have in tl
expensive process the
sented to serve, brief
professor, his involv
University and in nei
president of the City
courtly, frail thirty-e
lived in the same boal

Although he was po
experience in busine:
Company (formed to
block of stock. Such l

to Townsend and the other directors for "value received" shortly after he took office.
Townsend had arranged the stock deal because he believed it did not look good for a
banker to be openly attached to a venture as risky as an oil company. Drake went along
with it because his annual salary would be $1,000. Believing it imparted a certain respect
both to Drake and to the company, Townsend also gave Drake the title "Colonel."

As president of Seneca Oil, Drake arrived in Titusville in May 1858 and set about
hiring a drilling crew—a much more difficult task than might be expected. Titusville was
a tiny, out-of-the-way village, and Drake's crew could not even purchase picks and
shovels. On a borrowed horse, Drake rode to Hydetown for a single pick, to Pleasantville
for spikes, to Enterprise for chain, and to Erie for two shovels. Then he traveled by
stagecoach to Pittsburgh to consult with salt-well owners and to hire a driller—who
promised to show up in July and never arrived. This driller later told friends he thought
Drake's plans for a thousand-foot-deep well were insane and that he'd agreed to take the
job only to shut him up. A second driller did mean to do the job but then got itchy feet
and headed west.

Even after Drake managed to obtain equipment, nobody in the area knew how to
operate it. Summer turned to fall, the third driller he hired proved useless, and the
bonfires the farmers used to clear their fields of corn stubble made him recall a childhood
dream in which he started a fire that got out of control. When he awoke screaming, his
mother comforted him, saying, "That just means someday you'll set the world on fire."

An ailing Edwin Drake sat out the winter worrying about money. The beginning of
April 1859 marked the end of his contract. Company directors had lost interest in the
project and refused to put any more money into it. But Drake persisted, revealing a
vision and commitment that the others lacked. He got Townsend to make a few small
loans, local store owners to give him credit so he could feed his family, and his best
friend, Peter Wilson, a druggist, to co-sign a loan for him at a Meadville bank. Then he
sent a local teamster to Tarentum to pick up William Smith, a new driller he'd heard
about, and hired Smith and his son for $2.50 a day.

Known as "Uncle Billy," William Smith could not have been more opposite the lanky
and frail Drake. Short, broad, hefty, and laconic, Smith might have passed for the poet
Henry Wadsworth Longfellow. But, like Drake, he believed. When offered a blacksmith's
job in Franklin for $4 a week, he said only: "I can't quit Drake now."

From the moment Smith arrived on the scene, problems began to disappear. A
derrick that had proved impossible to raise the previous year went up in a single day. Dr.
Brewer was so happy he passed out cigars to all the workers, telling them: "Have one on
me. They didn't cost me a cent. I traded oil stock for them." During a single trip to Erie,
Smith obtained pipe Drake had never been able to find and then drove down thirty-two
feet before hitting rock. He continued to progress through the rock at the rate of three

feet a day until, in the afternoon of August 27, 1859, the bit hit a depth of sixty-nine feet and dropped into a crevice. It being late, the crew removed the drill and went home.

No work was scheduled for the next day, Sunday, but Smith was a compulsive tinkerer, so he and his son decided to stop by the well. Peering down the drill shaft, he noticed a dark fluid glistening on the surface of the water he was accustomed to seeing. Hurriedly, he fashioned a dipper out of a piece of drainpipe and ladled out some of the liquid. It was oil. He and Drake had always expected to find oil, but much farther down. He sent his son running into Titusville shouting: "They've struck oil! They've struck oil!" The next day, when Drake came to work, he found Smith and his son guarding the first well in the world ever drilled specifically for oil, and a variety of tubs and barrels brimming with crude.

Today Colonel Edwin Drake rests in Woodlawn Cemetery in Titusville under a cut stone monument on which stands a bronze figure, "The Driller," erected in his honor in 1901 by John D. Rockefeller's Standard Oil Company. A collection of his personal effects, as well as pieces of the first well, can be seen in the Drake Well Museum. His steadfast partner, Uncle Billy, lies under a granite obelisk in Pape Cemetery west of the Allegheny River near Saxonburg in Butler County.

As the California Gold Rush did ten years earlier, news of Drake's well soon began drawing fortune hunters to Titusville, Franklin, Oil City, and other small towns around the Allegheny. And among them was, again, like Johnny Appleseed, a famous name in American history: John Wilkes Booth.

One of the nation's best-known actors, Booth was earning some $20,000 a year when John Ellsler, manager of the Cleveland Academy of Music, suggested that he invest in an oil well in Venango County. With Ellsler and Cleveland gambler Thomas Mears, the actor arrived in Franklin early in 1864, purchased three and a half acres of land on the river about a mile below town, and formed the Dramatic Oil Company.

Almost immediately after launching this venture, Booth headed south for an engagement in New Orleans, where he was applauded as a genius and might well have stayed if he had not lost his voice. But instead of resting, as a doctor advised, Booth went to Boston, where his performance was panned by the critics. The oil business suddenly looked more appealing. Accompanied by Joseph Simonds, a Boston banker who had helped him with investments in the past, Booth returned to Franklin at the end of May 1864.

Darkly handsome, charming, and dashingly attired in the most fashionable clothes, Booth quickly made friends throughout the oil country. Local ladies were particularly taken with his style on horseback and on the dance floor, his recital of dramatic speeches at parties, and his habit of kissing their hands. Even more captivating were his sad eyes and pensive ways.

171

Booth was never a real oil man, but he often went through the gestures, riding out into the country to inspect his driller's progress and stopping at the real estate office, where oilmen gathered to exchange gossip and check the New York papers for market quotes. Spurred on by the war, the price for refined petroleum was between 71 and 73 cents a gallon, making it a highly profitable time to be sinking new wells.

While in Franklin, Booth was careful to avoid making any overt or threatening remarks about Abraham Lincoln to his new pro-Union friends. He did say, however, that he had a personal dislike for the president because Lincoln had gone back on his word. Although it is doubtful he ever knew Abraham Lincoln, Booth claimed that a Confederate spy named Beall captured on the Canadian border was a friend whom Lincoln had promised to spare and then went back on his word. "I'd rather cut off my right arm than see Lincoln renominated," Booth told friends.

Although it is impossible to prove Booth made the scratching, circumstantial evidence was strong when later that summer a maid at the McHenry Hotel in Meadville was cleaning Room 22, where Booth had stayed on one of his trips to town, and found a note scratched on a windowpane: "Abe Lincoln departed this life August 13, 1864, by the effects of poison." She called the manager, who dismissed the inscription as the work of a practical joker "while partially intoxicated."

Other hints that Booth was thinking about something other than oil arose from time to time in things he did and said but, as often happens, fell into place only after the fact. During one meeting of the drama and literary society he had formed with about a dozen other young men in a saloon on Doe Street, he got carried away with a recitation of the Sermon on the Mount, especially the passage that reads "But he that heareth, and doeth not, is like a man that without a foundation built an house upon the earth; against which the stream did beat vehemently, and immediately it fell; and the ruin of that house was great." Another time, on a ferry trip across the Allegheny, he got into a violent argument with a local carpenter, Titus Ridgway, who was reeling off a string of oaths against Robert E. Lee. When Booth responded by attacking Lincoln in a similar manner, Ridgway called him a liar, grabbed a spiked pole, and went after the actor. Booth drew his gun, saying he would "shoot any man who calls him a liar." The ferryman was barely able to stop the argument before blood was spilled.

As summer progressed toward fall, Booth began drinking more and talking about fighting. Once he even started a barroom brawl in which he ended up being thrown out by a group of oil-field roughnecks. Like a man who knows the end is near, he also took steps to put his affairs in order. He signed over property to his brother Junius and sister Rosalie and gave his sister Asia a bulky envelope with instructions that it be opened only in the event of his death. Then, on September 28, he left Franklin for good. He said he was going to play an engagement in Washington, D.C., but instead he went to Canada, where he met a group of Confederate sympathizers in Montreal, and then on to New York for a one-night performance of *Julius Caesar* at the Winter Garden Theater.

John Wilkes Booth

On Inauguration Day, March 4, 1865, eighteen-year-old Roe Reisinger, a Franklin native who won the Congressional Medal of Honor as a member of Pennsylvania's Bucktail Regiment during the Battle of Gettysburg and who was serving as an honor guard, reported seeing Booth on the platform with Lincoln. The actor had charmed an invitation out of the plump daughter of a New England senator who thought he was going to marry her. From Washington he went to Boston to see his brother Edwin. Then, on April 12, he was back in Washington on the lawn of the White House listening to Lincoln talk about reconstruction. Two days later he made his final public appearance when he leaped from the box where Lincoln was sitting to the stage of the Ford Theater and broke his leg.

Rumors that Booth was hiding in Franklin quickly circulated after the assassination. Friends of his in the town were questioned, and one, Joseph Simonds, with whom he had arrived in the area, was taken into custody. John Cain, a bank teller who resembled Booth and had just taken a job in Franklin, was actually arrested and held as the assassin until the bank president came to the jail and identified him.

About two weeks after the assassination, Booth was found hiding in a barn in Port Royal, Virginia, and died in a gunfight with federal troops. Six weeks later a well on Pithole Creek in which Booth owned a share struck oil. "Probably the most productive well in the oil region of Pennsylvania" the *Titusville Herald* called it, and Booth's memory was soon lost to the booming of Pithole City.

In her book *The Great Oildorado*, Franklin native Hildegarde Dolson provided a suitable metaphor for the mood of the United States after the Civil War when she wrote that Pithole "was more than a city; it was a state of postwar euphoria." After four years of the bloodiest conflict ever fought on American soil, followed by the assassination of the president who had preserved the Union, the nation was eager to find a new direction. Paper currency flooded the banks, leaving businessmen anxious to see the good economic times war brings to the marketplace continue, while the breakup of the army left tens of thousands of discharged soldiers in need of work. When word of the discovery of oil along Pithole Creek reached both groups a stampede was unleashed. "This once benighted but now flourishing region is the Mecca of the Oil World or the 8th wonder, I don't know which," a reporter for the *Venango Spectator* noted. "Even while I write, buildings are going up and some are put up and have groceries in them in six hours."

Pithole Creek was given its name by early travelers to the region who encountered sulfurous fumes escaping from rock fissures along its banks. According to one story, a hunter was sitting on the edge of a pit one winter afternoon warming his legs when he was overcome by the gases and had to be carried home by his companions. Word spread quickly about "sulphur and brimstone pits inhabited by the Evil One." Such superstition, combined with a real lack of road and water access, made land surrounding the stream almost impossible to sell when the Holland Land Company, the original owner, placed it on the market around 1800. Even after the company offered one hundred extra acres to any buyer, few takers came forward. As late as May 1865 there were only four log cabins standing along the stream, among them one belonging to the Rev. Walter Holmden, who agreed to lease sixty-five acres of his property to the U.S. Petroleum Company.

Ian Frazier, president of U.S. Petroleum, was a shrewd wildcatter who had already earned a quarter of a million dollars as partial owner of a well along the Oil Creek tributary of Cherry Run. He became interested in Pithole after a diviner he sent out reported feeling oil in the area. Ignoring scientists who called the method "a cheat, an art abhorrent to nature," Frazier went to the property and followed the diviner until his

Triumph Hill, Tidioute

forked twig dipped and pointed down, then ordered his crew to begin drilling. That first well proved to be dry, but Frazier persisted until, in January 1865, he struck oil.

The Frazier Well entered the world sprouting 250 barrels a day. In April a Boston company drilled another hole, the Homestead Well, only a hundred feet beyond the boundary of the U.S. Petroleum Company property. It too began producing oil at the rate of 250 barrels per day. Soon those figures climbed to 1,200 barrels a day at the Frazier Well and to 500 a day at the Homestead. The U.S. Petroleum Company subdivided its property and began selling its land for $3,000 a half-acre, and the rush to Pithole was on.

In May 1865 Thomas Duncan and George Prather, two fast talkers who purchased the Holmden farm for $25,000 at about the time the Frazier Well hit, laid out Pithole City in five hundred lots along twenty-two streets on a hill above Pithole Creek. The lots, which measured just thirty-three feet in width, could not be purchased but had to be leased for a period of three years, after which the owner of the building could either remove it or sell it to the owner of the property. If a five-year lease was desired, buildings had to be surrendered to the landowner at the end of the period. Lots rented for as high as $14,000 a year.

175

At the same time Pithole City was being built, exciting things were happening on the flats around Pithole Creek. On June 17, 1865, U.S. Petroleum sunk a well that began flowing at the rate of eight hundred barrels a day. Two days later another well struck, spewing four hundred barrels a day. These twin wells alone gave the company a daily income of $2,000. The same day the second well hit, a storage tank connected to the Frazier Well burst and poured more than twenty-five hundred gallons of crude into the creek. Two boys playing on the banks touched a lighted match to the oil. It took more than two hundred men to put out the fire. "No Smoking" signs sprouted like weeds all along the stream but did little good—the fire was the first of dozens to strike the town.

Oil City pileup, 19th century

By the end of June, Pithole was producing two thousand barrels of oil a day, one-third of the region's total output. Long processions of tank wagons moved back and forth from Pithole to Titusville, Oil City, and other shipping points. The heavy traffic quickly destroyed roads leading into the town. Conditions got so bad that, by July, many teamsters refused to haul oil out of Pithole. Worried merchants and shippers in Titusville hurried to put together a fund to repair the roads. Teamsters were required to contribute one dollar a week out of their own pockets. The price of shipping oil out of Pithole rose to three dollars a barrel, the same price crude was selling for in town.

Pithole was at a fever pitch by September, just nine months after the Frazier Well hit. Production rose to six thousand barrels a day. Duncan and Prather sold the Holmden farm, which was accounting for about four thousand barrels of the total, to three Titusville investors for $1.3 million in July, took it back when the buyers failed to meet the terms of the sale, and resold it in August for $2 million. About the same time, the Homestead Well stopped flowing and another well on the Holmden farm caught fire. Then, in October, fires destroyed $1.5 million worth of property on the flats, and in November the Frazier Well went dry. January 1866 saw a sharp drop in production, February and March witnessed major fires, and then in April six fires sent a large portion of the town up in smoke. The end was near.

Pithole hung on as a town into 1867, but by 1870 only a handful of people remained on the site. In 1878 the Holmden farm was bought by Venango County for $4.37 and resold to a private owner in 1886 for $83.76. The last building to be torn down in Pithole was the Methodist church, in 1939. All that remains on the site today are street grades along which photographs have been erected showing what the town looked like and a few foundation scars. A small museum above Pithole Creek tells the town's story through photographs, slides, and pieces of equipment.

Although Pithole may have been a flash in the pan as far as towns are concerned, its legacy lives on in no less a form than the Alaskan pipeline, for it was at Pithole that the world's first commercially successful oil pipeline was built. Designed by Samuel Van Syckel, the line ran from Pithole to a railhead on a nearby farm and cut the cost of moving crude from Pithole to the marketplace from three dollars a barrel to one dollar.

Busy Route 8/62 rims the west side of the Allegheny with discount stores and fast-food restaurants between Franklin and Oil City. At Reno a refinery stands as a sign that the region continues to produce oil. Between the bridges at Oil City appears the only "whitewater" along the river, a two-tenths-of-a-mile stretch that during high-water periods forms a series of large standing waves popular with local canoeists and kayakers.

Lying near the whitewater is the mouth of Oil Creek, which, along with all of its historical significance, marks the location of one of the most successful attempts to control Allegheny River ice. Almost as long as people have been living along the river

"Little crystals of frazzle ice begin to latch on to the pontoons and cable and then start attaching to each other," explains Corps Public Relations Officer John Reed. "Before you know it, you've got an ice cover going upriver above the junction of the river and Oil Creek. You still get ice formation below, but it's not as thick and you don't have as much slush ice underneath. It's worked beautifully so far."

Oil City, with its large buildings and string of oil storage tanks and other industrial facilities, stands in sharp contrast to quaint Franklin. Built on land once owned by the Seneca Chief Cornplanter, Oil City derived its name from Oil Creek. As far back as the Revolution it was a prominent rafting point along the river, and its location at the confluence of Oil Creek and the Allegheny made it the natural center for the early oil industry. Between 1860 and 1870 an estimated seventeen million barrels of oil were floated in barges from Oil City to refineries in Pittsburgh. Through its oil exchange, the town controlled world oil prices during the late nineteenth century. Over $1.5 billion worth of oil was sold on the exchange in 1885.

"Whew! what smells so?" one traveler to Oil City wrote in 1864. "The gaseous wealth of the oily regions . . . pigs . . . mud . . . I walked between walls and oil yards, barns and pens, keeping my bearing as I could. . . . I found the main street . . . too thick for water and wholly too thin for land. . . . The hurrying men, muddy and eager, pushed by . . . used to it."

Fire, the greatest threat to the early oil towns, destroyed most of Oil City on May 26, 1866. Near Route 8 north of the town, however, stands one remnant of the old days. McClintock Well No. 1 was drilled in August 1861 and is still pumping oil, making it the oldest producing oil well in the world.

Celebrating oil's heritage

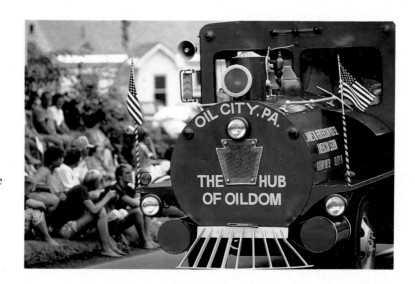

Nuptials, Oil City

Local oil companies have already experimented with displacing the petroleum with water, steam, gas, air, and chemicals, with only varying success. Each type of sandstone is different, Harper points out. Crude-oil-bearing sandstone in the Oil City–Franklin region does not react well to water as a displacement agent, while that found in McKean County is excellent for water flooding. On the other hand, oil in the Oil City–Franklin area responds well to injections of natural gas or air, while Bradford oil does not. "What technique you use depends on the rock," he says. "But nobody has yet come up with anything that will get another 20 or 30 percent of the oil out of the ground."

The thought is astonishing. Since 1859, longer than anywhere else on earth, oil has been regularly pumped from the fractured sandstone bedrock of the upper Allegheny Valley, and still, despite the best technology of the late twentieth century, more than half of it remains inaccessible. The idea makes me want to cheer for the earth and hope we finally begin to develop sources of energy that are less polluting. But at the same time, I know that some way will eventually be found to extract the crude, refine and burn it, and add to the earth's blanket. Humans are nothing if not ingenious when it comes to making money. Once they even managed to barge oil down Oil Creek, a feat that does not sound difficult until a person looks up the stream, which except during runoff periods does not look as if it can float a canoe.

The way the early oil men brought crude down Oil Creek was nothing less than an environmental nightmare. A dam was built across the stream near the spot where Drake drilled his well, and horses and mules would haul empty barges upstream from Oil City. After the barges were filled, a large hole was knocked through the dam and a torrent of water three or four feet high was sent thundering downstream. "The cry of 'Pond freshet!' went up from thousands of throats and frequently as many as two or three hundred craft of all descriptions were turned loose at the mercy of the raging flood," wrote Captain Way, who as a young man in the 1930s heard the event described by ninety-year-old Captain Dan Fry, one of the last oil-barge workers living.

> Well drillers, oil-field hands, teamsters, every able-bodied man available, dropped his chores and climbed aboard a boat to help "navigate" it out to Oil City.
>
> The art of navigating these craft consisted of making a herculean attempt to keep them in motion. This meant that the loaded boats frequently rammed the bank, turned end for end, rammed one another, collided with bridge piers, jammed on gravel bars, sank on protruding rocks and otherwise acted like a pile of straws racing pell-mell down a street gutter after a summer shower. On a particular freshet staged in May 1864, no less than 20,000 barrels of crude were lost in a "jam" on the Oil City bridge pier alone. One of the leading boats caught the stone obstruction broadside, hung there, and the latecomers, unable to halt, piled down upon a general scene of destruction. As many as one thousand men were engaged in these artificial splashes.

A model of the May 1864 pileup at Oil City can be seen at the Drake Well Museum near Titusville. Visitors can also view numerous photographs from the period showing an Allegheny River thick with a dirty coat of crude and full of floating planks and other debris.

From the time Colonel Drake drilled his well through Pithole's boom and bust, the Allegheny's oil country was largely the domain of independent dreamers, inventors, and innovators, rugged individualists who did not believe any real American worked for wages and who in the great American myth pushed back the wilderness and created a nation. But such fast wealth as could be had in Oil City, Titusville, and other nearby towns soon caught the attention of a new type of adventurer—the robber baron capitalist.

It is said that after John D. Rockefeller first set eyes on northwestern Pennsylvania's oil region just before the Civil War, he went back to his Cleveland home complaining about "chaos and disorder, waste and incompetence, competition at its worst." At the same time, though, the austere, devoutly religious, and reserved twenty-one-year-old grocer ("that bloodless Baptist book-keeper," one independent oil man would later call him) saw in all the frenzied activity a unique opportunity. In 1863, along with Maurice Clark, his partner in the grocery business, two of Clark's brothers, and Samuel Andrews, a candlemaker who had experience working with lard oil, Rockefeller became a partner in

John D. Rockefeller

Andrews, Clark & Company and opened the Excelsior Refinery near the Cuyahoga River. Then, in February 1865, anxious for far bolder growth than the Clarks were willing to undertake, he and Andrews bought out the Clark brothers, formed the Rockefeller & Andrews Company, and immediately began to expand. By November of that year the two men were owners of the largest of Cleveland's thirty refineries.

Avoiding the speculation, waste, and guesswork that characterized the get-rich-quick early oil industry in favor of efficiency and stability, Rockefeller and Andrews, aided by the best business minds they could buy, among them a young Cleveland entrepreneur named Henry Flagler, prospered into the 1870s. Then the chaos and competition that raged in a different industry presented them with another interesting opportunity.

In 1850 the railway system of the United States contained just over 9,000 miles of track, located mostly in the Northeast. Driven first by the Civil War and the need to transport troops and supplies to the front, and then later by the push to settle the West, by 1870 that total had grown to more than 85,000 miles of track, and by 1890 to almost 164,000 miles. To finance such growth and to ensure large profits, the railroads were hungry for customers and hatched all sorts of schemes (from buffalo hunts in the west to tropical vacations in then mosquito- and malaria-ridden southern Florida) to increase ridership. To entice freight, rebates and special rates, though illegal under federal law, were commonly offered to shippers.

When the expansion Rockefeller envisioned proved impossible with the private firm of Rockefeller, Andrews & Flagler, he and Flagler incorporated a joint-stock company, the Standard Oil Company of Ohio on January 10, 1870. Soon after Standard Oil's founding, the Pennsylvania Railroad cut its shipping rates and launched a fierce rate war. Business from the upper Allegheny's oil region began heading south to Pittsburgh in such amounts that Cleveland seemed doomed to be wiped out as a refining center. Rockefeller and Flagler were able to survive only by working out a deal with the New York–Lake Shore Railroad. The following year a depression hit the oil industry. Petroleum producers, refiners, and the railroads all were hit hard. A debate arose about how to end the boom-and-bust cycle that always afflicted the oil business, and the South Improvement Company was created.

John D. Rockefeller was at first a reluctant partner in the conspiracy known as the South Improvement Company, but once he joined he worked hard for it. The plan was actually the brainchild of Thomas Scott, vice president of the Pennsylvania Railroad and Andrew Carnegie's patron, Cornelius Vanderbilt of the New York Central Railroad, and Jay Gould of the Erie Railroad. "It was as ruthless and ruinous to nonmembers as anything ever devised by rogues," wrote Dolson in *The Great Oildorado.* "The gist of it: all the railroads would raise oil-freight rates anywhere from 100 per cent to 250 per cent. Refiners who belonged to the conspiracy would get enormous rebates over everything they shipped, and also *on every barrel their competitors shipped.* The railroads would divide their own share of the spoils evenly."

Stock in the South Improvement Company was issued on January 2, 1872. When independent oil producers in the Allegheny Valley got wind of the plan, they organized a boycott of the railroads involved. Meetinghalls in Franklin, Oil City, and Titusville were draped with banners proclaiming proud American mottoes—"Don't Give Up the Ship!" "No Surrender!" "United We Stand!"—and rocked with angry speeches denouncing the South Improvement Company and the outsiders who wanted to take over the oil business. Vigilante groups roamed the countryside, threatening producers who sold crude oil to the South Improvement Company and burning railroad cars bearing the company's name. The uproar was so great that, only three months after its first stock issue, the charter of the South Improvement Company was revoked by the Pennsylvania legislature.

Although the South Improvement Company scheme fell apart, Rockefeller's desire to control the nation's oil industry did not end with it. The independents soon found themselves being squeezed in a different manner when Standard Oil agreed to purchase all their oil and then reneged on the contracts, leaving the market awash in petroleum for which there were no customers.

Among the many independent oil men who suffered at the hands of the South Improvement Company and John D. Rockefeller was a man named Franklin Tarbell. By turns a teacher, farmer, river pilot, and joiner, Tarbell lived in Titusville and was a descendant of a family whose roots went back almost to the Pilgrims. He was never a very astute businessman, but he still managed to make a small fortune and provide for his wife Esther, a descendant of Sir Walter Raleigh, and his family in comfortable style when he invented a wooden tank capable of storing more than a hundred barrels of crude oil.

Although Franklin Tarbell's business survived the battle with the South Improvement Company and Rockefeller, the experience changed his personality. From an energetic, gregarious, intense individual who liked to relax by telling stories, playing the Jew's harp, and singing to his children, he turned inward and seethed at the injustice and underhandedness he saw perpetrated by the South Improvement Company gang and Standard Oil. It was a change that would not escape the notice of his daughter Ida, and one that more than thirty years later would help fill her with indignation and drive her to expose what may have been the most powerful monopoly in U.S. history.

Ida Minerva Tarbell was born the eldest of four children of Franklin Summer Tarbell and Esther Ann McCullough Tarbell in a log cabin in Hatch Hollow, Erie County, about four miles south of Wattsburg on November 5, 1857. Her father was planning to move his family to Iowa when oil was found in Erie County and he decided instead to stay and seek his fortune in northwestern Pennsylvania. He moved the family in 1861 to an oil encampment at Cherry Run and then to Rouseville, a few miles up Oil Creek from the

Ida Tarbell

Allegheny River, where he invented his storage tank. Following the flow of oil, the Tarbells moved from Rouseville to Pithole and then, in 1870, to Titusville, where Franklin Tarbell built a home on the main street using lumber from the Bonta House. Once among the grandest buildings in Pithole, the Bonta House was built for $60,000 during the town's boom period. After the bust, the owners were glad to accept Tarbell's offer to buy it for $600.

As a high school student in Titusville, Ida Tarbell developed an interest in science that called into question what she had been taught about the creation of the world. When her parents, who had originally been Presbyterians, became ardent Methodists, she began to question her own religious beliefs further. "Upset to have been deceived by the matter of the Six Days of Creation," says Kathleen Brady in her biography of Ida Tarbell (1984), "fretful over where she fit in a chaotic cosmic scheme, the girl had decided to trust only what she could discover for herself."

In 1876 Ida entered Allegheny College, an early coeducational school in Meadville, Crawford County, about thirty miles from her home in Titusville. She planned to study biology, but soon discovered science offered no opportunities for women, so after graduation in 1880 she took a post as a teacher at the Union Seminary in Poland, Ohio.

Feeling oppressed as a teacher, Ida left Poland after her two-year contract ended, turned down an offer to teach French and German at Allegheny College, and returned to Titusville, where she went to work in the editorial offices of *The Chautauquan*, the monthly magazine of the Chautauqua Society, a former Bible study institute housed in a camp on the banks of Lake Chautauqua near Jamestown, New York. Although *The Chautauquan* was founded by a religious organization, the magazine explored issues in science, history, and literature and seemed heaven-sent to the culturally starved residents of the oil region. And through this magazine Ida Tarbell found her true calling. She remained with the magazine until 1891, when she felt she had outgrown it, gathered her savings, and moved to Paris.

Living with friends in the Paris Latin Quarter, Ida divided her time in Paris among lectures at the Sorbonne, research at the Bibliothèque Nationale on the role of women in the French Revolution, and writing stories, at $6 each, for a group of midwestern newspapers. While in Paris she also met Samuel McClure, publisher of *McClure's* magazine, who when she returned to the United States in 1894 hired her to write a serial biography of Napoleon Bonaparte. The series was an immediate success and led Ida to tackle a biography of Abraham Lincoln, a man she revered and a subject to which she would return again and again over the next forty years.

By the 1880s the American public was beginning to rebel against the monopolies and trusts that since the end of the Civil War had nearly destroyed competition and taken control of the nation's beef, sugar, steel, coal, railroads, oil, and other industries essential to daily life. Workers struck for better wages, the eight-hour day, and union representation. In May 1886 a mass protest against the killing of strikers in Chicago's Haymarket Square ended as one of the bloodiest days in U.S. labor history when a bomb was thrown at a line of police officers and the police fired into the crowd.

Protests against monopolies and trusts continued through the 1890s with mixed success (the Sherman Antitrust Act was passed in 1890, but in Pittsburgh Henry Clay Frick beat back an attempt to organize the steel industry during the Homestead Strike of 1892). *McClure's* entered the fray in 1901 when it published an article entitled "What the U.S. Steel Corp. Really Is" and then decided to go even further by publishing a series on one trust that would show how an industry went from ownership by many to control by a few. After extensive debate among the staff, Standard Oil was chosen as the subject and Ida Tarbell as the author.

Driven by the same desire to know the truth that caused her to question what she had been taught in Sunday school, and by a knowledge of what John D. Rockefeller's efforts to control the oil industry had done to her father and her neighbors in Titusville,

court agreed. Standard Oil appealed the decision until the U.S. Supreme Court finally ruled against it in May 1911 and the company was ordered dissolved.

Ida Tarbell's reporting also helped lead to the passage of some much-needed laws regulating business. In 1906 the Hepburn Act established controls over railroad freight rates and classified pipeline companies as common public carriers that must treat all customers alike. The act was further strengthened in 1910 by the Mann-Elkins Act, which gave the Interstate Commerce Commission greater power to control pipeline rates. Then, in 1914, the Federal Trade Commission was created to police business practices, and the Clayton Act, which prohibited unfair competition that tended to promote monopolies, became law. Thus, within a decade of the publication of *The History of the Standard Oil Company*, virtually all the abuses Ida Tarbell wrote about had been addressed by the federal government.

From the appearance of her first articles on the Standard Oil Company in *McClure's*, Ida Tarbell was hailed as a heroine by independent drillers in oil fields not only up and down the Allegheny River but also across the nation. In the Kansas outback, thirty to forty wildcatters serenaded her as she sat talking with a local newspaper editor. In Kansas City she was the first woman to speak to the Knife and Fork Club, a dining club of the city's rich and powerful. But she never gloated over her victory, for even though Standard Oil was ordered dissolved, the thirty-eight companies into which it was broken up continued to function in concert. The octopus, as political cartoonists of the time had depicted the Standard Oil Company, remained alive.

As it marked the peak of the muckraking journalism era, *The History of the Standard Oil Company* also marked the acme of Ida Tarbell's career. She would continue to write prolifically for the rest of her life, but her reformist zeal never lasted very long and her stands often confused her early supporters. Even though she took on Standard Oil, she was always a believer in capitalism, and even giant corporations—as long as everyone was given a fair chance to compete in a business. And even though she never married or had any children of her own, she was a strong believer in traditional family values. Members of the women's suffrage and women's rights movements were put off when she criticized the assertiveness of their members and bewailed their inattention to the values of home and family. Progressives abandoned her when she fell under the spell of Henry Ford and became a believer in "welfare capitalism," Ford's plan in which corporations would see to the needs of their employees like welfare states. Other earlier admirers abandoned her when she wrote an adulatory biography of steel magnate Elbert H. Gary and praised Italian dictator Benito Mussolini for his national industrial policy. She made something of a comeback to her old ways in the 1930s when she supported Franklin Roosevelt's National Recovery Administration and the Social Security Act.

Ida Tarbell died of pneumonia in a Bridgeport, Connecticut, hospital, not far from the Redding Ridge farm she bought in 1906 with royalties from *The History*, at age eighty-seven on January 6, 1944. As was her wish, her body was taken back to Titusville, where it was buried in Woodlawn Cemetery not far from the grave of Colonel Edwin Drake and less than 150 miles from her old adversary John D. Rockefeller, who had died just seven years earlier at age ninety-seven and was buried in Cleveland.

Indian Days, Tionesta

Barely beyond Oil City the Allegheny becomes once more a wild and scenic river of empty pools and riffles, and scattered cottages collected in places with names like Ahrensville, Walnut Bend, Olepolis, and Henry's Bend, and reachable only by a few back roads, boat, or foot. The riffles here are a little livelier and the pools shallower than below Franklin. The eddy at Walnut Bend was once a popular overnight mooring spot for rafters floating timber to the mills at Pittsburgh and on down the Ohio. "About sundown, rafts can be seen rounding into the eddy thick and three-fold," notes the 1855 edition of *The Allegheny Pilot*. "Both eddy and shore are literally alive with the Allegheny's 'Hardy Salts,' landing and securing their rafts for the night."

Across the river from Eagle Rock, Route 62, which had taken a shorter, overland path than the winding river, rejoins the Allegheny. It rushes past President, opposite

Tionesta

Baum, and then crosses the river at Hunter, near where Holeman's Ferry once ran and Holeman's Eddy once served as "a very good landing place for several fleets." Then it hurries on to Tionesta.

A majority of Forest County is in the public domain of Allegheny National Forest or State Game Lands, so it has the smallest population of any county in Pennsylvania—about four thousand people. Tionesta is the county's only official borough and takes its name from Tionesta Creek, which after being temporarily restrained by Tionesta Dam enters the Allegheny on the south side of town. At various times the Delaware Indian name "Tionesta" has been translated to mean "it penetrates the island," "it penetrates the forest," "home of the wolves," and "there it has fine banks." Before the appearance of whites, three Indian villages stood in the area. Goshgoshing, "place of hogs"—one wonders how hogs could live in the "home of the wolves"—was probably located a short distance upriver from Hunter. Lawunkhannek was erected at about the mouth of Tionesta Creek, and Cuscushing somewhere between Tionesta and Little Tionesta creeks.

David Zeisberger, a Moravian missionary who explored northern Pennsylvania before the Revolution, found his way to the vicinity in 1767. Two years later he built the first Protestant church west of the Allegheny Mountains in Tionesta, but his quest for converts was strongly resisted by both the Delawares who lived at Goshgoshing and the Senecas who controlled the territory. The Delawares were not interested in the strange preacher's restrictive and threatening religion, which would have them work when their needs were satisfied and sought to interfere with their lovemaking. The Senecas were suspicious that the appearance of whites would lead to construction of a fort and a British takeover of the region. The trials Zeisberger faced preaching to Tionesta's Native Americans were so great that they were immortalized in an 1862 painting by C. Schussele. This painting now hangs in the Moravian Society Archives in Bethlehem, Pennsylvania.

Zeisberger also was probably the first white to record the presence of oil in the area. He noted in his journal that the Native Americans used it "medicinally for toothache, rheumatism, etc.," and added, "Sometimes it is taken internally. It is of a brown color and burns well and can be used in lamps."

In his diary on July 17, 1768, Zeisberger also noted the presence of "a fine large island" opposite the mouth of Tionesta Creek. The following year, he further described the island as a place on which the Indians had a "plantation . . . about 20 acres in size, right opposite to us and very good land." In 1855 *The Allegheny Pilot* warned rafters ferrying their logs to market about thirteen islands in the river at Tionesta, noting that "some of them are under a high state of cultivation and are owned by different individuals."

Islands are as common to the Allegheny as mountains, fog, and gravel. They occur all up and down it, even within the city limits of Pittsburgh, but nowhere in such

Schussele's "Power of the Gospel," depicting David Zeisberger preaching at Goshgoshing

abundance as between Oil City and Warren. According to a study by the U.S. Forest Service, there are 109 islands in the fifty-four-mile-long stretch between the two towns—leftovers from when the glaciers turned the Allegheny and forced it to cut a new path to the south.

Travelers following Route 62 close along the river north of Tionesta find that the islands come to their attention in a scenic and vaguely mystical sort of way. Even an island separated from the bank by a channel only fifteen yards wide is still an island—conveying the same sense of a higher power, adventure, mystery, solitude, and refuge that any land surrounded by water seems to elicit in the human soul.

But the Allegheny's islands mean far more to the river than the scenic beauty and metaphysical stirrings they awaken in a single species. The islands are ecologically unique. They contain stands of uncut, riverine forest generally found in more southern climates. Pondweed and riverweed are two rare plants found on the islands or banks of the river. Channels around the islands are also home to eight rare species of darter minnows, including the bluebreasted darter and the spotted darter, as well as eighteen species of mussels, among them the northern riffleshell and the clubshell, the latter of which is being considered for listing under the U.S. Endangered Species Act.

In fact, some of the best mussel habitat left in the United States can be found in the Allegheny. Because these soft-bodied mollusks have a low tolerance for pollution, their presence in the river also is a sure signal of high water quality. Charles Bier, a biologist with the Western Pennsylvania Conservancy, points out that the Mississippi River drainage, of which the Allegheny is considered a part, holds the highest diversity of fish

Thompson Island

Turk's-cap lily

and mussels in North America. While a few other sections of the drainage have held and still hold larger numbers of mussels than the Allegheny, no place holds a greater diversity—because, as Bier notes, "they have been destroyed almost everywhere else."

To help ensure that the scenic beauty and wildlife habitat of the Allegheny remains as undisturbed and free of development as possible, and that access and campsites remain available to canoeists and other recreational users, the Western Pennsylvania Conservancy began acquiring property along the river in the early 1970s. "In the late sixties we looked at the Allegheny from the standpoint of a recreational resource in western Pennsylvania," says Paul Wiegman, the Conservancy's director of natural services and stewardship. "The broadest concept developed at that time was a trail that would begin in Warren, at the base of Kinzua Dam essentially, and extend all the way to Pittsburgh."

Because green hillsides, open fields, and wooded mountains make for a much more pleasant trip for hiking or canoeing than refineries, mills, and strip mines, the Conservancy set about creating a green corridor by purchasing not only islands and land along the banks of the Allegheny, but also the country above and beyond the river. At first the state helped with the project, even drawing up plans for three state parks along the river, but by the mid-1970s state funds had dried up and interest had waned. Land in the Kennerdell area purchased for a park became Kittanning State Forest, and the Conservancy decided to go it alone. It pared down its plans and concentrated on the river between Tionesta and Warren, where it could resell the land to the federal government for Allegheny National Forest or the Pennsylvania Game Commission for its State Game Lands system.

198

Even though most of the Allegheny above Tionesta has now been saved from development, cabins and homes will continue to be built along the river, because individual lots are far too expensive for the Conservancy, and even the state or federal government, to acquire. But, Wiegman cautions, less development does not necessarily mean less pollution. Rivers are repositories for everything found on the land they drain. And the wild and scenic Allegheny still has problems with sewage from the small towns that cannot afford first-rate treatment plants and from runoff from fertilized fields, mines, and oil wells.

Mussel reserve

The Western Pennsylvania Conservancy, aided by the Northern Allegheny Conservation Association and other groups, has been fighting to save as much as possible of the Allegheny between Tionesta and Warren from the "progress" that once saw the forests around the river clearcut and deserted of wildlife, and the river's waters flowing dark with spilled crude oil. But busy Route 62, lying tight on the bank, keeps the stretch from being anywhere near a wilderness experience. The views of the mountains and river, though, are usually pleasant, disturbed mainly by collections of hunting camps. In a few places, for brief moments, when the road is angled just right and only the river, mountains, and sky appear outside the windshield, it is even possible to imagine what the country might have looked like when Céloron passed through. Father Bonnecamps wrote:

Tidioute Overlook

We marched all day between two chains of mountains, which bordered the river on the right and left. The Ohio [both the French and the English at first called the Allegheny the Ohio] is very low during the first twenty leagues; but a great storm, which we had experienced on the eve of our departure, had swollen the waters, and we pursued our journey without any hindrance.

Monsieur Chabert on that day caught seven rattlesnakes, which were the first that I had seen. . . . They are, I am told, very large ones. None of those which I have seen exceed 4 feet. The bite is fatal. It is said that washing the wound which has been received, with saliva mixed with a little sea-salt, is a sovereign remedy. We have not had, thank God, any occasion to put this antidote to the test.

Canoe camper

After Tionesta and its neighbor West Hickory, Tidioute is the only town of any consequence on the Allegheny before Warren. Another Indian name, "Tidioute" has been translated to mean "seeing far," "straight water," "cluster of islands," and "on the great river." Because there are quite a few islands near the town, it sits on the river, and Tidioute Overlook on the mountain opposite the town provides a view worthy of mention in the 1979 Geological Survey's *Outstanding Scenic Geological Features of Pennsylvania*, it's easy to understand how the word earned those translations. "Straight water," however, takes a little more imagination, as Tidioute sits on a near right-angle bend in the river that turns it from west to south.

The first settlers in Tidioute were members of the Harmony Society. At odds with his church, the lay preacher George Rapp disposed of the property he owned in Württemberg, Germany, in 1803 and sailed for the United States, where he purchased

Tidioute Bridge

Tidioute

five thousand acres of land on the Ohio River twenty-five miles below Pittsburgh. The next year about six hundred of his followers arrived in western Pennsylvania. A year later they formed the Harmony Society.

Under its tenets of hard work and simple living in harmony with God and the earth, the Harmony Society quickly prospered and spread up the Allegheny to Tidioute. Along with tens of thousands of acres of land, it also came to control a bank, several factories, coal mines, oil pipelines, and oil wells. By 1825 it controlled such a large volume of trade in western Pennsylvania that people began calling for its dissolution—a call that was not needed because the society's rule of celibacy doomed it from the start. The celibacy requirement caused more than 250 Harmonists to leave the sect as early as 1832, and few new converts were attracted. The last two Harmonists dissolved the society in 1906.

In 1860 the Grandin Well, the world's first free-flowing oil well, just below Tidioute Bridge, was tapped by the Harmonists. During the 1870s, Tidioute was the focal point of the richest oil pool in Warren County and, as the 1940 Works Progress Administration book *Pennsylvania: Guide to the Keystone State* noted, "played second fiddle to no town in Oildom for intelligence, enterprise and all-round attractiveness." The small collection of businesses on the main street today makes it difficult to believe that the town was once home to five thousand people. But remnants of Tidioute's glory days are still evidenced by the town's many large Victorian homes.

Magee, Cobham, and Althom pass as colorful settlements of hunting camps and second homes across the Allegheny from Route 62. The floodplain below the road, and to a much lesser extent the mountains above, also holds scatterings of cottages. Indian Paint Hill, with its large deposits of red ochre and adjacent petroleum springs that once furnished the Indians with face and body paint, is announced by a historical marker.

A few miles upriver, another historical marker announces the presence of Thompson Island. It was on the west bank of the Allegheny opposite Thompson Island that Colonel Daniel Brodhead's troops, part of an expedition General Washington sent to put an end to British-encouraged Indian raids on settlements in western Pennsylvania, fought a skirmish with a party of Senecas on August 15, 1779. "Discovered between thirty & Forty warriors coming down the Allegheny River in seven Canoes," Colonel Brodhead wrote in his report to Washington. Immediately the Indians, who favored fighting naked so that bits of cloth or buckskin would not enter a wound and cause it to become infected, "stript off their shirts & prepared for action, and the advance Guard immediately began the attack."

By the time Brodhead arrived on the scene with the main body of his troops, the Indians were in full retreat, "leaving their Canoes, Blankets, Shirts, provisions and eight guns, besides five dead & by the signs of Blood, several went off wounded. Only two of my men & one of the Delaware Indians [who were accompanying Brodhead] were

wounded & so slightly that they are already recovered & set for action."

Later, one of Brodhead's men, Joseph Nicholson, became a friend of the Seneca Chief Cornplanter. In October 1790, Cornplanter petitioned the state to reward Nicholson for his services by giving him a six-square-mile tract of land at the forks of the Allegheny and Brokenstraw Creek. The Indian village of Buckaloons (an English—or rather Irish—corruption of the Delaware "Poquihhilleu") stood on that site until it was destroyed by Colonel Brodhead the day after the Thompson Island engagement.

During the time Buckaloons was an Indian village, Céloron had stopped there and spoken with the inhabitants, saying he was "surprised, my children, to see raised in your village a cabin destined to receive English traders. If you look upon yourselves as my children you will no longer receive the English in your homes." Outnumbered and outgunned, the Indians took the only sensible course, telling the Frenchman, "You have invited us to discontinue this work. This is what we promise you, and this house which is almost finished, will serve only for a recreation place for the youth." And so the first youth recreation center was opened in western Pennsylvania, a tradition that has been continued in the form of a campground the U.S. Forest Service now operates on the site.

Almost directly across from Buckaloons and the mouth of Brokenstraw Creek stands one of the buildings of the New Process Company, the largest direct-mail retailer of clothing and home furnishings in the nation. The company was founded in 1910 by John Blair, a twenty-year-old undergraduate law student at the University of Pennsylvania.

Contemporary explorers

Perry Magee Run

Fossils, Buckaloons

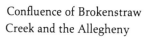

Confluence of Brokenstraw
Creek and the Allegheny

"His roommate in college had a father who manufactured raincoats," says Marilyn Oberg, executive director of Travel Northern Alleghenies, the local tourist promotion agency. "They were black raincoats that they rubberized. It was a new processing method, which is where the company—New Process—got its name. For a summer job, John and his friend decided to sell raincoats for his friend's father, but they didn't find much of a market for black raincoats. When John went back to school and got to thinking about the situation, he decided that if he could get the names of every mortician in the United States he could probably sell a black raincoat to each of them. So he spent the school year obtaining the names of all these morticians, and the rest was history. The next year, John and his friend started a mail-order business for the black raincoats with the 'new processing,' and it went from there."

Around Buckaloons and the New Process Company facility (the clothing manufactured there is labeled "Blair"), the Allegheny makes another of its right-angle turns, leading Route 62 to merge with Route 6 and hem the river in with multiple lanes of concrete. And then come more and more businesses, industrial plants, homes, oil tanks, and traffic until the river is swallowed by Warren—a town that, with its picturesque Victorian center and smelly refinery, might be described as a cross between Franklin and Oil City.

Like Buckaloons, Warren was also once the site of an Indian village—Kanaongan, better known as Conewango—that was visited by Céloron and destroyed by Colonel Brodhead. Having followed a route out of Canada that took him along Lake Ontario and Lake Erie and then down Lake Chautauqua and Conewango Creek, Céloron first laid eyes on the Allegheny on July 29, 1749, at Warren.

"As I was not far from the village of Kanaongan," wrote Céloron, "and as the savages were informed by M. de Joncaire of my arrival, they were anxious to find me. As soon as they had discovered my canoes they sent a deputation to invite me to visit their villages and there receive the compliments of their chief." He continued:

> I treated them well—the envoys. I gave a cup of brandy, for them to drink to their father Onontio, and gave them tobacco. They returned to their village; they saluted me with several discharges of musketry; I returned them, and formed my camp at the other side of the river. M. de Joncaire collected the chiefs in one tent, I received their compliments and felicitations, and as this village has from twelve to thirteen cabins, I invited them to go to la Paille Coupée [Buckaloons] to hear what I had to say to them on the part of their father Onontio; the women brought me a present of Indian corn and pumpkins. I responded suitably with other little presents. M. de Joncaire assured me that it was time he should have come to dissipate the terror which had seized on the spirits of the savages, that several had retired to the woods and that the others had made their packs to do the same. I sent M. de Joncaire to la Paille Coupée.

Refinery, Warren

It was at Warren—"at the foot of a red oak, on the southern bank of the river Oyo and Kanaougon, and at 42 degrees, 5' 23"''—that Céloron buried his first lead plate claiming the "Ohio Country" (as the Allegheny and lands to the west were known) for France. Almost as soon as the French departed, the Indians dug up the plate and carried it to the British Indian agent Sir William Johnson, who, seeing a way to enlist the Indians as allies, happily informed them that the writing claimed their land for the king of France. He then passed the plate on to Governor George Clinton of New York.

Today a power line crosses the confluence of the two waters, and houses stand on the south bank of the Allegheny at the mouth of Conewango Creek where Céloron buried his plate. Warren has not forgotten its past, however, and a copy of the plate stands bolted to a rock in Heritage Park across the river from the town's business district and under the flags of France, Great Britain, the United States, and the Seneca Nation of

Cornplanter mosaic, Heritage Park, Warren

Indians. The plate from Warren disappeared long ago, but a similar one buried by Céloron near the mouth of the Kanawha River in West Virginia was found by some boys playing along its banks in 1846. A reproduction of that plate is housed at the Fort Pitt Museum in Pittsburgh. The original belongs to the Virginia Historical Society.

"This is where I was when those guys came up to me and asked me if I could identify the ducks on the river," Jim Schafer tells me as we sit on the bank eating cinnamon rolls and drinking coffee during one of our trips upriver. "They were the ones complaining about the duck eggs floating down the river when the Corps of Engineers lets water out of the dam."

Mention of the ducks—the "Allegheny Navy" as locals call them—and of the Corps leads Jim to talk about his father. He was forever writing the Corps complaining that creation of the Allegheny Reservoir had made the river through Warren too cold for smallmouth bass and had destroyed some of the best fishing for that species in all of western Pennsylvania. It's an accusation that many anglers who knew the river before the lake often repeat, and one that Ron Lee, the Fish Commission's fisheries manager for the upper river, readily confirms. He says good smallmouth fishing on the Allegheny now does not begin until below Oil City.

But complaints about duck eggs and smallmouth bass are only two of many still heard about Kinzua Dam, the most controversial project on the Allegheny River since lock and dam construction at East Brady ended in the 1930s.

Spring flood, Allegheny tributary

12

WHERE THEY GOBBLE

The Allegheny River drains an area of almost twelve thousand square miles and at low flow discharges some 650 cubic feet of water per second into the Ohio River, more than four times what the Monongahela contributes. It has twenty-three major tributaries and dozens of smaller ones, which means that in the Allegheny system floods occur on one stream or another almost every year, and have since the glaciers created the river half a million or so years ago. The Johnstown Flood of 1889, the most famous deluge in American history, came out of the Allegheny basin, as did the region's last great inundation brought by Hurricane Agnes in June 1972.

When whites first arrived in the Allegheny Valley, the Senecas, who had moved

Saint Patrick's Day Flood, Pittsburgh, 1936

their villages from the river to smaller streams, warned them about floods by pointing to the tops of trees to show them places where they had once tied their canoes. But settlers disregarded the warnings and built close to the river, where water was abundant and access to markets was better. In fact, the pioneers often welcomed high water because it covered rocks, snags, and shoals and made it easier for them to get their crops to market. "Pumpkin floods," they called them, since the main loss was bottomland crops.

But there were always bigger floods too, such as that recorded by trader James Kenny at Fort Pitt on January 9, 1762:

> This Morning ye flood increasing still we had ye Bato up to ye Door, by Noon ye Street fronting our door undr water; many People brot Goods to us for preservation; got going with Canoes between ye Houses & Batoes, I set to work & got all our peltry up stairs & ye Wollings &c up about Dusk ye water got to power into our Celler increasing with ye Same progress as at first ye Celler having no Wall but mud banks we conclud'd to shut all ye Doors fast & make our escape, ye Ice

driving thick between us & ye Fort—some fellows waiting with a Canoe gave umbrage to us so that Josiah return'd out of ye Batoe & stay'd some Houres but fell out twice & had to swim till taken up several Indns stay'd till I went out having difficulty to get thro ye Ice.

The following spring, Kenny again had to flee his trading post and home when on March 8 "ye Water was got so high that they had to break in ye Roofs or Gable Ends of ye Houses to get them away in Battoes." That flood crested at about 40.9 feet, or just a few inches below the second-floor gunports of The Blockhouse in Point State Park.

Other Allegheny floods of record that have struck include one that crested at 28 feet on April 6, 1852, and another that crested at 34.9 feet thirteen days later, on April 19, 1852. "The entire surface of the river was thickly dotted with unbroken rafts, fragments of rafts and isolated logs and boards," said an unnamed reporter quoted in Leland Johnson's *Headwaters District*.

> Some of the rafts had three or four men on board, some two, some one, and many were guided only by the current of the stream. The latter were almost sure to strike a bridge pier, and the collisions invariably separated them into still smaller fragments. We saw probably a dozen that were manned strike upon the piers, and in several instances the courageous raftsmen were compelled to leap from one fragment to another to avoid being hurled amidst the crashing timbers. The coolness and self-possession of the hardy raftsmen was marked and admired by the hundreds who witnessed the unusual scene from the bridges and shores.

The "Barrel Flood" of March 17, 1865, brought one of the strangest deluges. Oil Creek swept its banks clean of thousands of barrels, derricks, and drilling rigs and sent it all cascading down the river to knock out the Pennsylvania Canal aqueduct at Freeport. And in the Johnstown Flood on May 31, 1889, more than 2,200 lives were lost when eight inches of rain fell on the Allegheny Mountains and caused the South Fork Dam on a tributary of the Conemaugh River to fail. The "Fifty Million Dollar Flood" of January 15, 1907, and the Ides of March Flood of that same year were two other major floods. The March flood crested at 38.5 feet, or about a foot above the door of The Blockhouse. It covered 52 percent of the Golden Triangle and closed one hundred office buildings, thirty-three miles of streets, seventeen miles of railroad tracks, and nine miles of trolley tracks. Steamboats tied up on Wood Street. But as far as the Allegheny River itself is concerned, all those floods were only a prelude to what happened in March 1936.

It started near noon on Saint Patrick's Day, when the water began to lap over the banks of Stony Creek and the Little Conemaugh River into the streets of Johnstown. By dark, pianos were floating in the streets, automobiles were driven into each other by the current, and people were seeking refuge atop streetcars and houses. Nearly 30 people lost their lives in the city, 77 buildings were destroyed and another 4,500 were damaged, and 16,000 people were left homeless. "A scene of inconceivable desolation, following devastation by a flood that rivaled the deluge caused by the historic dam break in 1889" is how a reporter for the *Engineering News-Record* described Johnstown when the water receded the next morning.

By the time the flood reached Pittsburgh on March 18, 1936, it was flowing at a rate of roughly 366,000 cubic feet per second and crested at 46 feet, about a third of the way up the roof of The Blockhouse, surpassing the previous record flood of 1763 by more than five feet. It inundated 62 percent of the Golden Triangle, claimed two hundred lives, drove tens of thousands of people from their homes, and brought industry to a standstill. On March 27, Pittsburgh Chamber of Commerce President H. B. Kirkpatrick organized a Citizens Committee on Flood Control and dispatched a telegram to federal authorities demanding that talk about flood control stop and something be done:

> Our organization representing the great industries of the Pittsburgh district as well as thousands of smaller business concerns most earnestly urges you come to Pittsburgh and survey for yourselves the shocking destruction worked by the flood in this great industrial area. Sober estimates made by men of experienced judgement calculate property damage in Allegheny County alone at one hundred fifty to two hundred million dollars. If the losses suffered by the industries which line our three rivers for a distance of forty to fifty miles beyond the city are included the figures reach a shocking total. By personal inspection you will be better able to make a rightful decision as to the extent by which the whole national interest is involved in this devastation of the most highly industrialized region in America.

In the wake of such destruction and urgings from business leaders and private citizens, the U.S. Congress passed a Flood Control Act on June 22, 1936. The act gave the federal government jurisdiction over flood-control projects on navigable waters and set the stage for the building of flood-control dams in the Allegheny basin.

But long before the Flood Control Act of 1936 opened the way for construction of a system of flood-control dams, people living along the Allegheny River were looking for ways to solve flooding problems. During the nineteenth century the predominant thinking was that floods were caused by the cutting of forests along the river. According to that theory, the removal of forest cover increased runoff rates and therefore flooding, and in the summer led to rivers drying up. "For generations, armies of settlers have been occupied in cutting the timber along the banks of the Tennessee, Ohio, Monongahela, and Allegheny rivers," an 1884 issue of *Southern Lumberman* noted. "The mountain

216

first the idea of reforestation to control floods—Allegheny National Forest was created in 1923 as part of that plan—and then, in 1898, sent a representative to the National Board of Trade convention to lobby for federal construction of flood-control reservoirs, as had recently been proposed for the upper Missouri River basin. The Board of Trade won approval of the idea from President Theodore Roosevelt and saw enactment of the National Irrigation Act of 1902—which authorized funding for reservoir construction, but only in the arid West.

After the Ides of March Flood of 1907 inundated half the Golden Triangle, a desperate Pittsburgh began entertaining all kinds of solutions to the flooding problems. A riverman suggested that, when floods were threatening, stern-wheel riverboats should be sent to tributary headwaters and pointed upstream with their paddle wheels at full steam to push the water backward. Several people proposed digging huge gutters alongside the Allegheny and other rivers to catch the spillover from floods and carry the water harmlessly to the ocean. An oil man recommended drilling a series of ten-foot holes deep into the earth and sending the floodwaters underground, where they could either join the groundwater or be converted into steam when they reached molten rock. A disciple of Thomas Edison wanted to hang electric wires over the rivers to boil away floods.

Though entertained by some of the ideas, engineers in Pittsburgh were a bit less imaginative when it came to solutions. Instead of pushing floods backward or boiling them away, they decided the city might best be protected by constructing small reservoirs upstream and levees around the Golden Triangle and other low-lying areas.

In spite of the recommendations of engineers and the Pittsburgh Flood Commission, however, plans for a reservoir and levee system were vigorously opposed. In November 1912, Pittsburgh voters rejected a bond issue to fund construction of levees around the city, and the following month engineers from the Corps determined that such a system would not benefit navigation—the Corps' main responsibility at the time—and reported that the federal government should not aid local interests in the plan. Then lumbermen, farmers, railroad owners, and people living near proposed dam sites vigorously voiced their disapproval. Debate over a reservoir system would continue for another twenty-four years—until the Saint Patrick's Day Flood and the federal government's support behind such a system, which led to passage of the Flood Control Act of 1936.

Tionesta Creek, Crooked Creek, and Mahoning Creek were the first three sites chosen for dams in the Allegheny basin. Construction began at Tionesta and Crooked Creek in 1938 and was completed in 1940. The Mahoning Creek dam was begun in 1939 and completed in 1941, when Pearl Harbor brought an end to almost all such civilian projects.

Although the Flood Control Act was not passed until 1936, the Corps first looked at building a dam on the upper Allegheny River in 1928. Congress approved Kinzua Dam

Kinzua before the dam

for a site nine miles upstream of Warren in 1936 and then modified the project in 1938 and again in 1941. From the start there was opposition.

At first, the fight against Kinzua Dam (the name "Kinzua," according to early Pennsylvania explorer John Heckewelder, is a corruption of "kentschuak," meaning "they gobble") was led by rivermen who did not want to see navigation to Olean blocked. "What is proposed for the river above Warren is a very poor substitute for the navigation dams we are entitled to," complained Harold Puttman, an opponent from Warren. The rivermen wanted locks in any dam that might be built, but the engineers did not believe there would ever be enough commercial traffic on the river to Olean to justify adding locks.

Soon the rivermen were joined by the residents of Kinzua and Corydon and by the Seneca Nation of Indians, all of whom would have their homes or land drowned by the reservoir. The opposition of the Senecas presented a particularly difficult legal problem because their rights were guaranteed by treaty. In recognition of Seneca Chief Cornplanter's efforts to maintain peaceful relations with early settlers, Pennsylvania had in 1791 granted the chief about 860 acres on the Allegheny above Warren. The land had been passed down to Cornplanter's descendants after his death in 1836 and was still occupied by them. In the Pickering Treaty of 1794, named for Timothy Pickering, superintendent of the Six Nations of the Iroquois Confederacy under Washington, the federal government granted the Senecas more than thirty thousand acres along the river in Cattaraugus County, New York:

> [The] United States acknowledge all the land within the aforesaid mentioned boundaries, to be the property of the Seneka Nation; and the United States will never claim the same, nor disturb the Seneka in the free use and enjoyment thereof: but it shall remain theirs, until they choose to sell the same to the people of the United States, who have the right of purchase.

From their first meetings with the Corps in 1940, the Senecas made it plain that they had absolutely no interest in selling any of the land they were to own "as long as the grass shall grow." Testimony before Congress on the issue maintained that, as a state grant, the Cornplanter lands in Pennsylvania could be acquired through eminent domain, but Seneca lands in New York came from a federal treaty and would therefore probably require an act of Congress to obtain. There the situation stood when the United States' entry into World War II overrode everything else in importance and all negotiations stopped.

After the war, the Corps turned its attention to dams on the East Branch of the Clarion River and Conemaugh Creek, and Kinzua remained on the back burner. Then, in October 1954, Hurricane Hazel struck, sending down the Allegheny and the Monongahela floodwaters that without the ten reservoirs already in operation would have been the second greatest deluge in western Pennsylvania on record. The Corps estimated that the reservoirs, which controlled about 23 percent of the watershed above Pittsburgh, lopped 8.7 feet off the crest at The Point, but the water still reached a depth of 32.4 feet, 7.4 feet above the flood stage (25 feet) and enough to drown a large portion of the Golden Triangle once again.

After Hazel, leaders of Pittsburgh and other river communities began an intensive lobbying campaign for Kinzua. The pressure was increased even more when, in March 1956, a flood caused some $2 million worth of damage to Warren. That same year, President Dwight Eisenhower approved funding for Kinzua Dam, and condemnation proceedings were begun to obtain the parts of the Seneca Nation needed for the reservoir. Most of the Cornplanter grant and slightly more than nine thousand acres in New York—holding 177 homes and between two hundred and three hundred Native Americans—were involved.

The Senecas immediately sought an injunction to stop the proceedings. The fight continued until the U.S. District Court for Western New York ruled in January 1957 that Congress had been informed of the Seneca treaty rights but could take lands for the project regardless of the Pickering Treaty of 1794, a decision that the U.S. Supreme Court let stand in June 1959.

The idea that the federal government might break yet another treaty with the Indians brought a wave of sympathy for the Senecas. The Society of Friends, which helped the tribe establish its own republic in 1848, threw its support behind the Indians, as did literary critic Edmund Wilson. In his book *Apologies to the Iroquois*, Wilson called the relocation a disaster almost comparable to the 1838 dispossession when the Ogden Land Company swindled the Senecas out of most of their land:

> Public confidence has received a coup de grace since it was learned that genuine flood control has never been the object of the Kinzua Dam, but has merely served as a pretext for putting through at public expense a particularly costly contrivance intended to serve the interests of a group of industrialists in Pittsburgh, who now appear as its principal advocates. Though Pittsburgh itself is not seriously in danger from the flooding of the upper Allegheny, certain Pittsburgh manufacturers have their reasons for wanting the river diluted at the seasons when it is running low. The sulphurous drainage from the coal mines is from their point of view deleterious because it ruins their boilers by rusting them.

Wilson claimed that pollution could be stopped by the industrialists themselves for a cost of $300,000 or $400,000, instead of the $150 million proposed for the dam. Country singer Johnny Cash joined the fray singing lines from Pete La Farge's "Senecas":

> On the Seneca Reservation there is much sadness now.
> Washington's treaty has been broken,
> And there is no hope, no how.
> Across the Allegheny River, they're throwing up a dam.
> It will flood the Indian country,
> A proud day for Uncle Sam.
> It has broke the ancient treaty with a politician's grin.
> It will drown the Indian graveyard.
> Cornplanter can you swim?

Meeting failure in court, the Senecas retained Arthur E. Morgan and Barton M. Jones, prominent engineers who had designed the Miami River flood-control project in Ohio and were principal organizers of the Tennessee Valley Authority, to study alternatives to Kinzua Dam. The pair devised a plan to divert floodwater from the Allegheny through a canal to the Conewango basin, where it would be stored in a reservoir and later emptied into Lake Erie or the Allegheny during periods of drought. It was a variation of a plan that had actually been proposed three other times, going back to 1911.

The Morgan-Jones plan was reviewed by a New York consulting firm approved by both the Corps and the Senecas. The report they issued in April 1958 said that alternative projects would cost at least 25 percent more than Kinzua Dam, require at least 51 percent more land, and relocate 150 percent more people. Morgan attacked the report after he learned that three members of the consulting firm had worked for the Corps in the past, and he proposed another alternative. But it too was rejected.

At the same time the Senecas were fighting the dam, Pittsburghers and residents of other towns along the Allegheny were putting the pressure on the Corps to get the

Hydroelectric facility, Kinzua Dam

Conewango Creek

project moving. The *Pittsburgh Press* complained that the Senecas deserved no more consideration than the whites who would be adversely affected by the dam. The "Indians were so poorly treated by white men that we shouldn't take their land now," said one editorial, "—even to save ourselves from flood disaster—as if tender solicitude now could wipe out the ancient injustices." The *Pittsburgh Post-Gazette* said: "This project has waited long enough. Flood waters are not nearly so patient." And so the people of Kinzua, Corydon, Cornplanter's Grant, Onoville, and Quaker Bridge were forced to move.

225

This is the goddamn truth. I don't have much time for engineers. The ones down at the dam—now, we're very friendly. They're good guys. Of course, they didn't have anything to do with what happened."

"But when they came into town," he continues, "they went around buying up all these old ladies. I remember one—she had a nice house, kept it up very well—she took the offer. 'What am I going to do?' she said. 'I've got to get out.' They got the people who didn't know any better and were getting old first."

The last few people in town put up a bitter struggle to save their homes. The Tomes' scrapbook of Corydon is full of news clippings of legal battles and threats that included the use of force. "When they got down to the last two, three, four—people who did have some money—boy, they had to pay then," Harry Tome says. "Those people just had the money to hire the good lawyers to fight, while other people didn't."

For three or four months the Tomes were packed and waiting for the money to move out of their home (a painting of which hangs in their present living room), the two-story brick structure, dating back to the 1830s and probably originally belonging to one of Philip's daughters. During the period, U.S. marshals from Pittsburgh visited the family on at least three different occasions, according to Harry: "They said, 'When you going to move?' I said, 'Where the hell's the money? I don't have nothing.'"

So bitter were the feelings of many locals toward the federal government, and so tense were the relations, that on one visit a young marshal even moved for his revolver when he saw Tome reach into his back pocket for a handkerchief. They were standing in the couple's living room at the time. Harry relates: "I thought, 'You sonofabitch,' when the guy touched his gun. Then the head marshal said, 'Hey! Hey! Hey! You just cut that out. He's okay.'"

Corydon

Kinzua Dam

The Tomes finally had to borrow money for the move. Then Harry jacked up the small house across from the family's barn, and another small building, and moved them both to property the couple had purchased above Willow Creek about four miles east of the reservoir. That small house, with a new addition, remains Harry and Marion's home. The other building was made into a cabin the couple rents to deer hunters from the Kittanning area. Those buildings are probably the last two surviving houses from Corydon.

As two of the stubborn ones who resisted the move, Harry and Marion Tome managed to have the Corps up its purchase price for their home on three different occasions. By the time the sale was final and the couple were ready to move in November 1964, their house was the last one standing in Corydon, according to Harry. Everything else—trees, houses, businesses—had been knocked down and burned. And the Corps wasn't taking any chance on the Tomes changing their minds. While it was still waiting to close the deal, bulldozers moved into place. As soon as the couple were finally out of the door, the dozers attacked the house.

Most of the four hundred people who once lived in Corydon scattered through Bradford, Warren, Jamestown (New York), and other towns and villages around the upper Allegheny. But the memories remain. "I'd rather see the town there than the water," Harry Tome says. "You talk to people from Kinzua, and the majority of them will say that—people right on up through the valley. There are a few who say, 'It's a good thing. We're better off.' But, hell, I'm not better off!"

"Never a place like it," adds Marion.

229

Ground-breaking for Kinzua Dam took place on October 22, 1960, under a colorful canopy of autumn leaves in the yard of Blanche Brownell, whose family had operated a ferry and hotel for raftsmen along the Allegheny since about 1826. The last train from Oil City to Kinzua brought fourteen hundred people to the site—among them a "tickled" Captain Way, who could not help but laugh when someone stole the silver ceremonial shovel to be used to turn the first sod.

"Kinzua Dam was going to flood out the graveyard where Cornplanter was buried," Captain Way also remembers about the dam. "They didn't know what to do with him. So I offered to go up there with my boat and bring him down and bury him on The Point in Pittsburgh. It seemed a logical place to put him. But that all fell through. The Indians finally prevailed on the powers-that-be up there to give them a hillside site above the new pool level. So they reburied Chief Cornplanter over there."

Continued dislike of the Kinzua Dam project led to scattered acts of vandalism and mysterious fires. Once two carloads of armed men who had been drinking came searching for Colonel James Hammer, the Corps project engineer. They never found him, but the episode points up how deep the feelings against the dam were among some people in the area. Another time Albert Jones, a leader of the Senecas' longhouse religion (founded by Cornplanter's brother Handsome Lake on the banks of the Allegheny), predicted that the "little people," the gremlins of Seneca lore, would prevent construction of the dam. "We Indians got something to protect us," he said. "We'll do some little things and there'll be a lot of people dead down there at the dam, without anybody touching them."

But work on the $108 million dam, the largest civil works project in the history of the Pittsburgh District U.S. Army Corps of Engineers, continued. And Kinzua was dedicated on September 16, 1966, creating behind its earth and concrete breast a twenty-four-mile-long lake with a 12,000-acre surface area and ninety-seven miles of shoreline.

Without an idea of where to look, it would be difficult to find the Riverview-Corydon Cemetery—where the graves of both Philip Tome and Cornplanter were moved to make way for Kinzua Dam. There is no marker or sign along the highway, and the access road, hidden between trees and brush, is easy to miss. But that is just as well, because in the late 1970s vandals entered the cemetery and knocked over many of the headstones. Jim had gone looking for it shortly after I gave him a copy of *Pioneer Life* to read, however, so we knew the location and were there soon after leaving Harry Tome's house.

Cornplanter clan members were unhappy about the relocation of their cemetery to its present site. They would have preferred another location, away from the graves of whites that had been moved from Corydon Cemetery, and with space for reunions and other communal affairs. The federal government had agreed to another site, but that plan was dropped when the Corps refused to build an access road. Once again the Senecas took the issue to court and lost. Relocation of the Cornplanter Cemetery began on

Cornplanter monument

August 24, 1964, with several descendants of the old chief, a former president of the tribe, and an archaeologist on hand to ensure that the bodies were handled with proper respect. Despite all the witnesses and the archeologist's identification of the remains as those of an elderly man afflicted with rheumatism, a disease from which Cornplanter suffered, a story that the body of the old chief had been spirited away for secret interment began to circulate.

"This is where I was standing when Harry Tome snuck up behind me and said I was going to have to pay to take a picture of that marker," Jim tells me as we stare down at the grave of Philip Tome. It is a new marker, placed there in 1989 by Harry and other members of the family. The original marker was broken when the grave was moved, and thrown into the weeds near the old Corydon Cemetery—where a hunter found it and returned it to the family. It now belongs to the Warren County Historical Society. Philip's old friend Cornplanter lies maybe thirty yards away across an asphalt drive under a fifteen-foot-high obelisk erected by the state of Pennsylvania some thirty years after the chief's death on February 18, 1836. Moved to this new site when the cemetery was moved, the much weathered and stained stone carries a eulogy:

> Chief of the Seneca tribe and a principal chief of the Six Nations from the period of the Revolutionary War to the time of his death. Distinguished for talent, courage, eloquence, sobriety, and love of his tribe and race, to whose welfare he devoted his time, his energy, and his means during a long and eventful life.

Gi-en-gwah-toh, the Cornplanter (who was also known by his white name, John O'Bail), was born about 1731 at Conewaugus on the Genesee River to a Seneca woman and the first John O'Bail, a Dutch trader from Albany, New York. Little is known about his boyhood except that he learned about his white father from his mother when his Indian playmates questioned the "different color" of his skin. After his marriage, Cornplanter traveled to Albany with his wife to visit his father, who was living with his white wife and children at the time and treated him with only the barest civility. Cornplanter's friend Philip Tome, in his *Pioneer Life* (1854), quotes the chief as saying: "He gave me victuals while I was at his house, but when I started to return home, he gave me no provision to eat on the way. He gave me neither kettle nor gun, neither did he tell me that the United States were about to rebel against the government of England."

Although he strongly argued that "it was better not to take sides in a civil war among white people," Cornplanter followed the decision of the Six Nations and fought on the side of the British during the Revolution. Anthony F. C. Wallace's 1969 book *The Death and Rebirth of the Seneca* quotes the chief's speech on going to war:

> Every Brave man Show himself. Now hereafter for we will find an many Dangerous times during the action of the war, for we will see many Brave man amongst the American Soldiers which we Shall meet, with their sharp adge tools, I therefore Say you must Stand like good Soldier against your own white Brother Because just as soon as he fined you out an us, I therefore Say Stand to your Post when is time come Before you But agreed yourselves. . . .

During the war, Cornplanter fought in many battles and raids in both Pennsylvania and New York. In one raid in 1780, Seneca warriors laid waste to miles of the south bank of the Mohawk River and took numerous prisoners, including the elder John O'Bail, Cornplanter's father. The capture of O'Bail was something of an embarrassment to his

Seneca relatives. Cornplanter immediately apologized for the burning of his father's house and offered to take him into his own home and support him for the rest of his life. O'Bail demurred, however, and as a show of respect for Cornplanter the Senecas decided to release him and the other whites taken in the raid.

In an address to President Washington in 1790, Cornplanter explained his reasons for fighting against the Americans. In the beginning, he said, the colonists told the Indians they were all the children of the king of England and invited the Indians to accept the king's protection. "What the Seneca Nation promise," he told Washington, "they faithfully perform. When you refused to obey that King, he commanded us to assist his beloved men in making you sober. In obeying him, we did no more than yourselves had led us to promise. We were deceived; but your people teaching us to confide in that King, had helped to deceive us, and we now appeal to your heart. Is all the blame ours?"

Like other reservations, Cornplanter's Town (Jenuchshadago), along the Allegheny, was a "slum in the wilderness." As Anthony Wallace explains, reservations were established as asylums where Indians who had lost their hunting grounds could remain peacefully apart from the white community "until they became civilized." In reality, though, the reservations were situated on some of the least desirable lands available, where no traditional Indian culture, such as hunting, could survive and where only the worst aspects of white society—frequently whiskey and disease—could easily penetrate.

Seneca resident of Cornplanter's Town

Although Cornplanter's Town had all the negative aspects of other reservations, its location in the deep and rugged forests above the Allegheny made it difficult to reach and allowed the clan to maintain a greater measure of autonomy than the Iroquois living on reservations near Buffalo, Niagara, and along the Genesee River. In 1798 only three or four whites resided within fifty miles of the grant. Clan members could hunt, fish, grow corn on a few pieces of bottomland, and continue their religious traditions without outside interference. A large wooden statue of Tarachiawagon, the Good Twin and Creator of the Seneca way of life, even stood in the middle of town and was the center of the harvest festival of Green Corn and New Years, when it was lavishly decorated with skins, handkerchiefs, ribbons, feathers, and the white dog sacrificed during the celebrations.

The town itself consisted of about forty houses scattered in a loose line through a meadow about thirty yards from the river's edge. The population numbered approximately four hundred, so between five and fifteen people occupied each house. The average house consisted of one room about sixteen feet square. Cornplanter's home was the largest in the town. It had two separate apartments connected by a porch and was about sixty-four feet long and sixteen feet wide. Nearly all the houses were made of logs and covered by a bark roof. In the center was a smoke hole for the ever-present fire and for interior light. On either side of the house ran two tiers of bunks. People slept on the lower bunks on beds of buckskin and stored food and household goods on the upper level.

The Indians having been cut off from their old ways, Cornplanter lived out his days in the town, mediating disputes with whites, dispensing favors, and watching his people slide into despair. Gradually he became morose and withdrawn. In December 1820 he experienced the first of a series of visions in which the Great Spirit told him to have nothing more to do with white people or war. "White people were crazy and the Indians were doing very wrong to follow their customs," he warned, preaching that it was wrong for Indians to own cattle, cows, and hogs—especially cows, because children who drank their milk when they were young would suffer misfortune throughout their lives. "If we would quit our old way we should get into confusion," he told his people, "and something would happen or befall us so that we should lose our lives."

Despite bouts with insanity and personal disappointments—his daughter died after a witch put a curse on her, and his wife ran off with another man—Cornplanter is said to have remained an imposing figure even at the time of his death in 1836. "Nearly six feet tall, gray-haired, bearded, with one eye missing and the empty socket covered by the drooping brow, a limp hand rendered useless by a severed tendon, one earlobe torn and hanging down on his shoulder like a rag, he stood like a scarred oak among saplings," writes Wallace.

Standing at the obelisk at the Riverview-Corydon Cemetery, we are saddened to think the old chief was not even permitted to rest quietly after his death. "After more than a hundred years of most varied life—of strife—of danger—of peace—he at last

234

slumbers in deep repose on the banks of his own beloved Allegany,'' says Philip Tome, quoting Sherman Day's *Historical Collections of the State of Pennsylvania.* Now he lies among the whites he first sought to accommodate and then escape. Still, looking past the stone at the shimmering surface of the Allegheny Reservoir stretching away through the mountains below like some mystic Norwegian fjord, we find it impossible to believe Cornplanter would not love the view. The only disturbance comes from the speedboats in the distance, at least until two women appear with a collection of children and picnic paraphernalia. Treating the sign prohibiting access to the reservoir through the cemetery as if it did not apply to them, they stroll past and down the bank.

"It's a real shame," I say.

"A real shame," Jim echoes.

Riverview Cemetery

the couple had stolen away to the reservoir. "The first night," she says, "millions of stars were out, and I remember thinking, 'If there's anywhere you are at peace or really out of pain or really out of misery, it's up there.' I said to myself, 'Please don't suffer anymore. I hope everything is okay.' And 'okay' didn't have a true meaning at the time, actually what okay meant later was that he had gone on to a better place. The next day I found out he had passed away." The Fish Commission had tracked them down to notify them of Ronnie's death.

"Most people can't understand how I can even want to go back up there," she continues. "Yet when I'm up there I feel so much more at peace with myself. I think the stars have something to do with it, because when you're up there the sky is just full of stars. It's all you can see, and it makes you look up and makes you realize there's more to this life."

All the controversy, joy, and sadness surrounding the Kinzua project aside, the primary reason for Kinzua Dam is flood control. And within six years of its dedication on September 16, 1966, it proved its worth by helping to lop twelve feet off the flood brought by Hurricane Agnes. Without Kinzua and the other flood-control dams of the

Cutting a wake, Allegheny Reservoir

Tailwaters, Allegheny Reservoir, New York

Red Bridge Campground,
Kinzua Bay

Allegheny basin, that deluge would have topped the Saint Patrick's Day Flood of 1936 by two feet and become western Pennsylvania's greatest flood of record.

Agnes slammed into the Gulf Coast of Florida on June 19, 1972. At the time, the danger to Pennsylvania seemed remote, but the next day the storm's winds began to force moist Atlantic Ocean air inland while a cool front approached Pittsburgh from the west. The cool air stalled along the Ohio and Pennsylvania border on June 21 as Agnes moved into North Carolina and poured an ever-increasing amount of rain into the Allegheny watershed. By the time the storm reached New Jersey on June 22 the hurricane winds had gone, but the rain continued. Then, the following day, Agnes moved west to center directly over the upper Allegheny. In three days she dumped as much as eleven inches of rain over parts of the basin in a fifty-mile-wide band along the western slope of the Allegheny Mountains from south of Pittsburgh to New York.

At Coudersport in Potter County the water roared so fast through its concrete chute that the ground shook. In McKean County, Eldred soon found its main street seven feet under water. In New York, just over the Pennsylvania border, the Allegheny at Portville was eight inches from the top of the dikes, and at Olean, New York, it was within a foot. West of Olean, in Salamanca, the river was seven and a half feet higher than ever recorded. The reservoir on the east branch of the Clarion River was soon completely filled, and other reservoirs in the basin were 90 percent full. The water climbed to within three feet of the top of Kinzua Dam.

The Hurricane Agnes flood crested on June 24 at 35.85 feet on the Pittsburgh gauge, or at the top of the door frame of The Blockhouse. Without Kinzua and the other dams of the Allegheny basin, it would have covered The Blockhouse. According to Corps estimates, flood-control projects in the Pittsburgh district had prevented more than $1 billion in flood damage—more than four times what all the projects cost to construct. Kinzua Dam alone, built at a cost of $108 million, is believed to have saved people downstream of it about $247 million in damages.

Morning mist, Buckaloons

Salamanca

13

IN ANOTHER COUNTRY

Sure enough, fifteen minutes after the 11:00 P.M. deadline, a pair of headlights momentarily brightens the darkness around Jim's van. I raise myself up from the lowered seat to see a patrol car cruising the perimeter of the lot. No overnight parking is permitted, but we are backed close enough to the line of used vehicles in the car dealership next door that it looks as if the van is for sale, and the cop on duty takes no notice.

"We made it," I tell Jim after the patrol car is gone. We congratulate ourselves on our shrewdness, then recurl on our seats for a night of tossing and turning catnaps.

If we had made a reservation, we could have been sleeping in my tent in the campground at Allegany State Park—or even in a motel room if we'd planned far enough ahead and weren't so cheap. But neither of us ever imagined Salamanca would fill up for the powwow.

In the morning our first move is across the parking lot to the fast-food restaurant on the other side, where we quickly find the restroom and wash the sleep and grime of yesterday off our faces. Then we order breakfast with large coffees to help speed away the near-sleepless night and settle into stuffing our faces and scanning the local newspapers.

Salamanca, New York, was the first stop for Captain Way on his 1938 trip down the Allegheny. Wet and cold from a steady rain, the captain and his partner had opted for a hotel room instead of a campsite. They left the *Lady Grace* tied just above the highway bridge, he reported, "with a congregation of curious spectators, holding umbrellas over their heads, looking at a skiff which had actually been on the Ohio River—200 miles away—and was bound to see it again a week later." Captain Way continued, "We sent a telegram: 'Arrived Salamanca at five, all is well.' "

Only after they were back on the river, "fifty miles from nowhere," did they realize all was not well. Somebody had stolen their food from the *Lady Grace* during the night. At Quaker Bridge they had to beg the owner of the local store, a Mr. Holt, to open on Sunday. An old raftsman from the lumbering days, he "had floated big white-pine rafts clear out to Parkersburg, West Virginia, down the Ohio," reported Captain Way. "He had a gleam in his old eyes. 'For a nickle I'd go along with you boys,' he said."

The story makes me think of how many people have said they'd like to come along with us—or at least that was the way they talked, because when they actually get the opportunity to tackle a trip, most people beg off with one excuse or another. It also reminds me of the people who look at us skeptically when we tell them this is what we do for a living. "Yeah, sure," they seem to think. "Doesn't sound like work to me."

Finished with breakfast and sprawled disheveled and a bit dazed in our booth, we suddenly understand why there are no campsites or rooms available in Salamanca. One Native American family after another enters the restaurant and lines up at the stainless-steel counter. They've arrived in cars, trucks, vans, and campers bearing license plates from Arizona, Oklahoma, Michigan, Florida, and at least a half-dozen other states. The sight of people from so many different tribes both surprises and fascinates us, and we become anxious for the powwow to start even though we don't know what to expect.

Although it is Saturday and not yet nine o'clock in the morning, Broad Street in front of the restaurant is whining with traffic. Businesses are hurrying to open, and souvenir peddlers empty their trunks of T-shirts and toy drums, headdresses, tomahawks, and all other sorts of items people might consider "Indian."

Near Veterans Memorial Park, where the powwow is to take place, we detour left in

Coaling towers, Salamanca

search of the personal-care home that Carson Waterman, a Seneca artist Jim had heard about, decorated with mosaics. Jim wants to take some photographs of the mosaics, but when we find the home the light is wrong and the most colorful part is blocked by a shrub. The gates to the park aren't scheduled to open for another hour, so we decide to look around Salamanca, the only city in the world built on an Indian reservation.

In 1842, the Senecas, who still own all the land on which the town stands and who only lease it to the white residents, signed a treaty granting the railroads a right-of-way across the Allegany Reservation. The first train, belonging to the Erie Railroad, came through in 1851. Eleven years later, the Atlantic and Great Western joined the Erie tracks at a tiny sawmill settlement the Indians called Bucktooth. The junction where the lines met was renamed Salamanca in honor of Don Juan Salamanca y Mayol, a large stockholder in the railroad.

A crossroads for lines running to Buffalo, Erie, Rochester, Cleveland, and south along the Allegheny River to Pittsburgh, the settlement soon saw turntables, shops, and engine houses spring up. When more land was needed and the price proved to be too high, the railroads moved their operations to a swamp about a mile and a half away. Bucktooth became West Salamanca, and the new site became East Salamanca—until 1873, when the "East" was dropped.

Railroad Museum,
Salamanca

Like other towns along the upper Allegheny River, Salamanca has many picturesque old wood-frame homes and businesses with ornate facades, built during its boom days. Almost all that is left of the railroads, however, can be found in the Salamanca Rail Museum, a passenger depot built in 1912 by the Buffalo, Rochester & Pittsburgh Railroad and restored in 1980. Everything in the museum—train models, photographs, lanterns, tickets, and other railroad memorabilia—is either a restored original or a duplicate based on the original architect's plans. Jim and I have both been to the museum on other occasions, however, so we decide to visit the overlook in Allegany State Park instead.

Allegany State Park sits on land between the Allegheny River and the Pennsylvania border deeded to the state of New York by the Holland Land Company in 1814. The tract, called the "donation lands," was the company's contribution to the building of the Erie Canal. Soon afterward, New York sold the land to speculators, but then ended up taking most of it back for taxes. In 1835, Benjamin Chamberlain, an early lumber baron, bought the entire expanse and gradually sold it off to other lumbermen and farmers, who clear-cut its virgin pine and hemlock and sent the timber down the Allegheny to mills in Warren, Parker, and Pittsburgh.

Around 1920, after the land no longer was a source of timber, New York Attorney General Hamilton Ward, who had often fished and hunted in the area, began urging that the land be developed into a state park. Following a fund drive that netted $25,000 and was matched by the state, seven thousand acres along Quaker Run were purchased, and the park opened in 1921. Today, Allegany State Park covers some sixty-five thousand

Quaker Lake, Allegany State Park, New York

acres, making it the largest state park in New York. It is also one of the prettiest parks anywhere. (Across the Pennsylvania line into New York the spelling of everything called Allegheny, except the river, changes, for no known reason, but New York's spelling, "Allegany," appears only in a few places in Pennsylvania, such as the town of Port Allegany in McKean County and Allegany Township in Potter County.) "In the forests are sylvan trails, spring-fed brooks, rare flora and fauna," Arch Merrill appropriately noted in his *Southern Tier* (1986). "The bear and the deer roam the woods, safe from the hunter's gun. Beavers build their dams in its waters. There are strange geological formations, such as Thunder Rocks and the Bear Cave. . . . A man-made observation tower, at an elevation of 2,200 feet, affords a magnificent view, especially when the woods flaunt their autumnal colors."

Beaver dam, Allegany State Park

Merrill might also have added raccoons. The night we were searching for the campground at least a hundred of them must have crossed the road in front of the van. They were everywhere, a living mass venturing into the open they avoid in the daylight owned by humans. It was only by a light foot on the gas and quick response, mixed with a little luck, that we avoided hitting any. But not everybody was so fortunate, as the carnage along the edge of the road attested.

At the overlook, though, there are no raccoons. Below us spreads only a Salamanca looking like a model-railroad town cut by a dark and silver ribbon of river and enveloped by the rolling mountains of the Allegheny High Plateau. Born in a general upheaval 230 million years ago, the plateau around Salamanca caught the upper Allegheny when the glaciers turned it almost half a million years ago, joined it with the middle river, and sent it on its way south.

Above the town lies the oldest part of the river—the section that, since the building of Kinzua Dam, the fewest people seem to realize belongs to the Allegheny. To many people along the lower river, and certainly to most Pittsburghers, the Allegheny appears to end arbitrarily at the dam. They never seem to wonder where all the water in the reservoir comes from. We talk about that until we check our watches and find it's time for the powwow to start.

Caught in the stops and starts of traffic, we see a monument to Simon Bolívar where Kent Boulevard slants off Broad Street. What a western New York town is doing with a memorial to the liberator of Bolivia totally mystified me the first time I saw it. But I learned the monument was dedicated to that South American hero by the Cattaraugus

Allegany State Park

County American Legion in 1941 in recognition of the Spanish origin of the city's name—a rather tenuous connection, I think.

Traffic builds quickly after we pass the monument, until, at the entrance to Veterans Memorial Park, a police officer is required to keep things moving. We spot a large sign at the entrance warning "Absolutely No Drugs or Alcohol." It makes me think of the stereotype of the drunken Indian—and then how many gatherings of whites could use a similar sign.

Following the cardboard signs pointing toward parking, we cruise around Salamanca High School and back out to a spot along the entrance road. Then, once Jim is sufficiently loaded down with equipment, we head for the park, passing three small boys whose Mohawk haircuts make us smile.

"You know why they do that?" Jim asks. "That was the part of the hair they always took when they scalped somebody. To leave it there was a challenge to their enemies. Sort of like, 'Here it is if you're man enough come and get it.' "

Even though the gates have been open for less than an hour the park is already a bustle of people. Carried by the flow, we soon find ourselves surrounded by food booths selling corn-and-bean soup, ghost bread, venison, buffalo sausage, and fried bread with jam. The menu reminds us of the ethnic festivals around Pittsburgh, with their Eastern European dishes of pirohi and kielbasa and halushki. Stepping aside to avoid stalling the flow any longer, Jim tells me that corn-and-bean soup is an Iroquois traditional dish. We agree to try some, and then wonder what might be a ghost bread sandwich.

As at other ethnic festivals, the "Keepers of the Western Door Powwow" (named after the Senecas' old role as guardians of the western route into the territory of the Six Nations of the Iroquois Confederacy) is designed to help preserve the unique culture and traditions of a people. But not all the crafts, artwork, and souvenirs have to do with the Senecas, or even the Iroquois. The number of different state license plates we saw at the restaurant indicated that the booths encircling the single bleacher stadium at the park's center offer items from many western and southwestern tribes too: turquoise-and-silver jewelry from New Mexico and Arizona, Navaho rugs and pottery, Hopi sand paintings. There are also T-shirts with chiefs in the full-feathered headdresses of the Plains tribes, but the Seneca and other eastern tribes never wore such elaborate headpieces because of the dense forests in which they lived. Some of the work is exquisite, other pieces were designed only to earn a quick dollar, and, as at every such affair, many of the toys were made in Hong Kong.

When we have our fill of browsing, we drift into the stadium to watch a line of young girls in elaborate dresses with brightly colored beadwork perform a dance the Senecas were doing even before the United States was ever imagined by Washington, Jefferson, and the rest. For a moment it's difficult to believe we are on the same river as Pittsburgh. Many people on the lower river seem to be only vaguely aware of the Allegheny beyond Kinzua, and even less aware that Native Americans still live along the

250

backwaters of the Allegheny Reservoir. "I didn't even know there were Indians in this part of the country" many people say when we mention the Seneca Nation. "Do they live in teepees?" is often the next question.

The Allegany Reservation was set aside for the Senecas by the Treaty of Canandaigua in 1794. Made up of a strip of land about forty miles long and one mile wide on either side of the river, the area belonged to the Senecas by right of conquest long before the treaty. Fierce warriors throughout most of their history, the Senecas had wrested it from the Eries in the middle of the seventeenth century. But prior to the Revolution, only a few people lived in scattered villages along the river. The heartland of the tribe was the Finger Lakes region and the Genesee Valley to the east. The rugged country around the Allegheny became a refuge for the tribe in 1779 after General John Sullivan devastated the Seneca homeland.

As the dancers get ready for their next performance, I leave Jim with his camera and head back for the food booths, where I buy a bowl of corn-and-bean soup. Made of ash-soaked corn, beans, and a bit of salt pork, it is probably one of the most healthful things I've eaten on the trip—but it does require a little extra salt and pepper to give it flavor. The ghost bread sandwich I buy from another booth across the way is something else entirely. About the size of a large biscuit, it is a nutritionist's nightmare: a flat piece of dough fried in lard and then cut in two, smeared with butter, and stuffed with a mixture of mashed beans and salt pork. It must weigh a pound. And it tastes great.

But the sandwich also makes me think about the food being served. Venison, corn, and beans have always been staples of Seneca life, but flour, lard, and salt pork are the "white man's" castoffs, the cheapest food available. This brings to mind stories and movies in which Native Americans were cheated out of food after they were forced onto reservations. Heart disease is a great problem among Native Americans today, and it's little wonder with a diet of so much fat and salt. Yet I have to admire the fact that they did the best they could with what was available to them, and survived. Now they celebrate, or at least recall, those days when flour, lard, beans, and salt pork were all they had to live on. Serving foods from the past at festivals is not unusual. The descendants of the many ethnic, national, and religious groups in the United States all do that too. But Native Americans have suffered as much or more than any group. Close to eight hundred treaties were signed with the Indians, more than half of them were never ratified—and all of them were broken by the white man.

After Jim returns and also tries a ghost bread sandwich, we head back toward the bleachers to hear the announcer talking about fancy dancers, feather dancers, and traditional dancers. The feather dance, I know, has something to do with a thanksgiving celebration, but the other dances are a mystery to me. Jim drifts along the bleachers searching for a better angle, fires a few shots, and then returns. We are trying to decide

Young Nation Singers

Trophy bucks

Keepers of the Western Door Powwow, Salamanca

Carson Waterman

how to find Carson Waterman, who had told Jim to meet him at the powwow, when a quiet voice rises behind us.

"Are you Jim?" we hear. "You must be, with all that equipment."

Tall and stout, but soft-spoken like many other Senecas we encountered, Carson Waterman has been a professional artist for twenty-five years. A graduate of the Cooper School of Art in Cleveland, Ohio, he has taught art at Cuyahoga County Community College, the Cleveland Museum of Art, and with the Seneca Nation of Indians Education Program. In addition, he has worked as a coordinator at the Seneca-Iroquois National Museum, where many of his works are on display, and produced a mosaic pyramid for Warren's Heritage Park. After seeing his work in Warren's park, Jim had made arrangements to meet him—a fortunate decision, we realize as soon as we enter his studio above the Allegheny in downtown Salamanca and he begins to show us some of his work.

"My paintings at this point," he tells us, "range from conventional landscapes—depicting the serenity of nature, with which I combine the traditional life-style of the Iroquois people during the Post Trade Goods Period—to very early design motifs from prehistory, which I combine with modern materials to end up with an abstract."

Waterman is carrying on in stainless steel, acrylic paints, holograms, and laser etching a tradition that began in stone and bone, grew to porcupine quills and moose hair colored with natural dyes, and then became the beadwork of the Trade Goods Period of the seventeenth and eighteenth centuries, when Europeans appeared on the scene with their metals and colored glass. The result is paintings of modern Senecas in ceremonial dress engrossed in traditional activities, such as dancing or beating turtle-shell rattles in the longhouse, before backgrounds holding ancient beadwork designs of plants, animals, and various symbols, such as diamonds and circles.

Waterman's work marks him as both a preserver of Seneca culture and a symbol of a resurgence, or reawakening, of interest in traditions he says came about in the early 1980s after about fifteen years of neglect. The neglect started with the building of Kinzua Dam and the relocation of many tribal members from lands they had occupied for generations. It was fueled by the rebelliousness of the late 1960s and the passing of the railroads, which employed a large number of the Senecas at about the same time. The changes led to a sense of confusion, even defeat, among the Indians. Interest by the young in tribal traditions waned and did not begin to recover until the mid-1970s, when tribal elders began pushing for more Indian education programs in local schools and Congress passed the Indian Education Act.

"Our people have been living on its banks dating back to prehistory," Waterman says about the importance of the Allegheny in the Senecas' history and in his own work, in which the river sometimes appears. "There are still legends or stories about our people confronting a mastodon in this area. So a lot of our artifacts date back to the glaciers that formed the river. That in itself is very significant to our people. There must be some very deep and spiritual reasons for them to have stayed here that long."

Kinzua Bay, Allegheny Reservoir

Although the land along the upper Allegheny River was not the original heart of the Seneca Nation, it came to play an important role in Seneca mythology, and especially the Seneca Nation's rebirth out of defeat and despair after the Revolution, through a new religion.

Among the Senecas there are two major versions of the tribe's origin. The first myth of Seneca creation starts with a heaven inhabited by man. In front of the chief's longhouse grew a great tree, a symbol of his power. One day, in a dream, the chief was told to uproot the tree and, when he did, light shone through the holes where the roots had grown. Curious about the light, the chief's pregnant wife walked over to the hole, peeked into it, and fell from heaven.

When the animals below saw the woman falling, the birds rushed up and made a blanket of their interlocked wings to catch her. The earth then being completely covered by water, the water animals hurried to get earth from the bottom of the sea so the woman would have something on which to stand. A muskrat was the first to successfully

Quiet cove, Allegheny Reservoir

bring earth to the surface. It placed the earth on the back of the great snapping turtle, who had agreed to be the base for the earth. More wet earth was brought up and added to that carried by the muskrat, and grew to become the earth that is known today.

Soon after landing on the new earth, the woman gave birth to a daughter, who grew up to become miraculously pregnant with twin boys. One twin, the "Father of All Good on Earth," was born normally, but the other twin, the "Father of All Evil on Earth," chose to be born through the woman's left armpit. The abnormal birth killed the mother and launched the contest between Good and Evil on earth.

After his wife fell to earth, the chief was instructed to replace the great tree he had uprooted. He did so, and the great tree was never moved again, so man entered the earth only once from heaven.

The other major myth of Seneca creation begins at Bare Hill on Lake Canandaigua in the Finger Lakes region of New York. According to that myth, the Great Spirit caused Bare Hill to open and the first Senecas to emerge from it and build a village and plant corn on the sides of the mountain.

As time passed, population pressures on the land around the mountain made the Senecas desperate for room, but Bare Hill was surrounded by a huge two-headed serpent whose poisonous breath would kill any Seneca who attempted to leave. As the need for land worsened, the desperate Senecas armed themselves with spears and attacked the serpent. During the attack, all the Senecas were killed, except for a boy and girl who managed to escape and return to the village. There, filled with despair, the boy and girl grieved for their lost families and friends and called on the Great Spirit to help them. In answer to their pleas, the Great Spirit transformed himself into an owl and appeared to tell the children how to defeat the serpent. The boy then made a bow and arrow, dipped the arrow tip in a special poison, and with the girl went out to meet the serpent.

During the encounter, the boy shot the arrow and it entered beneath the serpent's scales. The serpent began to writhe and die, falling down the hill, uprooting trees, and vomiting out the skulls of the Senecas it had killed. The skulls fell into the waters of Canandaigua Lake and became the stones on its bottom. The water also revived the serpent and brought him back to life. He still lives now. The children grew to adulthood and became ancestors of the Senecas.

When the Senecas were forced out of their original homeland around the Finger Lakes and the Genesee Valley and onto the Allegany Reservation, the tale of the serpent also shifted. Today, some stories have the first Senecas emerging from a hillside along the Allegheny River and the giant serpent at home in the Allegheny Reservoir.

More significant than the shifting of the creation myth to the Allegheny were the visions that came to Cornplanter's brother, Handsome Lake, while he was living along the river. Through him the religion of the longhouse, or the Code of Handsome Lake, grew at the start of the nineteenth century and restored the morale of the Seneca Nation and the other nations in the Iroquois Confederacy after they had witnessed the breakup of their lands and the end of their heroic role in North America.

The Code of Handsome Lake, described by Wallace in his *Death and Rebirth of the Seneca* as an amalgam of ancient traditions, the innovations of Handsome Lake, and Christianity, grew out of a series of visions by its founder, beginning in 1799. Two centuries later it has no formal name, also being called, among other things, the Cult of Handsome Lake or the New Religion, but it nevertheless functions as a religion in almost every way. Its headquarters are on the Tonawanda Reservation northeast of Buffalo, New York, where Handsome Lake's wampum belts are kept. The belts are so sacred that no white person is allowed to see them, and even the religion's highest leaders may read them only once every two years on a sunny day when not even a cloud as large as a person's hand can be seen in the sky.

Handsome Lake had his first visions on June 15, 1799, when the once proud warrior lay ill in the grip of "some strong power" on his bunk in Cornplanter's Town and began pondering the cause of his sickness and the demoralized state of his people. Fearing he might soon die, he became depressed and melancholy and believed he was "evil and loathsome" because he had sung sacred songs while drunk.

Cornplanter was outside town with the Quaker missionary Henry Simmons when a runner came to say his brother was dying. The chief went immediately to Handsome Lake's cabin, where a crowd of people had already gathered. His niece told him she had been outside cleaning beans when her father suddenly shouted "Niio!" ("So be it!"), rose from his bed, with "yellow skin and dried bones," and started to walk outside. He fell, but she caught him and then sent for his nephew Blacksnake, who examined him and found no heartbeat, no breathing, and a body cool to the touch except for a warm spot on the chest.

About half an hour after Cornplanter arrived, Handsome Lake began breathing again and the warm spot spread. Two hours later the prophet opened his eyes and moved his lips as if he wanted to speak. "My uncle, are you feeling well?" Blacksnake asked. "Yes, I believe myself well," Handsome Lake replied. Then he began to describe what he had seen.

In his vision, Handsome Lake had heard his name called and left the cabin to find three middle-age men dressed in ceremonial robes with red paint on their faces and feathers in their bonnets. They were carrying bows and arrows in one hand and huckleberry bushes in the other. Handsome Lake collapsed from weakness, but the men, who said they were angels sent by the Creator to answer his calls for help, caught him. After being instructed to choose his sister and her husband as healers, Handsome Lake was told to join his kinfolk the next day at the Strawberry Festival. He was to say that the Strawberry Festival should always be held and that all the people must drink the juice of the berry. If he did not carry this message he would be buried in a hot, smoking place in the hollow between two hills across the Allegheny to the southeast—about where Handsome Lake Campground now stands.

In the vision, Handsome Lake was also instructed to preach against four evil practices, summarized as drinking whiskey, practicing witchcraft, participating in magic, and practicing abortion and sterility medicine. People guilty of such things should be told to admit their wrongdoing, repent, and never err again. Moderate sinners were to confess privately to Handsome Lake in a prescribed ritual, the relatively innocent could confess in public, and the worst sinners were to confess alone to the Creator. The angels of the vision then spoke in approval of the recent execution of a witch and warned that a male witch was still living in the village. The angels accused Handsome Lake of singing sacred songs while drunk but excused him because he had been suffering. After warning him he must not drink, they left but promised to return.

After describing his vision, Handsome Lake asked Cornplanter to call a council of all the people to tell what had happened. The tale had such a profound effect on the audience that Henry Simmons would later write that many of the Indians appeared to be "Solid and weighty in Spirit," and that he "felt the love of God flowing powerfully amongst us." Thus the new religion was born.

Over the next three years Handsome Lake had three other visions on which his followers would build the religion. The second vision, which would become the core of the new religion's teachings, occurred on August 7, 1799, when a fourth angel appeared to take him along on the Sky Journey, during which Handsome Lake was exposed to scenes representing the worst sins of humankind. He saw a woman so fat she was unable to stand, who represented the sin of stinginess and preoccupation with material things. He saw a jail with a pair of handcuffs, a whip, and a hangman's noose, which represented the false belief of some Indians that the white man was better than the teachings of *Gaiwiio*, the good word. He saw a church without a door or a window, which showed how difficult it was for the Indians to accept the confining discipline of Christianity. He saw two great drops of liquid hanging in the sky threatening to drop and spread death, the danger from which he was trying to save humankind.

On the journey, Handsome Lake also met George Washington, the good white man who told the Iroquois to live happily in their villages, and a nail-scarred Christ. When Handsome Lake complained that only half his people believed what he was preaching, Christ replied: "You are more successful than I, for some believe in you but none in me. I am inclined to believe that in the end it will be so with you. Now it is rumored that you are but a talker with spirits. Now it is true that I am a spirit and the one of him who was murdered. Now tell your people that they will become lost when they follow the ways of the white man."

During the Sky Journey, Handsome Lake also saw the paths to heaven and hell, and

260

Allegheny High Plateau

the eternal tortures devised to fit various crimes: the drunkard was forced to drink molten metal; the wifebeater was forced to strike a red-hot image of a woman; the quarrelsome couple was made to argue until their eyes bugged out, their tongues protruded, and flames shot from their genitals; the wanton woman was forced to expose herself naked, gaunt with rotting flesh and serpents in her pubic hair; and card players were made to handle red-hot cards.

Handsome Lake's third vision came on February 5, 1800. Once more the three angels asked him whether the Indians had given up whiskey and witchcraft. They deplored the fact that the whites had taken Indian land and that they were so arrogantly certain the Great Spirit was in their books only.

Handsome Lake was told to spread the word, and out of his visions eventually grew a moral code that restored the pride and confidence of the Iroquois. The prophet died during a visit to Onondaga in central New York on August 10, 1815.

Land disputes and treaty violations might be ancient history to most white people, but how alive they remain in the minds of the Senecas becomes clear when the traditional dancers on the field finish and the master of ceremonies asks for a moment of silence to "remember the very painful episode of Kinzua." He urges all visitors to stop and relive the story of the dam through a special exhibit at the Seneca-Iroquois National Museum down Broad Street.

"Kinzua split the community," says Michelle Stock, director of education for the Seneca Nation. "I feel it was because we were relocated. In the old days, when I was a kid, people were more communal, more social."

Before Kinzua, she explains, she and the other Senecas who resided in Onoville, Cold Spring, Red House, and Quaker Bridge along the Allegheny River might have lived in old farmhouses—and not the modern homes built for them when they were relocated—but the people had traditionally lived that way. The homes were scattered, giving each family plenty of room and privacy, yet still within walking distance for visiting. Socials were held every Sunday night in the longhouse, and the people were generally more self-sufficient, chopping their own wood, drawing their own water, and farming their own land.

After the relocation, Stock and her neighbors found themselves living in Jimersontown on the edge of Salamanca and Steamburg about twelve miles downriver. People who had lived together all their lives surrounded by the forest, mountains, and river were suddenly restricted to three acres in a housing plan little different from developments around Pittsburgh or Buffalo. The Sunday socials in the longhouse also ended. The twelve miles separating the people in Jimersontown from the longhouse in Steamburg may not seem like much in today's motorized world, but from a cultural point of view, to people accustomed to walking everywhere, it was devastating, especially for the elderly.

262

"Within a year of the relocation we lost about sixty or more elders just from the culture shock of having to move and not really being able to adjust," Stock says. "They just gave up."

The pain of Kinzua is revealed clearly in the museum exhibit, which includes photographs of tribal elders who were displaced by the dam, the plain wood-frame dwellings in which they once lived, a map showing the land lost, books, newspaper and magazine articles, and other documents of the battle. On one wall is a copy of the treaty deeding the land to the Senecas, and under it is a petition asking the U.S. Postal Service to produce a stamp commemorating it. In another place is a document on relocation, and near it one of the old cast-iron markers that once marked the reservation's border. A display case holds a letter from Senator John F. Kennedy expressing understanding of Seneca concerns and seeking their support in his coming drive for the presidency. As president, he assured the tribe, he would push for House Bill 1794 to "fund relocation, rehabilitation, and the further economic and social development of the Senecas." The predominant feelings conveyed by the exhibit are those of sadness, loss, betrayal, and anger—emotions Stock also shows when she talks about visiting the site of her old home along the Allegheny River.

"Those of us who lived through Kinzua and used to live in the Cold Spring area or along the river still feel very strongly that that is home—home being a place of comfort," she says. "We will go down there many times just to walk along the river or to be by the river or by the old homesteads."

Only a portion of the houses that stood in the Cold Spring area are under the waters of Allegheny Reservoir, but all the houses were razed and burned for the dam because the Corps of Engineers believed the sites would be subject to periodic flooding. The Senecas retain the right to hunt, fish, and farm the land but may not live on it.

"When I was growing up, everybody went fishing—everybody," Stock says. "The river in those days had no carp. The closest we came were suckers. We had trout and bass and all kinds of fish you don't catch there anymore."

"We also always enjoyed just going along the river," she continues. "You always could find artifacts. You could always find arrow points—projectile points they called them. It was really kind of putting you in touch with your past. We still feel strong ties to the river. Most people will tell you they like to go along the river. They say it's the old homeland. When I first married, I took my husband down there and tried to explain how painful it was for us to be relocated and then find out that the land of many of us wasn't going to be flooded at all—and then, within a few short years, to see so many tourists and campers setting up along the river that used to be our home."

In addition to the tourists and campers who flood the old Indian lands during the summer months, Stock also mentions that some of the areas have become illegal dumpsites, full of old mattresses, beer cans, kitchen appliances, and other such refuse common along the back roads of America.

"There are a lot of memories too, when the water goes down," she says. "There was a lacrosse field down there and a ball field, and they went way back. My grandfather and his father used to play ball and lacrosse down there, and I remember them. When the water goes down, a lot of times you get to see bits and pieces. It's a hard feeling. Yet it's a mixed emotion because you feel bad about how it's changed, but you still feel comforted being there."

River shroud

265

Ghost Flats, Allegany Reservation

Levee, Olean

14

ALONG THE LAZY RIVER

A reporter and a crowd of curious spectators sent Captain Way off from Olean on his 1938 adventure down the Allegheny, and a brass band greeted him on his return upriver with his miniature paddle wheeler in the 1950s. But nobody pays any attention to Jim and me as we walk along the top of the levee that walls the town off from the river— except perhaps the golfer shagging balls in the park below. But then Jim's van is much less of an attraction than an eighteen-foot yawl drawing ten inches of water that expects to negotiate a series of six-inch-deep rock-strewn rapids, or than the last paddle wheeler, the last motorized boat of any type, to make the trip all the way from Pittsburgh to Olean, a feat that can never again be undertaken because of Kinzua Dam.

Flatboat

Staring at the river below the levee, the brown rock bottom clearly visible through its shallow glass of July water, I find it hard to imagine a real steamboat carrying eighty passengers and sixty tons of freight so far up the Allegheny. It happened twice, though, the first time with the *Allegheny* in 1830, then with the *New Castle* in 1837. Cornplanter himself saw the *Allegheny*, concluding: "White men will do anything to avoid using their muscles."

Even more incredible than the trips by the *Allegheny* and the *New Castle* though (since they were more like stunts) is to imagine Olean and the little Allegheny before us, 260 river miles above Pittsburgh, once being the principal port of embarkation for settlers heading west. But less than a decade after its founding in 1804 by Major Adam Hoops, an engineering officer on Washington's staff, it was a frenzied port in the push west.

"The place is called Olean Point," said Tilly Buttrick in his *Voyages, Travels and Discoveries* (1831):

> It was much altered in appearance since my former visit here; instead of a few log huts as before, there were forty or fifty shanties, or temporary log houses, built up, and completely filled with men, women and children, household furniture thrown up in piles; and a great number of horses, waggons, sleighs, &c., &c.

These people were emigrants from the eastern States, principally down the Ohio river. Two gentlemen undertook to take a number of these people, and found it to be about twelve hundred of all ages and sexes. They had a large number of flat-bottomed boats built for their conveyance; these were boarded up at the sides, and roofs over them, with chimneys suitable for cooking, and were secure from the weather. There were also many rafts of boards and shingles, timber and saw logs, which would find a ready market at different places on the Ohio river. There are many saw-mills on the stream above this place, where these articles are manufactured from the fine timber which grows in vast quantities in this vicinity. The river at this time had risen full bank, and I should suppose was navigable for vessels of fifty tons burden; but was frozen over. . . .

I waited about ten days, which brought it nearly to the close of March. On Saturday night sat up late, heard some cracking of the ice, several of us observing that we should soon be on our way went to bed. Next morning at daylight found the river nearly clear, and at eight o'clock was completely so. The place now presented a curious sight; the men conveying their goods on board the boats and rafts, the women scolding, and children crying, some clothed, and some half clothed, all in haste, filled with anxiety, as if a few minutes were lost the passage would be lost also. By ten o'clock the whole river for one mile appeared to be one solid body of boats and rafts. What, but just before, appeared a considerable village now remainded but a few solitary huts with their occupants.

Olean's high tide as a migration center came in 1818, when 3,000 settlers followed the spring floods down the Allegheny, 350 of them on a single raft. After the Erie Canal was completed in 1825, the town ceased to be a point of embarkation and its importance as a port rapidly declined.

More than thirty years before Tilly Buttrick embarked from Olean, the flatboats on which he and the other migrants were traveling had been carrying commerce along the Allegheny to American troops down the Ohio and to the Spanish at New Orleans. "These boats are flat bottomed, with upright sides and stern, and the front turns up like a skate," Thomas Ridout noted in 1788. "They seldom use any sail, and are steered by means of a long oar from the stern, and two or three oars are occasionally used to conduct them, for the stream, which runs at the rate of about five miles an hour, carries the boat with great rapidity."

Flatboats could vary in size up to ninety feet, depending on the needs and abilities of the builders. The two most common types were the Kentucky and the New Orleans. Because it had a shorter distance to travel, the Kentucky type was smaller, less well built, and only partially roofed. New Orleans boats were fully roofed and stoutly built. But neither style was made for upstream travel, and when they reached their destination they were usually torn apart and the lumber used to construct cabins.

The impossibility of pushing such wide, flat-bottomed boats upriver led to the development of the keelboat. Built like a ship on a timber keel that made the hull rigid and enabled it to withstand collisions with rocks and logs, keelboats were forty to eighty feet long and seven to ten feet wide and drew about two feet of water when loaded. Their long, narrow hulls were ribbed and planked over, and the hold was covered by a cabin surrounded by a runway on which the crew walked when poling the boat upriver. Nobody knows exactly how the keelboat originated, but the idea probably came from the shipwrights who migrated to western Pennsylvania from the Atlantic Coast. The first boat of record to have the cleated runways common to keelboats was the *Three Friends*, built by George Morgan in Pittsburgh in 1768.

"A keelboat was generally manned by ten hands, principally Canadian-French, and a patroon or master," wrote artist and naturalist John James Audubon in 1809. "These boats seldom carried more than from twenty to thirty tons. The barges had frequently forty or fifty men with a patroon and carried fifty or sixty tons. Both of these kinds of vessels were provided with a mast, a square sail, and coils of cordage known by the name of cordelles."

On their downstream trips, flatboats were guided by one, two, or three men working long tiller oars. Keelboats were rowed by between four and twelve men and steered by a patroon with a long tiller oar at the stern on downstream trips. Those journeys could be quite pleasant in good weather and when there was plenty of water in the river. But upstream trips were always agony, as Morgan Neville related in an 1829 article entitled "The Last of the Boatmen" in the *Western Souvenir*:

> In ascending the river it was a continued series of toil, rendered more irksome by the snail rate at which they moved [about six miles a day]. The boat was propelled by poles against which the shoulder was placed; and the whole strength and skill of the individual applied in this manner. As the boatmen moved along the running board, with their heads nearly touching the plank on which they walked, the effect produced on the mind of an observer was similar to that on beholding the ox, rocking before an overloaded cart. Their bodies, naked to the waist, for the purpose of moving with greater ease, and of enjoying the breeze of the river, were exposed to the burning suns of summer, and to the rain of autumn. After a hard day's push, they would take their "fillee," or ration of whiskey, and having swallowed a miserable supper of meat half burnt, and of bread half baked, stretch themselves without covering, on the deck, and slumber till the steersman's call invited them to the morning "fillee."

Notwithstanding this, the boatman's life had charms as irresistible as those presented by the splendid illusions of the stage. Sons abandoned the comfortable farms of their fathers, and apprentices fled from the service of their masters. There was a captivation in the idea of "going down the river"; and the youthful boatmen who had "pushed a keel" from New Orleans felt all the pride of a youthful merchant after his first voyage to an English sea port. From an exclusive association together, they had formed a kind of slang peculiar to themselves; and from the constant exercise of wit, with the "squatters" on shore, and the crews of other boats, they acquired a quickness, and smartness of vulgar retort, that was quite amusing. The frequent battles they were engaged in with the boatmen of different parts of the river, and with less civilized inhabitants of the lower Ohio and Mississippi, invested them with that ferocious reputation, which has made them spoken of throughout Europe.

By 1800, keelboats were regularly hauling the necessities of life up the Allegheny and returning with agricultural staples. Some of the trips were nothing less than amazing, such as that of the thirty-five-foot keelboat that arrived in Pittsburgh from Oneida Lake in New York in 1822. The boat and its crew had navigated Oneida Lake and the Oswego River to Lake Ontario and the Niagara River. At Niagara Falls the crew portaged its boat to Lake Erie and then sailed west, until it was in the area of Chautauqua Lake, to which it portaged, and then floated down Conewango Creek to Warren and finally the Allegheny to Pittsburgh. It was on a fifty-five-foot long keelboat built in Pittsburgh that Meriwether Lewis and William Clark undertook the most famous expedition in American history on August 31, 1803—an unusual time for such an undertaking, for, as Lewis would write President Thomas Jefferson, "at this stage of water, oxen make the best sailors on the Ohio River."

Like the cowboys who would follow them and the leatherstocking frontiersmen who preceded them, the keelboaters who worked the Allegheny and similar rivers produced their share of legends and heroes, among them another of the most famous names in American folklore—Mike Fink.

Although Mike Fink has entered the realm of myth, he was, like Johnny Appleseed, a real person. He was born to Scotch-Irish parents at Fort Pitt in 1770, but most details of his life have been obscured by contradictory tales. It is known, however, that at the age of seventeen he joined a company of rangers in western Pennsylvania and served as a scout. His river career began after the Treaty of Greenville (1795) ended Indian hostilities along the frontier, and he spent most of his time on the Ohio and Mississippi rivers, though at times he almost certainly also would have worked at least the lower Allegheny.

In appearance, dress, and behavior, Fink was said to be the essence of the "half horse, half alligator" keelboatman. Accounts from the period portray him as Herculean in build, sunburned, and weathered, garbed in a loose blue jerkin with white fringe, a red flannel shirt, and coarse trousers held up with a leather belt, to which was attached a large hunting knife. On his feet he wore moccasins, and on his head of raven black hair a cap made of animal skin. His air was assured, relaxed, and jaunty. Boatmen hailed him as "Snapping Turtle" and "The Snag." Intellectuals dubbed him a "Western Lion."

In literature, Fink has often been described as a heavy drinker, savage fighter, coarse practical joker, and favorite of the ladies, though feminists today would dispute that assessment because he once sought to cure his wife's wandering eye by forcing her to lie down in a pile of leaves, which he then set on fire. No doubt he played all those roles at different times. They were indeed common attributes of the frontier and the people who worked the river. But stories about him also carry recurring themes showing him as being of good humor, a good heart, and good sense, along with a strong arm and straight eye. While still a boy, Fink became so skilled with a rifle that he was barred from the local shooting matches. It was his skill with "Betsy," as he called his rifle, that pitted him against an even more famous American hero.

"One night I fell in with him in the woods, where him and his wife shook down a blanket for me in his wigwam," said Davy Crockett, describing one incident in *Davy Crockett's Almanack for 1839.* He continued:

> In the morning say Mike to me: "I've got the handsomest wife, and the fastest horse, and the sharpest shooting iron in all Kentuck, and if any man dare doubt it, I'll be in his hair quicker than Hell could scorch a feather." This put my dander up, and says I: "I've nothing to say agin your wife, Mike, for it can't be denied she's a shocking handsome woman, and Mrs. Crockett's in Tennessee, and I've got no horses. Mike, I don't exactly like to tell you you lie about your rifle, but I'm damned if you speak the truth, and I'll prove it. Do you see that ar cat sitting on the top rail of your potato patch, about 150 yards off? If he ever hears agin, I'll be shot if it shan't be without ears."
>
> So I blazed away, and I'll bet you a horse, the ball cut off both the old tomcat's ears close to his head and shaved the hair off clean across the skull, as slick as if I'd done it with a razor, and the critter never stirred nor knew he'd lost his ears till he tried to scratch 'em. "Talk about your rifle after that, Mike!" says I. "Do you see that ar sow away of furder than the end of the world," says Mike, "with a litter of pigs around her?" And he lets fly. The old sow give a grunt but never stirred in her tracks, and Mike falls to loading and firing for dear life, till he hadn't left one of them ar pigs enough tail to make a toothpick on. "Now," says he, "Colonel Crockett, I'll be pretticularly obleeged to you if you'll put them ar pig's tails on agin," says he. "That's onpossible, Mike," says I, "but you've left one of 'em about an inch to steer by, and if it had a-ben my work, I wouldn't have done it so wasteful."

So I lets fly, and cuts off the apology he'd left the poor cretur for decency. I wish I may drink the whole of Old Mississip, without a drop of the rale stuff in it, if you wouldn't have thort the tail had been drove in with a hammer. That made Mike kinder sorter sorthy, and he sends a ball after his wife as she was going to the spring and knocked half her coomb out of her head and calls out to her to stop for me to take blizzard at what was left on it. The angeliferous critter stood still as a scarecrow in a cornfield, for she'd got used to Mike's tricks by long practice. "No, no, Mike," says I, "Davy Crockett's hand would be sure to shake if his iron war pointed within a hundred mile of a shemale, and I give up beat, Mike, as we've had our eye-openers a-ready, we'll now take a phlegmcutter, by way of an anti-fogmatic, and then we'll disperse."

It was Mike Fink's skill with the rifle that brought about his end. The arrival of steamboats on western waters in 1815 started a decline in the keelboat business. By the 1820s the industry was in its death throes. In 1822 Fink signed up with a group of scouts and trappers hired by Major Andrew Henry and William Ashley to go up the Missouri River to its source and open the Rocky Mountain country to the fur trade. The following year, in a "shooting the cup" match at Fort Henry on the Yellowstone River (a contest in which he would shoot a cup off a friend's head), Mike aimed a bit too low and killed a fellow trapper. The next time he entered the fort, the victim's friend, a man named Talbott, responded by killing him with a double-barrel blast to the chest.

From the few solitary huts traveler Tilly Buttrick knew in 1815, Olean has grown into easily the largest city on the upper Allegheny. Its past still shines through, however, in the well-kept downtown buildings with ornate facades dating back to the turn of the century, and in streets bearing the names Sullivan, Greene, Henley, and Laurens—all officers who served with Major Hoops in the Revolution.

Hoops and three associates contracted with the Holland Land Company in 1803 for the land on which Olean sits. The agreement stipulated twenty thousand acres at the junction of the Allegheny and Olean Creek, or, as it was known then, Ischua Creek. The settlement Hoops began in 1804 was the first in Cattaraugus County. Actually, when the county was established in 1808, all of its territory was listed as the "Town of Olean." Hoops created the name "Olean" from the Latin *oleum*, which means oil, after the famous Seneca oil spring near Cuba, New York, about which Jesuit missionaries wrote in 1627.

Despite all his high hopes and hard work, Major Hoops lost his tract only a few years after Olean came into being, when he fell in arrears on payments to the Holland Land Company and it foreclosed on the property. Hoops left Olean for West Chester, Pennsylvania, where he died a disappointed and broken man in 1845.

273

six miles of old dikes along the Allegheny and Olean Creek and building one and a half miles of new levees and a half-mile concrete floodwall. The project today stands as a veritable fortress guarding Olean from the power of the river.

Strolling atop a dike maybe fifteen feet above the barely moving summer confluence of the Allegheny and Olean Creek, we find it impossible to comprehend what the area must have looked like with water lapping a foot from our feet as it did during Hurricane Agnes. When a leak developed under the dike, six thousand people were forced to flee. The dikes and levees, aided by thousands of sandbags and bulldozers that hastily constructed an emergency dike around the leak, did the job they were built to do and saved the town. In the summer, though, when the river is so low and tame and looking beautiful with its fringe of trees on the opposite bank, it is difficult not to think there might have been a better way than to isolate the city from its birth source so completely. But that is only the passing thought of an outsider. People living along the river must certainly be grateful for the protection of the levee. "The Allegheny, ordinarily placid and always picturesque, can be a raging devil when swollen by rain and thaw," noted Arch Merrill in *Southern Tier*. "More than once Olean people living on its banks have had to flee their homes. Sometimes they left in rowboats."

On the edge of Olean lies St. Bonaventure University, the largest Franciscan college in the United States. The campus can trace its roots back to 1836, when Nicholas Devereux, a devout Catholic, bought from the Holland Land Company a tract of land that included the site on the Allegheny where the school now stands. Devereux's original plan called for construction of a town, Allegany City, on the site. It was to be the cultural and commercial hub of the area, served by the Erie Railroad, the Genesee Valley Canal, and a widened Allegheny River. But the routes of the railroad and the canal were changed, and the river was never widened. The paper city crumpled, and all that was built was a hotel called "Allegany City."

Although the Erie Railroad did not pass through as had been originally planned, its construction brought many Catholic workers from Ireland to Olean. Because there were no churches in the area, Devereux went to Rome to ask the Vatican to send a group of Franciscan missionaries to western New York. He offered $5,000 and two hundred acres of land. The pope sent four volunteers in June 1855. Devereux's son, John, provided a home for the friars in Ellicottville that served as a monastery, chapel, and school, with an excellent student-teacher ratio of one to one: four professors for four students!

The first building on the present site of the university, the first and only Franciscan educational institution in the seven-hundred-year history of the order to become a university, was completed in the fall of 1858. The following spring the college opened its doors to fifteen students. The building lasted until a fire destroyed it in 1930. A year before the fire, the university gained another bit of fame when the school became the

On the banks of the Allegheny, McGraw-Jennings Athletic Field, St. Bonaventure College

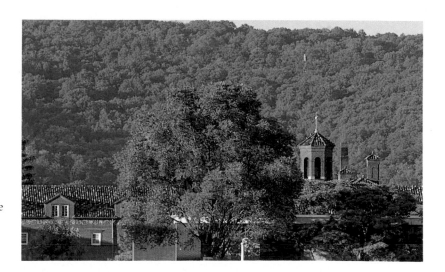

View of St. Bonaventure

owner of the shortest standard-gauge railroad in the world. The St. Bonaventure Railroad ran for only about a quarter of a mile. The school acquired it as a spur to connect the campus with the Pennsylvania Railroad line after the Olean Electric Railway ceased operation in 1929. It purchased a small engine, which ran until it broke down in 1940.

Driving through campus, we are still in awe of the golden glow that bathes the lush green mountains all around the city. A blank, gray overcast had filled the day since morning. Then, after a dinner of grape leaves and beer in a Lebanese restaurant, we step outside to find the streets of Olean literally aglow under a sky of scattered cotton balls. Immediately, we decide to head back over to St. Bonaventure and try for a photograph of the university, which on our first drive through had been completely deserted, except for a lone, elderly brother riding a rickety old bicycle.

"It's a miracle," Jim jokes, as we reach the rear of the campus and find a soccer field full of shouting, running high school kids. "This is great."

St. Bonaventure is a well-known college basketball power, but the two greatest athletes associated with the school, those for whom the athletic field where the kids are playing is named, come from the game of baseball. John J. McGraw, the immortal manager of Rodgers Hornsby and the New York Giants, began his professional baseball career in 1890 with the Olean club of the New York and Pennsylvania League. Two years later he was with the Baltimore Orioles and spending the off-season as the captain/coach of the St. Bonaventure team.

In 1893 McGraw persuaded his Orioles teammate, Hughie Jennings, to join him at the college. The pair attended classes in the fall and winter, coached the college team in the spring, and then headed for Baltimore in the summer. Jennings played for the Orioles until 1897 and then eventually moved on to manage the Detroit Tigers, including Ty Cobb. In 1927 McGraw and Jennings came back to St. Bonaventure for the dedication of the athletic field. McGraw brought his Giants with him to play an exhibition game against the St. Bonaventure nine. The Giants won 11 to 2.

Above Portville, the "Village of Colonial Beauty," and its well-kept, shaded clapboard homes, the Allegheny bends back south into Pennsylvania and once again changes character. From the quiet slackwater of the lower river to the primitive collection of pools and riffles between East Brady and Warren, and then the deep, still waters of Kinzua, it now turns into a meandering, near-swamp channel of mud banks and methane-bubbling bottom, broken stumps, and the stagnant odor of decaying vegetation.

"How would you like to paddle that to Pittsburgh?" I ask.

Having paddled more than thirty miles of seemingly endless pools from Franklin to Emlenton, neither of us is interested in the idea, or in the sore arms and shoulders the marsh of a river in front of us would surely produce. But that same stretch of river was once part of an incredible portage route. Pioneers from the East Coast came up the Susquehanna River, the West Branch Susquehanna, and then Sinnemahoning Creek and the Driftwood Branch of Sinnemahoning Creek to Portage Creek in Emporium. After paddling up Portage Creek as far as possible, they would then cross Keating Summit on foot to Allegheny Portage Creek and enter the Allegheny at Port Allegany, or, as the town was first called in recognition of its role in the scheme of things, Canoe Place.

Near the village of Turtlepoint—named, we assume, for the ideal turtle habitat the river appears to be in the area—we find a historical marker for Mount Equity Plantation. Because we find it tough to imagine the wide, level valley around us as ever being the site of anything important, we pull off the road to read the marker: "Governor Thomas McKean, for whom the county was named, purchased here in 1805 a 299 acre tract. Its name derived from the fact the purchase was made in part to give Pennsylvania equity in power in land settled by Connecticut." The river and land surrounding it had been part of a political move to counter claims Connecticut made to northern Pennsylvania around the time of the Revolution, claims that at one point actually had the two states fighting each other in northeastern Pennsylvania.

Port Allegany's past as "Canoe Place," a generic name once used to designate portage points throughout Pennsylvania, is touted by another marker at the square in the center of town. But it is even more evident by the Canoe Place Inn, a gigantic wood-frame restaurant and hotel on the edge of the square, where we stop for lunch and briefly discuss visiting the dessert-on-the-square festival scheduled for later in the day. We give up the idea because there are too many other things we need to do, and settle for a walk around the old mountain town and for glimpses of the river hidden behind a glass plant.

Fertile floodplain

Around Port Allegany the river begins to lose its swampy character and once more becomes a series of rocky riffles and pools. This time, though, it is only about the size of a large mountain stream. It is a type of water familiar to trout fishermen throughout Pennsylvania and New York. Standing on the bridge, I pick out likely-looking holding spots for trout and wonder how many people who cross the Allegheny in Pittsburgh every day know it leads such a double life. Not as many as might be suspected, I think, recalling anglers and boaters I know on the lower river who are only vaguely aware that the Allegheny in Potter County changes from a warmwater fishery to a very good trout stream. Those who know it has played a significant role in trout-fishing history are even fewer. I probably could count them on the fingers of both hands.

Coudersport—in Potter County, or "God's Country" as the locals call it—is the last town on the Allegheny River. Visited by the Moravian missionary David Zeisberger in 1767, it was laid out in 1808, before there was even a single white person in the area. The property belonged to John Keating, who agreed to give the land to the town and the county if the town would be named after his friend Judge Coudre. John L. Cartee of Massachusetts was the first resident. He arrived in 1825 and constructed a dam across the Allegheny with the idea of erecting a gristmill, but a flood ended those plans the following year. It's an old story all along the river.

The threat that even such a diminished Allegheny as that in Potter County has often posed to the people living on its banks is evidenced by the concrete trough in which the river makes its passage through Coudersport. Although the flood-control trough was built by the Corps of Engineers in 1954, it was, like the levees around Olean, mostly a response (delayed by World War II) to the near destruction of the town by an earlier flood, in July 1942.

"I'll tell you how quickly the water came up," says Tom Dewey, who was a boy at the time. "My father got up and looked out the window. He could see the water coming up over the bank of the river. By the time he got his pants on and got downstairs to get our car, which was in a garage between the house and the river, the water was in front of the house. He could not get out of the house. That's how quickly the water came up. It was a cloudburst."

Like Kinzua Dam, the Coudersport flood-control project did its job during Hurricane Agnes. "The water was lapping the top of the concrete," remembers Dewey. "The ground vibrated. It sounded like a fast freight express going through town for hours. The ground trembled all the way through town. But it worked. It held. It prevented what would have been a flood like in forty-two."

Although the flood-control channel worked when it was needed, it was, like many other Corps projects along the Allegheny, greeted with less than enthusiasm by some people. This was especially true among trout anglers such as Jim Bashline, noted outdoors

282

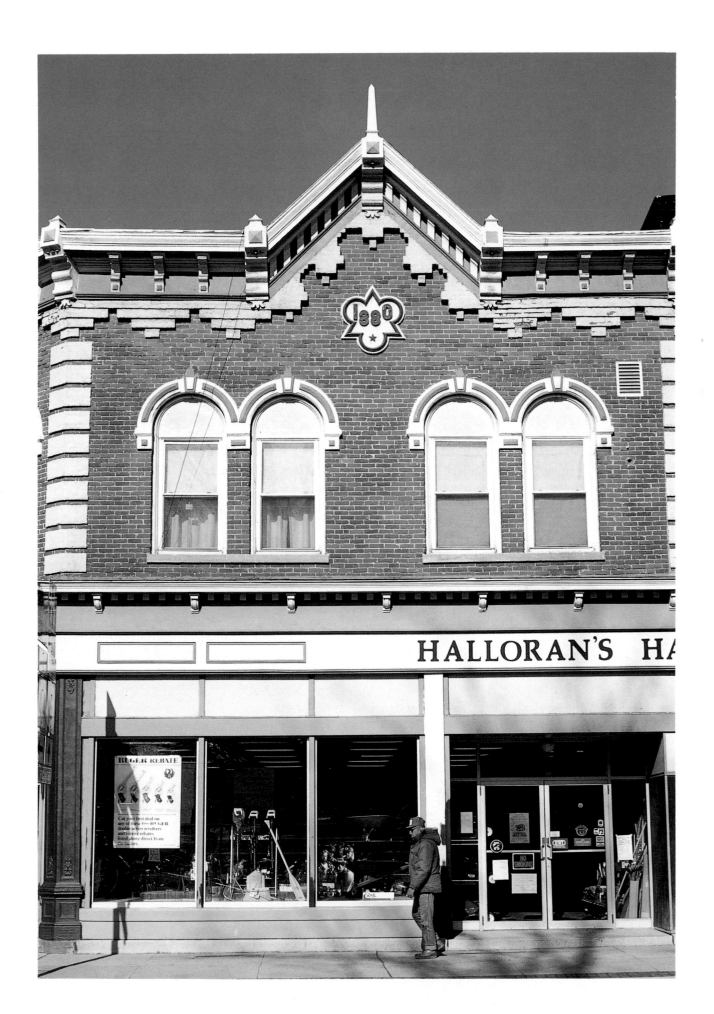

Flood-control project

writer and Coudersport native, who maintains that the Goodsell Hole, once laid at the juncture of the Allegheny and Mill Creek, was where night fishing for trout was first practiced. "The Coudersport city fathers, with considerable urging from the United States Corps of Engineers, decided to construct a concrete flood-control channel through the center of town," Bashline wrote in his 1972 book *Night Fishing for Trout:*

> There would have been other, far cheaper ways to handle the occasional flash flood that hit the Allegheny Mountains, but the Corps, in its doubtful wisdom, elected to do it the hard way. The Goodsell Hole and the other excellent pools that lay within the city limits became nothing more than concrete hog troughs. In a way it's a good thing I wasn't in Coudersport when the construction was going on. If I had been, I would probably be writing from the confines of a Leavenworth cell.

Night fishing for trout along the Allegheny River in Coudersport started before World War I. The brown trout had only recently been introduced to northern Pennsylvania, and anglers trying for the new fish found it to be much more wily and cautious a creature than the native brook trout it replaced. When methods developed for the brook trout produced only small browns, resourceful anglers—among them Dr. Samuel A. Phillips and Bob Pinney—began experimenting with new ways to offer their bait or flies.

Doc Phillips was a dentist who, in Bashline's words, "seldom practiced in the mouths of human beings. He was far more interested in attaching bits of steel to the jaws of trout." Doc's wife, Caroline Larrabee Phillips, was a flytier who not only fed her

284

husband's passion with her beautiful creations but also ended up providing the lion's share of the family's income by selling her flies. "An ideal arrangement," Bashline called it, and many anglers would agree.

When Doc discovered it was next to impossible to catch a brown trout of respectable size using standard brook trout methods, he turned to the night. Caroline Phillips aided her husband's quest by developing two classic night fly patterns: the Yellow Dun and the New Page. Bashline rated the Yellow Dun as "king of the night flies." Unfortunately, however, nobody has been able to duplicate Caroline Phillips's creation successfully. The gray duck-feather wings of the wet fly and ginger hackle are easy enough to copy. The problem is the body. When dry, it is a rosy pink mohair, but when wet it takes on the appearance of "a glob of bloody flesh."

Seven Bridges, above Coudersport

Doc Phillips might be considered the father of night fishing for trout, but it was a member of the next generation, Bob Pinney, who perhaps took the method to its height. Like Theodore Gordon, the godfather of dry fly fishing in America, Robert N. Pinney was a lifelong bachelor who lived with his mother until she died, and then with his sister. His work as the night clerk at the local hotel left his days and the hours before midnight free for fishing, something he did every day during the season when the weather permitted. "To say that Pinney liked to fish would be an insult," Bashline, who accompanied him on the streams for twenty years, wrote. "He *had* to fish."

After learning from Doc Phillips that big browns would strike a fly at night, Pinney, along with a small group of friends, turned to the Goodsell Hole to work out problems with tackle, flies, and presentation. Over more than fifty years of trout fishing he became

Opening day of trout season

so proficient that fifteen-inchers were commonplace for him, and eighteen-inchers brought only a muffled grunt. It was the two-footers he was after, Bashline noted, and he caught hundreds in the Goodsell Hole and others along the Allegheny, a civilized eastern trout stream that was not supposed to produce such fish.

"Fishermen just died," Dewey recalls about the end of the Goodsell Hole. "They were in tears. I came up the night they drained it. A few of the fishermen got together and cut a deal with the construction firm. The company said, 'Okay. We will schedule the bulldozing of the Goodsell Hole so that a few of you guys can be up there with nets and salvage as many fish as you can.' And they started opening it up with the bulldozer." He pauses and sighs. "You just would not believe the trout. Dozens and dozens of them. They took them upstream, but of course it was a futile gesture because they couldn't survive up there. It was just too small. But they felt they had to do something."

A collection of Phillips's flies, as well as a small assortment of cane rods from the turn of the century, now rests in the Potter County Historical Society headquarters in Coudersport.

The Goodsell Hole may be only a memory, but the Allegheny in Potter County remains a magnet for trout fishermen from throughout Pennsylvania, New York, Ohio, and other eastern states. People like Ken Igo of Latrobe and John Giesey of Ligonier have even made a yearly ritual of fishing the river on the opening day of trout season every April.

"It's unique," says Igo about his love of the upper Allegheny. "It's a nice little stream. I like the camaraderie. You see the same people at the same holes all the time, the same cars. Fishing is good."

With seventeen opening days on the river under his belt, Igo has amassed quite a collection of stories to go with the fishing. One of his favorites involves an incident that took place at the Seven Bridges area of the river in the early 1970s when the aerator on the Fish Commission's stocking truck broke and the truck's load of five thousand trout had to be released under the bridge. "That was the first stop," Igo says, "and the driver said they had problems with the pump and were going to have to decide whether to call for another truck or dump the fish in. They decided to dump the fish into the one spot. You can spit across the river up there too. People were lined up shoulder-to-shoulder across the bridge, shoulder-to-shoulder on both sides of the stream, up and downstream for probably a couple of hundred yards. The paper even came out and took pictures of everybody."

As with all anglers, though, the pair's favorite stories about the Allegheny are those in which they poke fun at each other.

"My buddy, Ken Igo, who has to be one of the best fishermen in Potter County"—Giesey starts—"he always lets me fish downstream first. He does it to find where all the fish are—he figures I'll miss them and then he'll know where they're at. But two years

Upper river

ago I was fishing in front of him. Of course, I like to leave a couple of fish for him, and I missed a real nice fish. But naturally, he never thinks I'd leave a big one for him. Anyway, I rolled a real nice brookie and yelled back to him—he was maybe a hundred yards behind me—'Hey, Ken! When you get to this section there's a real nice fish here.' He laughed, thinking I was just pulling his chain. When he gets down there, though, he hooks this big fish and I hear him screaming. 'Buddy! Buddy!' Of course, since that day he carries a net all the time. But he didn't have a net then. He's yelling, 'Please come up here and net this fish for me!' I went up and netted it for him, and now it's a nice trophy on his wall."

"Twenty-two inches," Igo says smiling.

"He bought a net when we went home Monday morning which he carries to this day," Giesey adds.

"It was funny," Igo says. "He was under a log jam. I hit him and he went downstream with the initial rush, under the logs. I couldn't get through and had to put my rod in the water and hand-feed it through the logs, then pick it up at the other end. Then it came back up and did the same thing again, and then went down again. It was opening day, and a whole crowd of guys were standing around clapping and applauding. They kept saying, 'That's good thinking. Good thinking.' But there wasn't anything else I could do."

Recreation, especially hunting and trout fishing, is the main reason most people visit the upper Allegheny. Considering the vast forests and mountains surrounding the river, that is readily understandable. What is more difficult to grasp is that the same rugged slopes also serve as a breadbasket for much of Pennsylvania and other parts of the East, producing potatoes both for supermarket shelves and for some of the best-known potato-chip makers in the nation.

Ferd Irish is one of the three largest potato growers in Potter County. He came to Pennsylvania from northern Maine, where his father was a farmer, in 1960 because of the larger market. He and his son, Wayne, are now one of eight or nine growers in the county who plant about 1,200 acres of potatoes a year. That may not sound like much, but the 250 acres kept in potatoes on the Irish farm annually produce about four and a half million pounds of Irish round white potatoes.

"It's good potato ground," Wayne says about the area. "Most of it is good draining soil. We have warm days and cool nights, and we get a fair amount of moisture through the growing season, so we don't have to irrigate at all. Because of the weather—warm days and cool nights and hard winters—we don't have an insect problem we have to spray a lot for here. Other areas in the state of Pennsylvania have a lot of potato-beetle problems. We don't have that here yet, and I claim it's because of the weather."

Although demand for potatoes in Pennsylvania is great, and the state has the largest

289

Wayne Irish, potato farmer

number of potato-chip makers in the nation, the number of growers fell by nearly half in the 1980s. The reasons include retirement of some older farmers (it's rare for a third generation, such as Wayne, to be in farming today), the general shakeup in the farm economy during the 1980s, and competition. Like every other business today, the upper Allegheny's potato farmers are fighting competition from some far-off places—in this case, Idaho, Colorado, and Canada.

"It's easy today for Idaho, Colorado, and other areas to get potatoes into our markets virtually overnight," Wayne says, "and Canada is becoming a big competitor in Buffalo, Pittsburgh, Philadelphia. I understand they can now put a ferryboat from New Brunswick and Prince Edward Island into New York Harbor and come down here. So we have competition from all over. But we feel we're so close to the market, just a gas tank away, and with the gobbling up of Lancaster and southern Pennsylvania by the cities pushing out, we can compete. It's hard to believe Potter County is a breadbasket for the state, but we're doing it."

On the eastern edge of Coudersport along Route 49, a scattering of gigantic maple logs, perhaps lost by one of the groaning trucks forever crawling out of the overlooking mountains, appears on the edge of the road as a reminder of one area in which the upper Allegheny region rules without serious challenge anywhere in the world. Hardwood timber—oak, maple, beech, chestnut—is easily the number-one cash crop of Potter County. Exactly how valuable are the forests above the river is revealed by the fact that buyers for companies in Europe and Asia have set up offices in sleepy, out-of-the-way little Coudersport so they can be on hand immediately when a new tract of forest becomes available for cutting.

But then lumbering has always been an important industry along the Allegheny. Through the nineteenth century, logs and cut lumber comprised by far the greatest tonnage shipped down the river. One hundred million board feet of forest products floated the Allegheny in 1838, and almost seven times that in 1857, when more than four hundred sawmills were shipping their output down the waterway.

Depending on the source, either Michael McKinney or Daniel Jackson is believed to have floated the first timber raft downriver to Pittsburgh. "We met the other day one of the oldest men now extant, Mr. Michael McKinney, of Warren County, Pa., who is 97 years of age," wrote a reporter for the *Pittsburgh Commercial Journal* in 1855 about McKinney's last raft trip.

> He lives near the town of Warren, and came to the city on Friday on a raft, himself pulling occasionally at the oar. He is vigorous and active and bids fair to live through a number of years yet. He informed us that he was the first man who ever piloted a raft of logs from Warren down the Allegheny to Pittsburgh. It was sixty-eight years ago [i.e., in 1787]. He is undoubtedly the "most ancient mariner" of the Allegheny alive.

Jackson, another early settler of Warren County, is credited with bringing the first raft to Pittsburgh by Lansing Wetmore, a Warren County judge of the early nineteenth century. "In 1799," Wetmore wrote, "he ran a raft of 30,000 feet of pine boards to Pittsburgh, the first raft of lumber that was ever known to descend the river, and considered of course at the time to be a very large raft and wonderful adventure." Jackson is also credited with operating the first sawmill along the river, about a mile above Warren near the mouth of Jackson Run. According to L. L. Schenck's *History of Warren County,*

Lumber rafts near Warren

Jackson's mill was completed about 1800 and it was related that the sawing of the first board was thought to be an event of sufficient importance to call for some unusual demonstration on the part of those present. Accordingly, it was placed on the ground, a bottle of whiskey brought out, and two individuals, after partaking of its contents sufficiently to give elasticity to their limbs, went through the primitive performance of dancing a jig.

Small rafts from the farthest reaches of the Allegheny would, on the first rise after the ice broke, jump mill dams and run rapids to collect at Warren, where a dozen of them would be tied together into "Pittsburgh fleets." These rafts were 60 to 70 feet wide and

292

250 to 300 feet long. Rafts not sold at Pittsburgh were joined in threes to continue their voyage to Cincinnati, Louisville, and even New Orleans. One record raft shipped down the Allegheny held one and a half million board feet of lumber and covered more than two acres of water surface. Sometimes a hundred rafts together would fill the Allegheny from Herr's Island to The Point, often breaking into jumbles on bridge piers. A reporter caught the sheer terror Pittsburgh's bridges brought to the hearts of raftsmen in an 1841 article for the *Pittsburgh Gazette*:

> As we wanted to run the right shore pier, we hugged in close as the wind which blew off strongly from Allegheny Town would let us. Every man was at his oar, with his coat off, when within twenty rods of the upper bridge. It was apparent that we should have a hard run. The footwalk that runs outside of the bridge was filled with people looking to see us through, while the rafts alongshore were covered with lumbermen, who were anxious spectators, and kept hallooing to us to change our course, but the pilot paid no attention, determined to go his way or drive down the pier. The wind blew hard, and the water chopped and foamed and flew into our faces so that it seemed as if our oars were hung to a breakwater, rather than a bundle of floating boards. We were within ten feet of the pier, and the inside of the raft was not yet outside of it, and the men were straining every muscle to the uttermost, but it seemed as if the thing could not be moved an inch to the right and must go to destruction. The pilot muttered to himself, "By God, we're stove," and shouted, "Hard up there, forward! Damn you, pull!" and the muscles of his neck rolled out into cords and the veins of his forehead and face and arms swelled almost to bursting. Fortunately, at the moment he gave the order, the wind lulled a little, the raft moved to the right, her head lopped by, she grazed on the pier, and rubbing and jerking along her middle, stopped! Every man held his breath, for one minute's pause there, and she would break around the pier, and then dash in pieces on those of successive bridges below. "Left, forward! Right, behind!" yelled the pilot, and quick as lightning, the pulling was reversed before, thus making a cross pull. She settled a little and halted, but her head was through, and the wind catching that, she started again and a few strokes more cleared her, when away she went, amid the shouts and greetings of hundreds who had watched her in breathless suspense. It was the narrowest escape ever made in Pittsburgh. We passed safely through the rest, and after rocking and tossing on the waves of the Ohio, landed a mile below town, so exhausted with fatigue as to be scarcely able to stand.

Such narrow escapes, coupled with a long winter in the backwoods, made the red-jacketed raftsmen and their Seneca companions (Cornplanter himself began operating a sawmill on the river a few years after he was granted his tract above Warren in 1794)

Lumberjacks

ready for a little fun, and they often wreaked havoc in towns where they stopped. "The Olean boys have scattered themselves in squads through the city," the *Pittsburgh Dispatch* noted in April 1856, "and knocked up rows at every point where four or five of them got together." When a tavern keeper at Manorville, between Ford City and Kittanning, tried to preserve some semblance of order in his establishment by cutting off the whiskey, the raftsmen went to their rafts, secured some ropes, and attached them to the tavern. Then they threatened to set their crafts loose and pull the building into the river if the tavern keeper did not continue to serve them.

White pine and hemlock bark for the tanning of hides were the first timber products shipped down the Allegheny. In the beginning, timber was cut only from around streams on which it could be floated to the river. Then, in the early 1880s, powerful locomotives capable of hauling logs from the most rugged and remote reaches of northern Pennsylvania were developed. The new technology, supported by an unfailing belief in free enterprise, unleashed a torrent of greed. From the number-one producer of lumber in the nation, Pennsylvania dropped to third by 1890. The year 1907 was the last time the state was recognized as a lumber-exporter, and by 1920 Pennsylvania was producing only one-third of its own lumber needs. Photographs from the period show a landscape as barren and scarred as any World War I battlefield. As beautiful and wild as the forests surrounding the upper Allegheny River appear today, it must be pointed out that they are only about one hundred years old, mere shadows of the primeval woodlands that once blanketed the mountains. It can only be hoped that we have learned our lesson and that the trucks now hauling logs out of Potter County to container ships in New York are not once again giving away the future.

Above Coudersport an ever-shrinking Allegheny parallels Route 49 to about Seven Bridges, where the road begins to climb and the river ducks around the face of Cobb Hill. Then, as the asphalt starts to level out once more, the river reappears as a trickle announced by a blue and yellow cast-iron state historical marker along the side of the road and a larger plywood keystone erected by the Potter County Historical Society in a corner of a pasture. Across the road, a farm pond surrounded by cattle at first gives the impression it could be the dammed origin of the river, the spring where it all begins, but a second look reveals a vague, sparkling thread running beyond the pond and pasture into a wooded hollow to the north.

Maybe fifty yards past the historical marker, Jim wheels the van sharply to the left onto a dirt drive running back to the farm with the pond, and then, at a huge mailbox labeled "R. Jones," adds a right and points us down a long, rutted lane toward a bluish-gray house surrounded by four-by-fours, dump trucks, and other instruments of the excavating trade. As we near the house, a big dog appears and runs alongside the van in typical farm country fashion. We hope he is friendly.

A first hint that the house might be home to someone of extraordinary talent comes in the form of an Indian bust carved out of a stump sitting on the corner of the porch. The hint is reinforced after the dog decides we're harmless and we get out of the van to ask permission to follow the river to its source. We spot an "Old Man Winter" face cut into the center of a log. The works are so good that it seems odd anyone would allow them to sit outside unguarded and exposed to the elements. In Pittsburgh, people would fight to have either of them standing next to their fireplace.

As soon as Nancy Jones opens her door, however, the reason the pieces are outside becomes clear. They are the experimental work, the crudest work, compared with the carousel horses, Christmas statues and ornaments, elaborate plaques with animals and faces, and a polished menagerie of pigs, rabbits, giraffes, snakes, and other creatures of

Nancy Jones

reality and imagination that fill the living room inside.

The sight of so many beautiful carvings makes us lose track of our objective almost immediately after we make it known, sends us drifting from windowsill to shelves to cabinet to coffee table, and unleashes an awed barrage of questions and remarks about the works. The tour ends with Jim mumbling, "This is wonderful. This is wonderful," and me fixated on two half-size carousel horses along a side wall and asking stupidly, "How long did it take you to do one of those?"

"This one has three hundred and fifty hours in," Nancy answers, pointing at one of the horses, "and then I made another that had four hundred hours in. After that I didn't keep track."

Lively and intense, Nancy began her wood-carving career twelve years ago while she and her family were living in New Jersey. It started one night after her husband, Bob, went to the library, checked out some books on wood carving, and began to whittle a rabbit. Sitting on the couch watching him, Nancy one day complained she was bored stuck at home with four kids. So Bob handed her the rabbit and a pocket knife.

Almost from the first slice, Nancy fell in love with the art and soon progressed far beyond her husband. Today, Bob's involvement in carving is limited mainly to gluing together the wood for her big pieces and rough-shaping on a bandsaw, while Nancy's work has earned her awards, appearances on television shows such as "A.M. Buffalo," teaching assignments at the Pennsylvania Lumber Museum and the Saw Mill Center for Arts in Cook Forest State Park, and an invitation to carve eight horse heads for the Empire State Carousel, the first wooden carousel to be built in the United States since the Great Depression.

Much of the maple and cherry Nancy uses in her carving comes from the woods and fields around her home. "These little faces on driftwood"—she says, pointing to an intricately rendered head with flowing beard and hair worked into the lines of the wood—"a lot of them we found in the woods. I'll send my son down to the river to get me pieces of driftwood."

The idea of a teenage boy living in the last house along the Allegheny and searching the banks of the river for "weird" pieces of wood for his mother to create works of art conjures up an exciting image of change: the Allegheny, a river above which the land was once stripped bare of trees and billions of board feet of lumber floated to market, now nourishing an artist whose medium is the wood found on its very headwaters. Jim begins talking to Nancy Jones about buying a piece.

Two and a quarter miles north of the spot where Allegany, Sweden, and Ulysses Townships join, at an altitude of 2,520 feet, lies a relatively flat hill about eight hundred feet long and four hundred feet wide. Known as the "Triple Divide" to geologists and as the "Watershed of the Nation" to locals, the hill marks the divide between waters

Like probably many other people who have heard about it, the idea of seeing Potter County's Triple Divide fascinated me for years. The thought of standing on a spot from which it is possible to venture forth by foot and canoe to lands where caribou migrate, watermen drag for oysters, and Cajuns waltz to accordions is powerful medicine for the romantic. Though my rational mind, armed with the bits I've read and pictures I've seen, tells me to expect only an open field crossed by a vague line of trees, my imagination argues that there must be something different about the spot, something to indicate what lies off in the distance.

As we enter the woods behind the Jones home, Jim begins to reminisce about the first time he searched out the source of the Allegheny. That was a couple of years ago. Then he had stumbled and struggled his way along the banks, simply following the water to its end without knowing for sure which of the springs pumping out of the mountain was the unfailing one, the one that ran even in drought years, the one considered the source of the Allegheny. This time, however, instead of fighting the rugged terrain of the banks, we move easily along the path Nancy told us about with the sound of the river off to our left hidden behind a cover of rhododendron, hemlock, and sprouting hardwoods.

A few hundred yards later, we spot a hunting camp and then turn down to the river, now nothing but a mountain brook clogged with rotting pieces of trees. We spot one spring and then another and another, and wonder whether they might be the Allegheny's source. But when we don't see the pipes we'd been told to look for, we decide they are not and push farther upstream, until finally two pieces of white plastic plumbing pipe catch our attention. "A high precipice, partly surrounded by trees, rose abruptly, and at its foot, underneath a moss-covered ledge of jutting rock layers, was the Spring, at journey's end," wrote Mary Welfling in a 1949 newspaper story about a hike with friends to the source of the Allegheny. Except for the addition of more trees and the pipes, the scene appears pleasingly the same, at least before we reach the pipes and discover they are the outlets for a concrete trough of sorts—and the wilderness spell is broken.

In her story, Welfling and her friends also accept the spring's "implied hospitality by drinking from its waters of icy coldness and delicious sweetness." Aware of the toxic changes that have occurred in the world since 1949, how even remote mountain waters can be a source of such diseases as giardiasis and loaded with acid runoff or long discarded chemicals, neither of us moves to sample the spring. Instead, Jim begins searching for angles from which to photograph the river, while I simply admire the skunk cabbage surrounding us.

Although the spring is regarded as the true source of the Allegheny, the water continues on out of sight through the woods. So when Jim is finished with the camera, we load up and start along the bank to find the place where the water finally stops. Weaving our way between branches and over rocks, we eventually reach the spot where

Mountain trickle, headwaters of the Allegheny, Potter County

the water stopped on Jim's first visit. But it has been a wet year, and the water runs on now. We accommodate the river's added length by pushing on to a flat, open area near the top of the mountain where the water spreads out and takes on a marshy character dotted by lumps of sod, heavy patches of skunk cabbage, and wild leeks. At one point where the skunk cabbage is particularly thick, Jim decides to shoot a few more photographs. Not really interested in watching, I tell him I am going on to the power line I see ahead and look for Triple Divide and the spot where the water finally stops.

Locals call the Triple Divide the "Watershed of the Nation" because it marks the starting point for three of the country's greatest river systems, and with them the first American frontier and the start of the march west. I am thinking about the name and how well it fits the Allegheny.

The history of the United States can literally be told through the story of the Allegheny River. Indians. Frontiersmen. Colonists. Washington. Iron. Oil. Steel. Glass. Aluminum. Railroads. Munitions for war. Destruction of the environment. Inventors. Idealists. Scoundrels. Rich. Poor. Keelboats. Steamboats. Immigrants. Sportsmen. Assassins. Everything good and bad about the country can be found along the Allegheny River, I think as I reach the power line and the water seems to end in an anticlimactic collection of grasses. I stand on the line for a moment feeling disappointed, and then decide to push across to the grove of trees on the other side and the open field beyond it that I think must hold the center of the divide.

Almost as soon as I am back in the woods, though, the water reappears as a loose collection of shallow potholes. Tiptoeing from dry spot to dry spot, I follow the water through the grove until a dirt and gravel road arises unexpectedly and its grade finally puts an end to the potholes and my search. I stare out at the open field in front of me, wonder whether it really is the Triple Divide, and wish I had my copy of *Outstanding Scenic Geological Features* along to compare the photograph in it with the field.

Then I turn around and look at the headwaters of the Allegheny River during the wet season. The Watershed of the Nation. It is surrounded by a collection of ancient, rusting farm equipment and discarded paint cans. I wonder exactly what it all says about our nation.

BIBLIOGRAPHY

The Allegheny River: Its Islands, Eddies, Riffles, and Winding Distances of Scenic Beauty. Emlenton, Pa.: Emlenton Chamber of Commerce, n.d. (The title page states that most information in the book comes from an 1855 book entitled *The Allegheny Pilot.*)

Allegheny River: Will It Be Part of the National Wild and Scenic Rivers System? Warren, Pa.: U.S. Department of Agriculture, Forest Service, n.d.

Baldwin, Leland. *Pittsburgh: The Story of a City, 1750–1865.* Pittsburgh: University of Pittsburgh Press, 1937.

Bashline, Jim. *The Final Frontier: Night Fishing for Trout.* Wautoma, Wisc.: Willow Creek Press, 1987.

Botkin, B. A., ed. *A Treasury of American Folklore.* New York: Crown, 1944.

Brady, Kathleen. *Ida Tarbell: Portrait of a Muckraker.* Pittsburgh: University of Pittsburgh Press, 1989.

Buck, Solon J., and Elizabeth Hawthorne Buck. *The Planting of Civilization in Western Pennsylvania.* Pittsburgh: University of Pittsburgh Press, 1979.

Darragh, William C. *Pithole: The Vanished City.* Privately printed, 1972.

Dolson, Hildegarde. *The Great Oildorado.* New York: Random House, 1959.

Donehoo, George. *A History of Indian Villages and Place Names in Pennsylvania.* New York: Lewis Historical Publishing House, 1926.

Dorson, Richard. *America in Legend.* New York: Pantheon Books, 1973.

Genoways, Hugh H., and Fred J. Brenner, eds. *Species of Concern in Pennsylvania.* Pittsburgh: Carnegie Museum of Natural History, 1985.

Geology of the Pittsburgh Area. Harrisburg: Pennsylvania Geological Survey, 1959.

Gertler, Edward. *Keystone Canoeing.* Silver Spring, Md.: Seneca Press, 1985.

Geyer, Alan R., and William Bolles. *Outstanding Scenic Geological Features of Pennsylvania.* Harrisburg: Pennsylvania Geological Survey, 1979.

Harbison, Francis R. *Flood Tides Along the Allegheny.* Pittsburgh: Buhl Brothers, 1941.

Harpster, John W., ed. *Crossroads: Descriptions of Western Pennsylvania, 1720–1829.*

Pittsburgh: University of Pittsburgh Press, 1938.

Johnson, Allen, ed. *Dictionary of American Biography*. Vols. 1 and 4. New York: Charles Scribner's Sons, 1936.

Johnson, Leland R. *The Headwaters District: A History of the Pittsburgh District U.S. Army Corps of Engineers*. Pittsburgh: Pittsburgh District U.S. Army Corps of Engineers, n.d.

Kidney, Walter C. *The Three Rivers*. Pittsburgh: Pittsburgh History & Landmarks Foundation, 1982.

Kussart, Serepta. *The Allegheny River*. Pittsburgh: Allegheny River Improvement Association, 1938.

MacCartney, Clarence E. *Right Here in Pittsburgh*. Pittsburgh: Gibson Press, 1937.

Merrill, Arch. *Southern Tier*. Interlaken: Heart of the Lakes Publishing, 1986.

Merritt, Joseph F. *Guide to the Mammals of Pennsylvania*. Pittsburgh: University of Pittsburgh Press, 1987.

Mulkearn, Lois, and Edwin Pugh. *A Traveler's Guide to Historic Western Pennsylvania*. Pittsburgh: University of Pittsburgh Press, 1954.

The Ohio River Basin. Washington, D.C.: League of Women Voters, 1964.

Oresick, Peter. *Definitions*. Albuquerque: West End Press, 1990.

Palmer, Tim. *Rivers of Pennsylvania*. University Park: The Pennsylvania State University Press, 1980.

Peterson, Edwin L. *Penn's Woods West*. Pittsburgh: University of Pittsburgh Press, 1958.

Polley, Jane, ed. *American Folklore and Legend*. New York: Reader's Digest Books, 1978.

Pratt, Richard, Bruce Sundquist, and Peter Wray, eds. *A Hiker's Guide to Allegheny National Forest*. Pittsburgh: Sierra Club Allegheny Group, 1982.

Schaaf, Gregory. *Wampum Belts and Peace Trees: George Morgan, Native Americans, and Revolutionary Diplomacy*. Golden, Colo.: Fulcrum Publishing, 1990.

Shepps, Vincent C. *Pennsylvania and the Ice Age*. Harrisburg: Pennsylvania Geological Survey, 1978.

Smith, Helene, and George Swetman. *A Guidebook to Historic Western Pennsylvania*. Pittsburgh: University of Pittsburgh Press, 1976.

Stotz, Charles Morse. *The Model of Fort Pitt: A Description and Brief Account of Britain's Greatest American Stronghold*. Pittsburgh: Allegheny Conference on Community Development, 1970.

Toker, Franklin. *Pittsburgh: An Urban Portrait*. University Park: The Pennsylvania State University Press, 1986.

Tome, Philip. *Pioneer Life; or, Thirty Years a Hunter*. Baltimore: Gateway Press, 1989.

Van Diver, Bradford B. *Roadside Geology of Pennsylvania*. Missoula, Mont.: Mountain Press Publishing Company, 1990.

Wallace, Anthony F. C. *The Death and Rebirth of the Seneca*. New York: Vintage Books, 1972.

Wallace, Paul A. W. *Indians in Pennsylvania*. Harrisburg: Pennsylvania Historical and Museum Commission, 1981.

Way, Frederick Jr. *The Allegheny*. New York: Farrar & Rinehart, 1942.

Weil, Roy, and Mary Shaw, eds. *Canoeing Guide to Western Pennsylvania and Northern West Virginia*. Pittsburgh: American Youth Hostels, Pittsburgh Council, 1983.

Wilson, Edmund. *With Apologies to the Iroquois*. New York: Vintage Books, 1959.

Works Progress Administration. *Pennsylvania: Guide to the Keystone State*. New York: Oxford University Press, 1940.

CREDITS

All color photographs in this book (with the exception of the illustration on p. 196) are copyright © 1992 Jim Schafer.

Front endpaper: Map by permission from *Early Maps of the Ohio Valley* by Lloyd A. Brown (University of Pittsburgh, 1959).

Back endpaper: Map courtesy of the Darlington Collection of the University of Pittsburgh.

Map following the Preface: Courtesy of the Western Pennsylvania Conservancy.

Lines from "The Senecas" by Peter La Farge (quoted on page 223) © 1963, 1991 by ESP-DISK', LTD. Used by permission.

Sources and credits for the black-and-white historical photographs are listed below with page numbers.

    Courtesy of the Archives of Industrial Society, University of Pittsburgh: pp. 15, 34
    Courtesy of The Carnegie Library of Pittsburgh: pp. 4, 35, 38, 41, 42, 44, 103, 178, 214, 268
    Courtesy of Chatham College Archives: p. 79
    Courtesy of Cincinnati Historical Society: p. 3
    Courtesy of the Drake Well Museum: pp. 135, 173, 175, 176, 185, 188
    Courtesy of the Historical Collections and Labor Archives, Penn State University: p. 292
    Courtesy of Historical Society of Western Pennsylvania: p. 94
    Courtesy of the Pennsylvania Lumber Museum: p. 294
    Courtesy of the Venango County Historical Society: p. 151 (1856 Eastman drawing)
    Courtesy of the Warren County Historical Society: pp. 221, 228, 233

The illustration on page 44 is an 1842 Denison Kimberly engraving after a painting by Daniel Huntington, courtesy of the Library of Congress.

The color illustration on p. 196 is courtesy of the Moravian Archives.

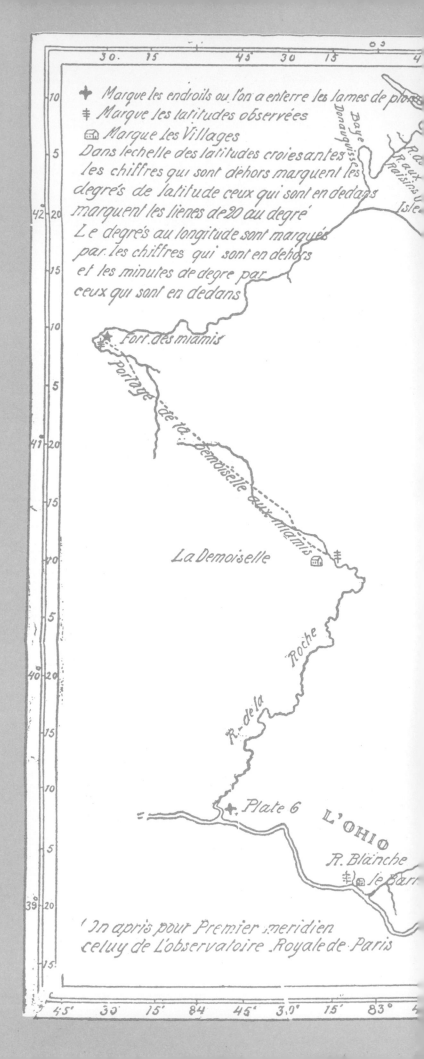

The Allegheny as Father Bonnecamps saw it, from Warren downriver. Plate 1 was buried at Warren, and Plate 2 was buried just downriver of present-day Pittsburgh.